SO-AYU-429

WHAT OTHERS ARE SAYING ABOUT
MARKING HUMANITY

"Before time and circumstance erase Holocaust survivors from existence, their tragic stories must be recorded. Even now, as we advance in the twenty-first century, we are confronted by deniers, dictators, bullies, and fiends who wish to destroy the Jewish people and our precious State of Israel. They accuse us of falsehood, despite the fact that the barbed wire, barracks, and gas chambers of Nazi hellholes still stand. In *Marking Humanity* it is apparent that the agony and suffering is real. The voices are eloquent. The enduring pain is horrific. We can only bear witness, but that is our duty to the martyrs and victims of hatred and brutality."

**—Vivian Jeanette Kaplan, author of *Ten Green Bottles:
Vienna to Shanghai—Journey of Fear and Hope***

"All of the memoirs conveyed in *Marking Humanity* are a poignant reminder of lives lost in the madness of the *Shoah*. This anthology unfolds under the deadly thud of the Nazi jackboot marching over the lives of Jewish mothers, fathers, sons, and daughters. A must read for a world once again on the cusp of descending into a new abyss of intolerance and ancient hatreds."

**—Ian Leventhal, Executive Director for the Toronto office
of the Jerusalem Foundation of Canada**

"A moving testimony to the power of creative expression in helping survivors of extreme trauma begin to heal their souls. In the words of Dora Posluns: 'Can one imagine Auschwitz? You must write!' "

**—Stephen K. Levine, author of *Trauma, Tragedy, Therapy:
The Arts and Human Suffering***

"Evocative writing. Political power. This compilation fusing history, essays, and poetry reminds us of some of the worst horrors of the Holocaust and of how many did not make it through. But over and over it testifies to the strength of the human spirit, as well as to the lives that survivors managed to create and their desire to be sure we know what happened. The editor reminds us that there are reasons for the hatred that infiltrates our world and much we still need to do to stop humiliation and hatred and to end and prevent genocide."

**—Ruth W. Messinger, President of
American Jewish World Service**

Marking Humanity

Marking Humanity
Stories, Poems, & Essays by Holocaust Survivors

Edited by Shlomit Kriger

Toronto
www.SoulInscriptionsPress.com

MARKING HUMANITY
Stories, Poems, & Essays by Holocaust Survivors
Edited by Shlomit Kriger

Toronto, Ontario
www.SoulInscriptionsPress.com

Copyright © 2010 by Shlomit Kriger

All rights reserved. No part of this publication may be reproduced or transmitted in any form or by any means, electronic or mechanical, including photocopying, recording, or by any information storage and retrieval system, without prior written permission from the publisher.

Cover Design and Illustration by Jim Zaccaria
Interior Design by Glenna Collett

Library and Archives Canada Cataloguing in Publication Data

Marking humanity : stories, poems, & essays by Holocaust survivors / edited by Shlomit Kriger.

ISBN 978-0-9864770-0-3

1. Holocaust, Jewish (1939-1945)—Personal narratives.
2. Holocaust survivors. I. Kriger, Shlomit, 1982-

D804.195.M27 2010   940.53'180922   C2010-901034-5

Printed in Canada

Permissions

"Holocaust Overview" reprinted courtesy of the United States Holocaust Memorial Museum, Washington, D.C.

Holocaust photographs featured with "Holocaust Overview" reprinted courtesy of Yad Vashem, Jerusalem, Israel.

(Permissions continued on page 273)

For my grandfather, Kusha Kriger,
whose parents, siblings, and other relatives
were killed in the Minsk ghetto in Belarus during the Holocaust,
while he was fighting for peace with the Red Army.
And for all other victims who were silenced
through this great atrocity.
May their memories be blessed (z''l).

Contents

Foreword

These words are being written as we enter a new decade of the twenty-first century. The passage of time holds meaning for all of us. It has ushered in a distinct sense of soul searching within the media and general public with reflections on the turbulent and disappointing first decade of the new millennium.

For those of us working in the field of Holocaust studies, time is not an ally but an enemy. We have attended many funerals. We have witnessed the passing of a generation. Each week it seems as if another survivor is lost and that those who remain, strong and valiant as they had once seemed, are growing older. They are more frail and giving way to the ravages of old age.

Those who were 18 years old at the time of the liberation are now well into their 80's. This year, the men among these survivors will celebrate their second *Bar Mitzvah*,[1] the 70th anniversary of their first *Bar Mitzvah*, which, if it were possible, would have been observed during the war in ghettos, under occupation, under siege, often clandestinely and illegally. (Lest women feel discriminated against, my point is historical. Rabbi Mordecai Kaplan introduced the *Bat Mitzvah* in the United States for the first time in 1922. It did not become common even in the U.S. until the post-war years; therefore, few, if any, European women were called to the *Torah*—Jewish Bible.)

No generation has left as voluminous a record of memoirs and testimonies as that of the Holocaust survivors. The USC Shoah Foundation Institute in the U.S. has more than 52,000 testimonies in 57 languages from 32 countries, and it is the largest of the many collections. Yad Vashem in Israel has collected testimonies for the entire post-war period. The

---

[1]A *Bar Mitzvah* marks the occasion when a Jewish boy comes of age at 13 years old. According to Jewish Law, he is then obligated to observe the Commandments. For girls, a *Bat Mitzvah* takes place when they turn 12.

Fortunoff Video Archive for Holocaust Testimonies at Yale University has been recording since 1979. The Holocaust Documentation and Education Center in Southern Florida began slightly afterward, and these are just a few of the collections worldwide. Memoirs come across my desk on a weekly and even daily basis. Most tell a story. Some are truly gripping. And even in the simplest of them, the stories they tell convey insight into the darkness that was experienced, as well as the world after the liberation.

But Holocaust survivors have done more than bear witness. As you will notice throughout the biographies of the featured survivors, over the past two decades survivors have become teachers throughout the world, speaking with students in schools that are large and small, secular and religious, public and private, Catholic, Protestant, Jewish, and in a few cases—too few cases—Muslim. Many connect with the rich mosaic of students from diverse ethnic backgrounds: black and white, Asian and Hispanic, those from lands touched by the Holocaust, and those in the rest of world whose ancestors barely knew what was happening.

Survivors have been surprised by the way in which they have been received in American classrooms, as well as in Europe and Israel. They speak of suffering and anguish, and students see in them symbols of resilience and even triumph. While they see themselves as defined by a past, youth are moved to discover that even after such a past, involving so massive a loss, one can look forward. No longer young, they are admired for their age. Representatives of the past who often trace their roots back to places that had barely entered the twentieth century, they are respected by those who grew up in the age of computers, digital music players, the Internet, and instant messaging—not because they are of the *here and now*, but because they lived *then and there*. The encounter is remarkable.

Shlomit Kriger has compiled the writings of survivors from the United States, Canada, and abroad, survivors of the Holocaust from urban centres and rural communities. Even though their offerings are diverse and their experiences are different, they seemingly speak with one voice, of one experience.

In the immediate post-war years, when the term "survivor" was used it meant only one thing: those who had been in concentration camps. Even then there was a hierarchy, because there was an absolute distinction between death camps and concentration camps. The former were places where Jews were systematically killed—gassed upon arrival. At three such

Dear Edith,
Thank you for being part of
this project. Enclosed are your
complimentary copies of the book.
Let's continue to do our part
to mark humanity with peace,

All the best,

Shlomit Krieger

camps, the *Aktion Reinhard* camps of Treblinka, Belzec, and Sobibor, almost all—99 out of 100—were killed upon arrival; only a few were kept alive to perform basic tasks of the camp: sanitation, sorting of valuables, disposal of corpses, and service to the German masters. Though about 1.5 million Jews were killed in these death camps, there were fewer than 200 survivors. (That is not a misprint; perhaps it is an exaggeration of the number of those who survived. We know of two survivors of Belzec, perhaps 100 from Treblinka, and about 50 from Sobibor who were found alive after the war.)

Auschwitz-Birkenau, which comprised three camps in one—a prison camp (Auschwitz I), a death camp (Auschwitz II or Birkenau), and a slave labour camp (Auschwitz III or Buna-Monowitz)—had many more victims as well as survivors. Some prisoners were kept alive to serve the Nazi industry that had invested heavily in slave labour and wanted to be its economic beneficiary. The Nazis presumed that a virtually limitless supply of slave labour would be theirs indefinitely.

Those who were not in camps were not regarded as survivors *then*, much as American World War II veterans distinguished between those who served in theatres of combat and those who did not. Child survivors were not considered survivors *then*. Their parents often protected themselves from fully feeling what happened to their children by saying, "What could they remember? What could they understand?" And refugees, children who had escaped on the *Kindertransport* (Children's Transport)—the children of Germany and Czechoslovakia who were fortunate enough to be sent to England and be received by the country just before the war began—were not considered survivors either. Neither were the Jews who survived the war in hiding by "passing" as "Aryans" or by being sequestered by others who often risked their lives and freedom to offer them shelter. Nor those Jews who in the days after the German invasion of Western Poland or following the German conquest of Soviet-occupied Poland in 1941 went counter to the Jewish experience of the nineteenth and early twentieth centuries and fled east to the Soviet Union. Many were sent to Siberia, where they experienced hardships, cold, disease, famine, even death—but *not systematic killing*.

That was *then*.

However, given the passage of time, *Marking Humanity: Stories, Poems, & Essays by Holocaust Survivors* includes—as it should—the writings of all who are now considered survivors. It features those who were children and others who were adults, those who were in camps and who found refuge in England or the United States, some who escaped eastward, and others who lived in hiding. Their writings and memories are varied; yet, their urge to bear witness and their sense of themselves as survivors with a unique tale to tell are the same.

One must welcome this testimony for its richness and diversity, for its inclusiveness and ingenuity. I have read prose far more than poetry and am far more confident in my assessment of an essay than a poem. Nevertheless, I find the contributors' poetry moving. The insights expressed in a few words leave me wanting more, greater exposition and detail. Still, poetry has the ability to say much with brevity and to bring language to the edge of what can be said and what cannot be said.

As we read and as we hear survivors' testimonies, we must think of what is said and what is left unsaid, of the spoken or written word and the silence between the words. We must also recognize how many have found healing through expression and how many of these survivors have used art and literature not only to share, but also perhaps to purge. This work offers them one such important opportunity, and we, as readers, can be part of that healing process. But we should also consider what Ludwig Wittgenstein, an Austrian philosopher of Jewish descent, once wrote: "What we cannot speak about we must pass over in silence."[2] And yet, survivors have chosen with increasing frequency and intensity to abandon silence and to speak of what cannot be spoken.

We who will all too soon live without that living memory of the past must be grateful for that breech of silence even as we are respectful of the unsaid.

Michael Berenbaum
Director of the Sigi Ziering Institute: Exploring the Ethical and Religious Implications of the Holocaust
American Jewish University
Los Angeles, California

---

[2]Ludwig Wittgenstein, *Tractatus Logico-Philosophicus,* 2nd ed., trans. D. F. Pears and B. F. McGuinness (New York: Routledge, 2001), Prop. 7.

Preface

Whoever destroys a soul, it is considered as if he destroyed an entire world.
And whoever saves a life, it is considered as if he saved an entire world.

—Talmud

I wish there was no need to produce a book based on such a dark period in history. However, considering the continuing spread of antisemitism and other acts of discrimination and violence that occur around the world, I felt compelled to facilitate this anthology's manifestation.

Throughout this book, you will gain further insight into the fears, sorrows, triumphs, challenges, personal reflections, dreams, and growth that the Holocaust survivors and their relatives, friends, and neighbours experienced—amidst the chaos that ensued and as they went on to rebuild their lives after the liberation. These courageous individuals survived some of the worst atrocities known to mankind, and there is much to learn from them and their experiences. They serve as an example for others around the world still struggling to be heard and to reach a place of love, peace, and healing.

These survivors could have easily allowed themselves to succumb to the ways of their oppressors, drowned in their sorrows, and projected nothing but anger and hatred onto the world. Instead, they remained resilient and rose above the hatred and tyranny of Germany's Nazi regime. They held onto their dreams, went on to lead productive lives, made positive contributions to their communities, and as survivor Susan Warsinger discusses in her story, rediscovered a sense of belonging.

Many Holocaust survivors have also turned their past into a force for positive change by giving lectures on war and tolerance to youth and adults of all backgrounds. They recognize that it is factors such as people's egotism and ignorance that form the roots of evil, not—as the Nazis claimed—an entire race or country. This understanding is key, because what has remained of great concern for many people is not only what has been learned from the Holocaust, but also the possibility that such an event could recur.

The Holocaust was not just a "Jewish problem"; it touched all of humanity. Along with six million Jews, millions of men, women, and children of other backgrounds and religions were also killed. As featured survivor Tamara Deuel notes in her piece "Memories and Contemplations," people must ask themselves, "Why?" What makes *anyone* worthy of such treatment, and how do perpetrators convince themselves that their actions are warranted? I urge you to then go beyond that and consider, "What now?" How far has humanity really come since the Holocaust?

According to the *2009 Audit of Antisemitic Incidents* released by the League for Human Rights of B'nai Brith Canada in 2010, 1,264 incidents from across Canada alone were reported to the League that year—an increase of 11.4 percent over the 2008 figures and close to a five-fold increase in a decade.[1] Furthermore, a Holocaust denial conference was held in Iran in early 2009 entitled "Holocaust? A Sacred Lie by the West," for which Iranian President Mahmoud Ahmadinejad gave a message of support, stating that "the Zionist regime is the 'illegitimate child' of the Holocaust phenomenon."

"His words are an example of the indelible thread running through both traditional antisemitism, which historically targeted the Jew as an individual deemed unworthy of the same basic human rights enjoyed by all others, and its newer variant, which disallows the Jewish people as a collective entity the same basic right to self-determination in its own homeland as all other peoples," stated the League in its 2008 Audit.[2]

While antisemitism played a significant role in the Holocaust and still haunts Jewish communities today, over the years there have also been numerous acts of hatred and violence targeting people of every

---

[1] "2009 Audit of Antisemitic Incidents: Patterns of Prejudice in Canada," Toronto: League for Human Rights of B'nai Brith Canada (2010), 4.

[2] "2008 Audit of Antisemitic Incidents: Patterns of Prejudice in Canada," Toronto: League for Human Rights of B'nai Brith Canada (2009), 2.

background. The ways in which these acts are committed does not make them more acceptable. On September 11, 2001 the event that came to be known as 9/11 took place when al-Qaeda terrorists hijacked four airplanes and crashed them in various locations in the United States, including the Twin Towers of the World Trade Center in New York. Many school shootings have occurred across the globe, some of the most prominent being at Columbine High School in Colorado, Virginia Tech in Blacksburg, Virginia, and Dunblane Primary School in Scotland. Some of the genocides that have transpired around the world involved Cambodia, Guatemala, Bosnia and Herzegovina, Rwanda, and—ongoing since 2003—Darfur in Sudan.

Many initiatives promoting global peace and wellness have also been implemented over the years, many in response to these atrocities. But I believe that it is essential for people to continue to delve deeper into the root causes of these destructive acts. We need to target the very basics of humanity if we are to establish positive solutions that may someday put an end to the ongoing societal issues we face.

According to many spiritual teachings, people are more than their names, emotions, physical appearances, earnings, "possessions," the ideas and beliefs that others feed them from birth . . . they have souls. The human body is a vehicle for the soul, allowing it to undergo various experiences on Earth aimed at facilitating its growth. Furthermore, every soul is a spark of the same "Source" or G-d. If this is the case, then what makes one person's life worth more than another's? The idea that people can benefit by harming others is merely an illusion. It is up to all people to work on themselves and to help care for the world. We are all on this journey together.

One of the fundamental issues that played a role in the Holocaust and connects the many incidents of discrimination, hatred, and violence across the globe is bullying. This form of abuse can often go unnoticed and be conducted in subtle ways. As a result, it can be difficult to prove. And yet, while a bully may not always be using a gun or fist to leave physical scars, words alone can aid in slowly murdering someone on the inside. The wounds inflicted by those who choose to inflate their own egos or try to solve their problems through dominance and aggression can last a lifetime.

Most people can likely say that they have at least witnessed some form of abuse at some point in their lives, whether at school, in the media, within their own families, or in some other time and place. They just may not call it that because they have learned to believe that it is "normal." But the first step toward addressing this issue is awareness. We must recognize the signs of abuse and not accept it. Furthermore, people should not have to wait until they see things happen to celebrities or hear of mass tragedies before they begin to take a deep, honest look at their own lives and surroundings and assess what could be changed.

In elementary school, I saw one of the girls in my class sitting alone in the lunchroom. She seemed like a nice person, so I decided to join her. It is not that I did not have other friends, but I did not feel comfortable seeing her all alone. We ended up becoming good friends. She was kind, intelligent, and loved to laugh.

Many of our peers, however, regularly made fun of her. I can still picture how at recess several of the boys in the schoolyard would push her onto each other and then yell, as if she was a piece of trash. As was the case with victims of the Holocaust, the bullies made my friend feel such helplessness and despair that resistance was difficult.

One day, I accompanied her to the guidance counsellor's office to report how she was being treated. I knew that she did not deserve this treatment. Who does?

The guidance counsellor soon invited a policeman to our school to speak to the students about bullying. This helped a bit, but it did not completely solve the problem. Regardless, it was too late. My friend was torn inside from all the abuse, and in the midst of all her pain, her parents were getting divorced. She fell into a deep depression and became suicidal. I saw the cut wounds on her arms, and I knew that inside she was crying out for help. Her parents sent her to some group homes to help her heal. Thankfully, I have heard that she is now doing well and pursuing a career that she enjoys.

I sometimes wonder what would happen if I could turn back time and show the students who teased my friend what their behaviour would lead to. Perhaps they would reconsider whether the bullying was worth it. According to Dr. Debra Pepler and Dr. Wendy Craig, scientific co-directors of PREVNet—a national network of Canadian researchers, non-governmental organizations, and governments committed to stop bullying—children who bully "are experiencing regular lessons in the use of power and aggression to control and distress others."[3] Furthermore, these children "do not just grow out of it" and may later get involved in sexual harassment, dating violence, gangs, domestic abuse, child abuse, and elder abuse.[4]

Still, when it comes to understanding and getting through to those who bully, the issue may not always be black and white. While victims of bullying can become depressed and vulnerable, some bullies may also be suffering. As Pepler and Craig note in their 2007 report *Binoculars on Bullying: A New Solution to Protect and Connect Children*, "Involvement in bullying is linked with numerous health problems, including anxiety, depression, and physical complaints such as headaches and eating problems, for both children who are victimized and those who bully" (Pepler & Craig, 3). In addition, both groups of children are "at higher risk of suicidal thoughts."[5]

In 2002 the United States Secret Service and the U.S. Department of Education released a report based on the Safe School Initiative, an examination of 37 incidents involving 41 school attacks that had occurred in the U.S. between 1974 and 2000. The report states that "incidents of targeted violence at school rarely were sudden, impulsive acts."[6] In addition, 71 percent of the attackers "felt persecuted, bullied, threatened, attacked or injured by others prior to the incident" (Vossekuil *et al.*, 21). Most attackers also "had difficulty coping with significant losses or personal failures," and 78 percent "exhibited a history of suicide attempts or suicidal thoughts at some point prior to their attack" (Vossekuil *et al.*, 22–23).

---

[3]Debra J. Pepler & Wendy Craig, "Binoculars on Bullying: A New Solution to Protect and Connect Children," Voices for Children (February 2007), 5. Hereafter cited in text.

[4]Debra J. Pepler & Wendy Craig, "Making a Difference in Bullying (Report No. 60)," La-Marsh Centre for Research on Violence and Conflict Resolution (April 2000), 5.

[5]Jennifer Lamb, Debra J. Pepler, & Wendy Craig, "Approach to Bullying and Victimization," *Canadian Family Physician* 55 (April 2009), 357.

[6]Bryan Vossekuil, Robert A. Fein, Ph.D., Marisa Reddy, Ph.D., Randy Borum, Psy.D., & William Modzeleski, "The Final Report and Findings of the Safe School Initiative: Implications for the Prevention of School Attacks in the United States," Washington, DC: United States Secret Service and U.S. Department of Education (May 2002), 11. www.secretservice.gov/ntac/ssi_final_report.pdf. Hereafter cited in text.

The incident at Virginia Polytechnic Institute and State University (Virginia Tech) in April 2007, when 23-year-old senior student Seung Hui Cho murdered 32 and injured 17 students and faculty before committing suicide, was the deadliest mass shooting by a single gunman in U.S. history. An examination of Cho's past reveals that he was deeply troubled. A report released by the Virginia Tech Review Panel notes that, according to Cho's parents, he became traumatized after doctors performed cardiac tests (possibly including a catheterization) on him in Korea when he was three years old.[7] Since then, he did not like to be touched and would rarely speak or make eye contact, even with his family (Panel Report, 32).

After the family moved to the U.S. in 1992, Cho's parents worked outside the home long hours, and Cho and his older sister felt isolated (Panel Report, 32). Cho became even more withdrawn; he had few friends and spent much time on hobbies by himself (Panel Report, 32). School peers teased him, but he did not discuss this with his family (Panel Report, 33).

Cho was in middle school when the mass murder at Columbine High School occurred in 1999. Shortly thereafter, he wrote a paper for English class, expressing "generalized thoughts of suicide and homicide," indicating that "he wanted to repeat Columbine" (Panel Report, 35). A psychiatrist soon ended up diagnosing him with "selective mutism" (a type of social anxiety disorder) and "major depression," and he received an antidepressant for about a year (Panel Report, 35).

During high school, Cho was identified as having special educational needs, and his school provided special accommodations that helped him succeed academically (Panel Report, 39). As the report states, these factors, combined with his continued work with an art therapist, "lessened his anger and frustration" (Panel Report, 40). However, when he applied to college, Virginia Tech did not obtain information about his condition or the treatment that he had received over the years (Panel Report, 38).

Beginning in 2005, Cho's professors and peers became concerned about his conduct, which included "violent writings, threatening behaviour, disturbing comments or e-mails to students," and "suicidal

[7]Report of the Virginia Tech Review Panel Presented to Timothy M. Kaine, Governor Commonwealth of Virginia, "Mass Shootings at Virginia Tech April 16, 2007," Official website of the Governor of Virginia (August 2007), 32.
www.governor.virginia.gov/TempContent/techpanelreport.cfm.
Hereafter cited in text as Panel Report.

behaviour."[8] Professors attempted to intervene, campus police investigated, and a judge ordered him to receive outpatient treatment (Gardner *et al.* 2007). Nevertheless, Cho, who had stopped receiving treatment when he completed high school, ended up contacting and visiting the campus counselling centre only a few times (Gardner *et al.* 2007).

—⁓—

It could seem simple to point fingers at perpetrators, or to assume that some people are purely evil or lost causes. More barriers, security, and stricter laws may be enforced. However, will that really get to the very core of the issues that afflict humanity?

I am not justifying or making excuses for any act of discrimination, hatred, or violence. People ultimately have the free will to make their own choices about their behaviour and how they respond to their life experiences. In Holocaust survivor Eva Brown's commencement speech to students at California's El Camino College, she recalls the fear that she saw in the eyes of a young Nazi guard as he "reluctantly carried out his orders." Yet, the Nazi officers, even under totalitarian rule, also had the choice to control their conduct. Just as someone who is handed a gun can decide to not pull the trigger, every moment in life presents an opportunity to think and act positively or negatively.

Nevertheless, it is worth considering that it is rare to hear about people engaging in significant attempts to harm others when they are truly happy with themselves and their lives. Like Cho, often it is those who find it very difficult to heal from past traumas and/or cope with unhealthy environments, life transitions, anger, resentment, regrets, etc. who may turn their pain and sorrow onto themselves or others—whether through substance abuse, eating disorders, criminal activities, or other means. Therefore, it is essential that—preferably from an early age—people obtain the necessary support and treatment to deal with challenges they face and learn healthy ways to build self-esteem and to express or defuse their emotions.

There should be no shame or fear involved when it comes to people working on themselves and their life situations. Nobody is perfect. All

---

[8]Amy Gardner, Debbi Wilgoren, & Howard Schneider, "Panel: Va. Tech Failed to Respond to Cho Warning Signs," *The Washington Post* (Aug. 30, 2007). www.washingtonpost.com/wp-dyn/content/article/2007/08/30/AR2007083000759.html. Hereafter cited in text.

people face different experiences—both positive and challenging—as their souls are on Earth to grow and learn throughout their unique journeys.

Some may argue that those suffering from mental illness automatically pose a danger to others since they cannot properly assess or even control their actions. However, it is important to recognize that there are varying degrees and layers to mental illness. According to Lillian Freedman, a Toronto social worker who has assisted many youth and adults through her work and provides public lectures on topics such as mental illness, it may be that "when a medical condition affects the way the brain functions there is no predictability regarding behaviour and decision making is not rational." Still, she notes that this is particularly true in conditions involving psychosis, which causes people to believe they are hearing voices telling them things that are not real and instructing them to act in ways they never would when healthy. They may also hold other delusional beliefs or experience hallucinations and act on some of their visions. "Extreme forms of depression can also make people do terrible things, in the false belief that they have no other choice left," she says.

Nonetheless, Freedman explains that these types of illnesses are also treatable. "Thousands of individuals with mental illness are successfully treated and move on and never have the potential or the urge to harm themselves or anybody else," she says. "The best form of protection for everyone—those afflicted, their loved ones, and society—is early education, early awareness that something might be wrong (even with a young child), early diagnosis and treatment by qualified professionals, and constant monitoring and support systems."

In an interview I did with Toronto Psychotherapist Annette Poizner for an article that appeared in the *Jewish Tribune* in December 2006, she said that people's memories can reveal and even determine their personalities. She explained that "young children have a more crude form of intellect, yet they are still forced to make some sense of the world around them. While they may have countless experiences, their unconscious minds will tend to hold onto certain memories that stood out for them and helped them make early generalizations. These early memories strung together make up a type of map of the world that establishes what the individual can expect from himself, from others, and from life."[9]

---

[9]Shlomit Kriger, "Memory Plays Central Role in Determining Personalities," *Jewish Tribune* (Dec. 7, 2006), 18.

What may seem to one person as a harmless incident could end up affecting many areas and stages of another's life. In addition, people's environment—which can include caregivers, friends, the community, and even the media—can have a major impact on their conduct and their responses to experiences.

Morty Lefkoe, president and founder of The Lefkoe Institute, developed a series of psychological processes called The Lefkoe Method based on the notion that people's behaviour and much of their emotions are the result of their beliefs, usually formed during childhood. The method "allows people to identify the beliefs responsible for their dysfunctional behavioural or emotional patterns and then eliminate those beliefs."[10] For example, in a 1995 *New York Times* article, Lefkoe explained that parents' behaviour and statements could affect their children negatively. "A lot of the ways we get children to stay off the furniture or finish their food leads them to negative self-images," he said. "They can think something is wrong with them."[11]

In 1994 Lefkoe completed a pilot research study testing his method's effectiveness on criminal behaviour. The 13-week study involved 16 criminal offenders at two Connecticut institutions. He said the study showed that "helping the criminal offenders eliminate negative beliefs, typically involving self-esteem and self-worth, allowed them to also rid themselves of angry emotions, violent behaviour, and possibly, future criminal tendencies" (*The New York Times* 1995).

—◊◊◊—

It may seem impossible to reach every troubled soul out there. And shifting the ideologies adopted by those surrounded by leaders and caregivers who advocate violence and oppression may appear unreal. But what type of world do we want future generations to discover? Let's focus on the possibilities rather than the obstacles. Every person helps to shape the world. We must strive to be positive examples within our own families and communities. In addition, we must make an effort to spread information on and methods for creating healing and peace. We owe it to ourselves.

---

[10]www.lefkoeinstitute.com

[11]Dieter Stanko, "Finding Positives and Removing Negatives," *The New York Times* (Aug. 6, 1995). Hereafter cited in text.

There are already numerous initiatives in place to help create such a global movement. Founded in 2002, Kids4Peace, an initiative of St. George's College Jerusalem with the cooperation of the Episcopal Diocese of Jerusalem, brings together Jewish, Muslim, and Christian faith leaders and children through programs aimed at building bridges and promoting cooperation and respect between people of the three faiths.[12]

The Motivating the Teen Spirit organization, based in the U.S., runs programs that empower youth of various backgrounds to love themselves, communicate more effectively, and make integrity-based decisions. Since renowned author, motivational speaker, life coach, and teacher Lisa Nichols launched the program in May 2000, it has served over 35,000 teens, assisted in preventing over 800 suicides, encouraged over 575 drop outs to return to school, and helped thousands of teens reconnect with families.[13]

Finally, Erin Gruwell has devised initiatives that have been helping to alter the face of education. When Gruwell became a teacher at Wilson High School in Long Beach, California, during the 1990s, she found herself facing students who struggled with feelings of anger and confusion, having dealt with abuse, homelessness, juvenile detention, or gang involvement. To better connect with them, she revised her teaching style, assigning them books on topics such as the Holocaust and racial discrimination—over time empowering them through characters to whom they could relate. The students penned diaries reflecting on the issues the characters faced as well as the issues in their own lives. They also participated in activities and field trips aimed at helping them learn respect and tolerance for one another.

Gruwell's teaching methods inspired and motivated the students. In 1998, 97 percent of her students graduated (150 teens). Coining a reference from a period during the civil rights movement, the students called themselves the Freedom Writers (named after the Freedom Riders of the 1960s). That name was also used for a book featuring their diary entries and experiences.

Gruwell and those students have since shared their stories with educators and youth across North America, promoting the Freedom Writers

---

[12]http://kids4peace.ca

[13]www.motivatingtheteenspirit.com

Method through the Freedom Writers Foundation in Long Beach.[14] Their story was also brought to life in the 2007 film *Freedom Writers*.

I, too, had the opportunity to discover the power of the written word in helping people express themselves, become empowered, and even heal. In 2005 I coordinated the 6th Annual Creative Writing Contest for the Homeless through Toronto-based humanitarian organization Ve'ahavta.[15] The contest allows the homeless participants to gain a voice in the community and to be recognized as more than mere statistics. It also helps people better understand homelessness and the experiences these people face.

Some of the participants told me how the contest assisted in motivating them to believe in themselves and take steps in positive directions. One of the winners decided to hold on to his money so he could pay his ex-wife for rent and buy food. He also checked into a recovery house for a 28-day alcohol and drug treatment program. The grand prize winner, Theresa Schrader, had stayed at various homeless shelters, battled a drug addiction, and wrote about her previous experiences working as a prostitute. Today she is studying social work, raising her three-year-old son, living in subsidized housing, giving lectures about her former experiences, and continuing to hone her passion for creative writing.

I also enjoy expressing myself through the arts and have been singing and penning poetry, songs, and short stories since I was nine years old. However, the Ve'ahavta contest allowed me to gain deeper insight into how transformational the arts really can be, and that led me to explore the field of expressive arts therapy.

I got the idea to produce this Holocaust anthology in the summer of 2008, after I met featured survivor George Scott, who has written numerous poems but had not previously had any published. While I felt that it was essential to provide the Holocaust survivors the chance to be heard and share their writings with others, I also hoped that they would possibly achieve some level of release and healing through the creative process. Many survivors have great difficulty talking about their experiences, let alone digging up memories they have tried to bury. I am glad that the contributors have been able to express themselves through writing.

---

[14]www.freedomwritersfoundation.org

[15]www.veahavta.org

Survivor Ruth Barnett explained to me how important creative writing has been for her from an early age. Her experiences during the war, including fleeing from Germany to England on a children's transport with her older brother and living with foster families and at a hostel, convinced her that she was "bad and unlovable for anyone to cope with for very long." But she found that she could delight her schoolteachers with her writings and paintings, and these activities made her feel as though she "could achieve something worthwhile at the same time as expressing [her] turbulent feelings (which nobody had explained to [her]) and lifting [her] mood." Having later worked as a psychotherapist, she said she realized that "some traumatized people can better use art and writing to process their feelings."

Barnett wrote her poem "Mother" when she was 16 years old. She explained that the poem embodies her emotional struggle to come to terms with her mother: "I was totally unable to relate to my parents, who were complete strangers to me after 10 years of separation."

—⋙—

As humanity progresses, may people recognize that they should not have to wait until, G-d forbid, children slit their wrists or join pro-violence groups, or mass tragedies erupt across the globe, before they stand up for peace, justice, and well-being. Not everyone has to give public lectures or devise large programs to make a difference. Even just spreading the word on positive values can go a long way.

Just as one individual like Nazi regime leader Adolf Hitler could bring about mass destruction, we must believe that one individual can also create great peace in the world. Everyone can help contribute to a chain reaction of positive actions.

G-d bless,

Shlomit Kriger

Holocaust Overview

The Holocaust was the systematic, bureaucratic, state-sponsored persecution and murder of approximately six million Jews by the Nazi regime and its collaborators. "Holocaust" is a word of Greek origin meaning "sacrifice by fire." Under their leader, Adolf Hitler, the Nazis came to power in Germany in January 1933. They believed that Germans were "racially superior" and that the Jews, deemed "inferior," were an alien threat to the so-called German racial community.

During the era of the Holocaust, German authorities also targeted other groups because of their perceived "racial inferiority": Roma (Gypsies), the disabled, and some of the Slavic peoples (Poles, Russians, and others). Other groups were persecuted on political, ideological, and behavioural grounds.

In 1933 the Jewish population of Europe stood at over nine million. Most European Jews lived in countries that Nazi Germany would occupy or influence during World War II. By 1945 the Germans and their collaborators killed nearly two out of every three European Jews as part of the "Final Solution," the Nazi policy to murder the Jews of Europe. Although Jews, whom the Nazis deemed a priority danger to Germany, were the primary victims of Nazi racism, other victims included some 200,000 Roma (Gypsies). At least 200,000 mentally or physically disabled patients, mainly Germans, living in institutional settings, were murdered in the so-called Euthanasia Program.

As Nazi tyranny spread across Europe, the Germans and their collaborators persecuted and murdered millions of other people. Between two and three million Soviet prisoners of war were murdered or died of starvation, disease, neglect, or maltreatment. The Germans targeted the non-Jewish Polish intelligentsia for killing and deported millions of Polish and Soviet civilians for forced labour in Germany or in occupied Poland, where these individuals worked and often died under deplorable conditions. From the earliest years of the Nazi regime, German authorities persecuted homosexuals and others whose behaviour did not match prescribed social norms. German police officials targeted thousands of political opponents (including Communists, Socialists, and trade unionists) and religious dissidents (such as Jehovah's Witnesses). Many of these individuals died as a result of incarceration and maltreatment.

In the early years of the Nazi regime, the National Socialist government established concentration camps to detain real and imagined political and ideological opponents. Increasingly in the years before the outbreak of war, SS and police officials incarcerated Jews, Roma, and other victims of ethnic and racial hatred in these camps. To concentrate and monitor the Jewish population as well as to facilitate later deportation of the Jews, the Germans and their collaborators created ghettos, transit camps, and forced-labour camps for Jews during the war years. The German authorities also established numerous forced-labour camps, both in the so-called Greater German Reich and in German-occupied territory, for non-Jews whose labour the Germans sought to exploit.

Following the invasion of the Soviet Union in June 1941, Einsatzgruppen (mobile killing units) and, later, militarized battalions of Order Police officials, moved behind German lines to carry out mass-murder operations against Jews, Roma, and Soviet state and Communist Party officials. German SS and police units, supported by units of the Wehrmacht and the Waffen SS, murdered more than a million Jewish men, women, and children, and hundreds of thousands of others.

Between 1941 and 1944, Nazi German authorities deported millions of Jews from Germany, from occupied territories, and from the countries of many of its Axis allies to ghettos and killing centres. Unlike concentration camps, which served primarily as detention and labour centres, killing centres (also referred to as "extermination camps" or "death camps") were almost exclusively "death factories." German SS and police murdered nearly 2,700,000 Jews in the killing centres either by asphyxiation with poison gas or by shooting. The SS considered the killing centres top secret. To obliterate all traces of gassing operations, special prisoner units (the Sonderkommandos) were forced to remove corpses from the gas chambers and cremate them. The grounds of some killing centres were re-landscaped or camouflaged to disguise the murder of millions.

In the final months of the war, SS guards moved camp inmates by train or on forced marches, often called "death marches," in an attempt to prevent the Allied liberation of large numbers of prisoners. As Allied forces moved across Europe in a series of offensives against Germany, they began to encounter and liberate concentration camp prisoners, as well as prisoners en route by forced march from one camp to another. The marches continued until May 7, 1945, the day the German armed forces surrendered unconditionally to the Allies. For the western Allies, World War II officially ended in Europe on the next day, May 8 (V-E Day), while Soviet forces announced their "Victory Day" on May 9, 1945.

When Anglo-American and Soviet troops entered the concentration camps, they discovered piles of corpses, bones, and human ashes—testimony to Nazi mass murder. Soldiers also found thousands of survivors—Jews and non-Jews—suffering from starvation and disease. For survivors, the prospect of rebuilding their lives was daunting.

In the aftermath of the Holocaust, many of the survivors found shelter in displaced persons (DP) camps administered by the Allied powers. Between 1948 and 1951, almost 700,000 Jews immigrated to Israel, including 136,000 Jewish displaced persons from Europe. Other Jewish DPs immigrated to the United States and other nations. The last DP camp closed in 1957. The crimes committed during the Holocaust devastated most European Jewish communities and eliminated hundreds of Jewish communities in occupied Eastern Europe entirely.

Camp inmates on bunks at the time of liberation in Buchenwald, Germany.

Children next to a barbed wire fence in Auschwitz-Birkenau, Poland.

Jews standing on the platform after alighting from a train in Auschwitz-Birkenau, Poland, May 1944.

A general view of the Bergen-Belsen concentration camp in Germany, April 1945.

Political prisoners in the camp yard in Oranienburg, Germany, 1933.

Roll call at a detention camp in Kistarcsa, Hungary, 1944.

MARKING HUMANITY

Prisoners demonstrating the transferring of bodies to the crematorium in Dachau, Germany, 1945.

German civilians forced to walk by a row of corpses in Volary, Czechoslovakia, May 1945.

IN THE SURVIVORS' OWN WORDS

I can see that in the midst of death life persists,
in the midst of untruth truth persists,
in the midst of darkness light persists.
—Mohandas K. Gandhi

Eva Brown

*E*va Brown was born in Hungary in August 1927. She was the middle child born to a rabbi and his wife, and she had three brothers and three sisters. During the Holocaust, her father was sent to a labour camp, while the rest of the family lived in the Putnok ghetto. They were later sent to the Auschwitz-Birkenau camp, where her mother and seven-year-old brother were sent directly to the gas chamber. Eva's identity was reduced to a number—A17923.

Following the war, Eva reunited with her father, but she learned that 60 members of her family had been murdered. In 1948 she immigrated to the United States. She was married for 50 years and has two daughters and one granddaughter. For the past eight years, she has served as a speaker at the Museum of Tolerance in Los Angeles. She lives in West Hollywood, California.

An Address to Students

Commencement Speech at El Camino College in Torrance, California, June 2006

Eva Brown

When I was asked to be a keynote speaker at your graduation, I was immediately overcome by amazement and dread. I was amazed that I, a foreigner with a Grade 6 education, was chosen to inspire you, but I dreaded that I would not be able to do so.

I have spent a lot of time worrying about what I could possibly say to you that would mark this momentous occasion. What would you take away from this? Our differences are so great. You are at least 60 years my junior and have at least 14 years of education. You have mastered the electronic world of computers, digital cameras, and cell phones. I can hunt and peck on a typewriter, take photos with my old-fashioned film camera, and would never give up my rotary phone. But the biggest difference is our education; you are graduating from El Camino College, and I graduated from Auschwitz. If your enemies are your teachers, then I have learned so much from the Nazis.

To understand my message, you must first know my story. Seventy-nine years ago, I was the middle child born to a rabbi and his wife in a very small town in Hungary. My childhood was spent with my six siblings. Life was simple and carefree; we played, went to school, and celebrated holidays. But in the midst of this normalcy, German boots were marching across Europe.

In 1944 Hungary was invaded and my life was turned upside down as my father was taken away to a labour camp. My mother, younger siblings, and I were sent to the Putnok ghetto. Struggling with hunger and exhaustion, we did not think things could get worse until the cattle cars came

MARKING HUMANITY

and took us to Auschwitz—a place of unimaginable horrors and atrocities and ferocious beauty and tenacity of the human spirit. It is a bizarre coincidence that this occurred on June 9, exactly 62 years ago today, on a Friday night.

As I watched my mother and seven-year-old brother go to the gas chamber, I could not understand the depravity and madness of human beings that was reflected in Hitler's "Final Solution." Everyone's past was erased. No distinction was made between doctors, lawyers, teachers, shoemakers, and honours students; each identity was reduced to a blue number tattooed on our forearms.

I found solace in the compassion of the Nazi guard that brought me food and a blanket to shield me from the bitter cold. I learned that to make myself valuable was to live. At 15 years of age, I had expected to be dating, going to school, and planning a dazzling future. Instead, I concentrated on discovering talents that would keep me alive: giving manicures, haircuts, and massages to my captors. I became an experimental scientist of my own body and mind. I learned to stay awake during the daily 4:00 AM head count that lasted three hours. I carefully balanced my food intake and energy output so I was able to finish all my work. Death was certain for those who fell asleep or fell behind in their assignments.

Even under these most dehumanizing conditions, we had choices. Some committed suicide by throwing themselves onto the electric barbed wires; others overcame starvation and sickness by sheer force of will in their determination to live. We prayed and comforted each other and vowed to make sure that one day the world would know what had happened to us.

I learned psychology—especially the art of denial and distance. I dreamt of my future; looking beyond the smoke from the gas chambers, I planned my life. I would find my family, get married, buy a house, and have children. I selected my wardrobe and menus; visions of shiny silk dresses, warm woolen coats, stuffed goose, and rich pastries filled my head as I removed gold teeth from dead prisoners. I named my smiling healthy children as I clipped the German officers' mustaches, and I danced with my dashing husband as I filed their nails. I designed my living room and chose wallpaper for my bedroom as I worked outside in my bare feet as icy rain and snow soaked me.

After the liberation, I reunited with my father and learned that 60 members of my family had been murdered during the war. At age 17

I was struggling to regain footing in a world that had been pulled from under my feet.

I left for America with nothing but a desire to rebuild. I had lost my family, my country, and an entire way of life. But I got married, raised two children, and learned to speak a new language. I worked, paid taxes, and gave money to charity. My fellow survivors and family never talked about our experiences. It was like a bad dream that we forgot after waking up in America.

In the media the Holocaust was sensationalized or sentimentalized—it did not ring true. I remembered the fear in the young Nazi guard's eyes as he reluctantly carried out his orders. In 1994 I saw the film *Schindler's List* and was transported back to that terrible time and place. As I watched the survivors pay tribute to the man who saved them, I vowed to break my silence. After waiting 50 years, I was finally ready to tell my story. While I could not speak for the dead, I would honour their memory by sharing my experiences. Thus, I became a teller of stories.

I volunteered to give testimony for the USC Shoah Foundation Institute and the Museum of Tolerance. Speaking as a Jew who comes from far away, I share my family's story with a diverse audience: Catholics, Muslims, agnostics, the young and old. I speak of loss and redemption and of the evil that people are capable of and the good with which they can heal. The Nazis taught me the power of forgiveness. This enables me to spread my message of tolerance and respect for everyone. People from all walks of life relate to my experiences. I have found that faith and age are not the common denominators. It is by being part of the human family with the realms of emotions that touch us all—grief, terror, despair, joy—that people embrace my determination to ensure that the world will never forget what happened over 60 years ago.

My story is also about the randomness of how we're placed in life and how we respond. The greatest lesson that I have learned is captured in a quote by renowned physicist Albert Einstein: "There are only two ways to live your life. One is as though nothing is a miracle. The other is as though everything is a miracle." The fact that I am celebrating here with you today confirms that I am living the latter.

Sixty years ago, the world ignored the genocide of the Jews. Today, in America, 25 State curriculum regulations require the Holocaust to be taught and 24 others implicitly encourage it. My life has come full circle.

I enjoyed so many opportunities here and always felt that I was riding on a train without a ticket. There was a larger debt to be repaid. For a family that journeyed to this country for freedom, I am finally paying the fare.

Therefore, my message to you is to never give up. Follow your dreams and always have hope. Be involved in your life through your family and friends and through public service. Play a role in making your community and country safe, so that every citizen may enjoy freedom just as I have.

Dora Posluns

Dora Posluns (née Shumska) was born in Berdychiv, a predominantly Jewish city in Ukraine. She was in her teens when World War II began. She and her family fled across Russia and ended up in Uzbekistan in a primitive poverty-stricken area, where they remained for the rest of the war. Her father, however, died of starvation.

Dora later married Wolf Posluns (originally Poslaniec), a Warsaw Jew who had entered Russia with the Polish Armed Forces. Because of her marriage, she and her mother were able to leave Russia for Poland. There, she gave birth to two children. The family later immigrated to Israel, where Dora first began to write poetry. They finally settled in Canada in March 1953.

Residing in Toronto, Ontario, Dora went on to volunteer with numerous organizations. She is, however, most famous for her performances, in which she sang, read her poetry, and generally made her audiences (as large as 200 people) laugh, cry, and feel good. Particularly moving were her annual commemorations of the Holocaust performed at geriatric care centre Baycrest and Baycrest's Joseph E. and Minnie Wagman Centre. She has three children and four grandchildren.

Write!

Dora Posluns

In front of our eyes they went to the gas chambers
Our fathers, our mothers, our brothers, our sisters
Together with the small children
In front of our eyes they went to the crematoria
They left us behind to testify as witnesses
Their eyes alone spoke in the silence
Their silence, trembling, the last cry from their speaking eyes shrieked
Remember us!
You survivors don't forget us
G-d did not send us to the gas chambers
A human being like you, like me
The unbelievers who deny the Holocaust
Say it couldn't have happened, it didn't happen
We the survivors are the last living witnesses
In front of our eyes, they were taken to the crematoria
The last silent scream in their eyes to us
Write!
Write our names as a witness
You child of a survivor, to the second generation
You child of a survivor, to the third generation
Write our names as a witness
Until the end of all generations
It's unbelievable . . . can a human being imagine Auschwitz?
You must write!
Let us write, brothers, in a new *Machzor*,[1] a new *Siddur*[2]
While their ashes are dispersed on the walkways

---

[1] The prayer book that Jewish people use on the High Holidays.

[2] Jewish prayer book.

In all our prayers, let us mention them
In all our memorial services, let us mourn them
In all our *Kaddish*[3] prayers, let us recognize them
May they lend beauty to each "Hatikvah"[4] that we sing
The death of millions of martyrs is the stuff of legends
Remember not to forget
Never again
Remember us
Write!

---

[3]Jewish mourners' prayer.

[4]"Hatikvah" ("The Hope") is Israel's national anthem.

Samuel Bak

Samuel Bak was born in Vilna, Poland (now Vilnius, Lithuania), in 1933. He loved to paint from a very young age. During the Holocaust, he and his family moved into the Vilna ghetto. There, at age nine, he held the first exhibition of his paintings. He and his mother managed to escape from the

Courtesy of Pucker Gallery, Photograph by Andy Abrahamson.

ghetto and sought refuge in a Benedictine convent. By the end of the war, they were the only members of his extensive family who had survived. The Nazis shot his father in July 1944, only a few days before Samuel's liberation. Samuel and his mother fled to Lodz and then travelled to Germany, where they lived in Displaced Persons camps.

In 1948 they immigrated to Israel. Samuel went on to attend high school and then the Bezalel Academy of Art and Design. He later served in the Israel Defense Forces. In 1956 he left for Paris to study at École Nationale des Beaux-Arts. Subsequently, he lived and exhibited his artwork in Israel, Paris, Rome, New York, and Switzerland. Then, in 1993, he and his wife settled in the United States.

The list of Samuel's innumerable exhibitions of the last five decades includes a 1978 Retrospective at the Germanisches Nationalmuseum in Nuremberg, a 2002 Vilnius Picture Gallery retrospective, and a 2006 Yad Vashem show that featured 60 years of his works. In 2002 Indiana University Press published Samuel's book *Painted in Words: A Memoir*.

Burlap Sacks

Samuel Bak

It was in the late summer of 1941. In June of that year, the German army had occupied Vilna. Mother, our Russian housekeeper, Xenia, and I were left in the large apartment that suddenly looked empty and haunted. The celebration of my eighth birthday in August had been postponed for an indefinite date. Our reserves of food were exhausted. It was dangerous for Jews to go out into the streets.

Luckily, Xenia was able to be of help. She had her resources, and although finding comestibles had become increasingly difficult, we managed. Getting news was another problem. Radios were forbidden. A few Jewish neighbours in our building were the only people we saw. They went on spreading various rumours, in which they hardly believed. We were on the receiving end. We did not know what the others did. The telephones of all Jewish households had been disconnected, and Xenia was our only go-between. It was difficult to have complete trust in her, given the complex history of our relations. She was often absent for long stretches of time, and this made us question her reliability. But we had no choice. We could not protest; we were totally dependent on her goodwill.

Not many days remained until our transfer to the ghetto. One morning, Xenia left early and came back after a few hours accompanied by a rugged man, who was carrying a heavy sack of patched-up burlap. The man smelled of straw and well-fertilized soil. Stiff flaxen hair partly covered his weather-beaten face. His worn jacket, heavy boots, and the sack were all shedding sawdust-like dirt. With an awakening feeling of joy I realized that the sack might contain potatoes and that soon we would be able to appease our gnawing hunger. Xenia gave Mother a quick sign with her eyes and directed the farmer to the dining room with a signal of her hand.

"Please take a seat," said the housekeeper in an unusually polite voice, of a sort that she had never used for addressing persons of his kind. With a quick and agile movement he let the sack fall to the floor, and it landed on the large Persian carpet in the center of the room. The sack came to a quick halt and remained standing there, slightly leaning to the side as if it was about to burst open and send the potatoes rolling under the table. A halo of thin soil surrounded it. More of the dirt was being shed with each of the man's steps. With an unusual gesture of self-confidence, he grabbed the back of Father's chair and sat down.

A tremor like a quickly passing wave of some mysterious explosion passed through my body. Never before had I seen anybody but Father sit in that chair. Why didn't they warn him that this was the master's chair and no other living person in the whole world had the right to sit on it? Few objects had such unquestionable sanctity in my eyes. I tried to interrogate Mother with a staring look. All I got back from her was a light shaking of her head that told me to be quiet.

The maid murmured something into Mother's ear. These must have been the pre-agreed conditions of exchange, which would give us the right to the potatoes. Early on that day, Xenia had taken it upon herself to go to one of the roads that led to the central market with the intention of stopping one of the few carts that were carrying comestible goods from the neighbouring villages. The adventuresome peasants, who preferred to leave their horses well hidden from the German authorities, pushed or dragged the carts into the city with the sheer force of their muscles and offered a limited choice of precious products. Vilna was hungry, and those providers who passed the various military roadblocks with their merchandise and managed to save them from confiscation expected a very lucrative barter.

When Mother reentered the room, she carried a well-upholstered hanger from which dangled Father's tuxedo, in all its glory of bygone days. If the satin lapels had mouths that could speak, they would have told many stories, some of them quite unfit for a child's ear. However, I knew that they had a life of their own. On certain evenings, being carefully hung with the rest of the garments on the back of one of my parents' bedroom chairs and facing my direction, the elegant lapels gave me the feeling that they observed me. I used to admire their delicate shine. There was a buttonhole that fascinated me, because it had no corresponding button and served uniquely for the purpose of displaying a white carnation.

I loved to prolong the evening hours before going to bed by assisting my parents' preparations for their festive outings. True, I felt proud to be able to contribute to the various stages of their dressing up, but the main reason for my desire to be with them in those moments was the sheer pleasure of admiring their star-like glory. Crawling on all fours I used to search for the special buttons that had to be inserted by Father's expert hands into his white shirt's over-starched plastron. They had the bad habit of popping out and getting lost under the bed. I loved to watch him struggle and get angry. My small hands returned to him the innocent objects, and their final insertion into the stiff material had the power to calm his rage. Father's Russian words of magic, very similar to the exclamations of the janitor who used to clean our staircase, helped him. Mother would tell him that he had a dirty mouth and that the little one was around. But I knew that she was wrong.

Father looked resplendent and absolutely clean, with no trace of dirt on his lips. His curly dark hair that had been pomaded and pulled for an hour with a special brush was perfectly smooth and shone as if it had been lacquered. His face, freshly shaved and sprinkled with a special powder, had an opaque marble beauty. The last move before putting on the jacket was the removal of any excess perfumed dust in order to save the marvelous lapels from invasion by the soothing after-shave powder.

Those glamorous days seemed far away. At present, I couldn't take my eyes off the dirty burlap sack and the mess on the precious carpet. My thoughts were elsewhere: "How does my Father look now?" I knew that he was in a labour camp cutting turf. I saw him once for a few minutes when an extraordinary chance permitted him to visit us for a whole 15 minutes. Father looked gray and smelled of earth. His clothes were encrusted with brown clay, and huge chunks of it seemed to be glued to his shoes. He appeared unshaved, as rough and as rugged as the peasant who was now claiming his throne. Yet, my parents, in that fleeting moment of reunion, were overjoyed. To me they seemed much happier with each other than they had on those magical evenings when they often used to complain and grumble while transforming themselves little by little from ordinary parents into royalty.

The scene of the potatoes' acquisition continued as if it were a silent film. The peasant gave a faint smile to the black garment. With dirty fingers he grabbed the satin lapels, which did not react with the contempt I had expected from them. With another hand he reached for a large piece of burlap that hung from one of his jacket's pockets, quickly wrapped it around the crumpled tuxedo, and turned the whole suit into a miserable bundle. He tucked it under his arm and was gone. I couldn't help myself. Tears were rolling down my cheeks.

I should have known better. I had already listened to many frightening stories. More than once I had been cautioned about the way times were changing. I was also told that in spite of the troubling nature of events, I was to be informed of everything as if I were a young adult. It was dangerous to remain a child. I had to grow up quickly. I tried my best, but the mind of an eight-year-old boy had its limitations.

Perhaps it was the potato-man's passage through our home that finally made these things clear to me. It was the first time I fully understood that nothing was going to be the way it had been. When I reflect about it today, I realize that must have been the moment during which I started to say goodbye to Father.

Two years later, it was again a burlap sack that entered mine and Father's lives and severed them forever. My last memory of Father is the image of his hands, once perfectly manicured but now rough from labour, holding open a large patched-up sack full of sawdust so I could step into it and be smuggled on his strong and loving back out of the labour camp from which there was to be no escape for him. This was, indeed, our final farewell. But I did not cry. I was 10 years old, and I was an adult.

Inge Heiman Karo

*I*nge Heiman Karo was born in Essen, Germany, in 1926. Along with her parents and younger brother, she fled to the United States in December 1939. Many of her relatives were murdered in the Holocaust.

Growing up in Philadelphia, Inge attended high school and went on to hold various jobs, including stenographer, bookkeeper, and legal secretary. In 1982 she graduated from Beaver College (now Arcadia University) with a degree in psychology. She was a member of the Junior Hadassah organization and the Abington Town Watch, and she volunteered in such positions as an aide in the physical therapy department

Inge Heiman Karo at age 11 in 1937.

of Abington Memorial Hospital and a cook for the Cook for a Friend program.

In 1997 Inge wrote and published the book *Joseph and His Daughter: From 1890–1980*, based on her family's experiences before, during, and after the war. This book includes a play entitled *The Library*, which is based on her experience of having to turn in her library card during the Holocaust. Students at Muhlenberg College created a theatre show based on this play and other pieces from her book that was performed at schools and Holocaust conferences throughout Pennsylvania.

Now retired, Inge does volunteer work for the Holocaust Oral History Archive at Gratz College. She also speaks to student groups about the Holocaust. She and her husband have one son and two grandsons.

The Library

Inge Heiman Karo

Rachel walked into the library, sat down at her desk in the children's section, and admired the shiny new nameplate that told anyone who cared to know: Here sat Rachel Klein, Librarian. She got an almost sensual pleasure from the rows upon rows of books. Books which she had read held memories of hours pleasurably spent, while books still unread promised more such hours.

A little girl wearing her hair in two long brown braids approached the desk and shyly asked for a book. After Rachel helped her, she had a strange sensation of having lived through a moment like this before. Something tugged at her memory. A sense of unease, which she could not define, intruded on the happiness she felt.

It was not until her mid-morning break that Rachel remembered just where she had seen a little girl like that before. In her mind, she returned to the Berlin of the 1930s, during one of her many trips to the library. She visualized an austere room, with a counter at one end, presided over by a forbidding-looking woman. Only by the sign outside could one know that this was a library. There was no aimless browsing here. The books were all hidden away. You approached one of the librarians, requested the books you wanted, and if she thought they were proper for you to read, she brought the books from the back to be checked out.

Rachel saw herself, a shy little girl with long brown braids, hesitantly approaching the counter, clutching a list of book titles in her hand.

During the girl's earlier visits to the library it went as follows:

"Back already Rachel? Did you really finish all those books in just four days?"

"Yes, Miss Schmidt."

"I find that hard to believe. Tell me what the books were about."

Rachel, forgetting her shyness, did just that, but Miss Schmidt was not yet ready to concede defeat. A few visits later, she tried again.

"Rachel, these books that you requested are for Grade 8 students, and you are only in Grade 5. You will have to bring a note from your teacher certifying that you are capable of understanding this kind of material."

After a while, the librarian's attitude mellowed a little. Miss Schmidt might even venture a smile as she said, "Good afternoon, Rachel. Let me see your list."

"Thank you, Miss Schmidt."

"I am only giving you three of the novels you requested, Rachel, and am including some science books. You have a good mind, and you must develop it."

"Yes, Miss Schmidt."

One day, the little girl was curiously reluctant to go to the library. She looked into all the store windows, carefully jumped over all the cracks in the pavement three times, and spent an extraordinary amount of time wiping her feet outside the entrance to the library. Even though she stood in the longest line and let a stout lady with a shopping bag full of books get ahead of her, it finally became her turn. There she was, in front of Miss Schmidt.

"Let me have the books you are returning, please."

She silently handed over the books.

"You are holding up the line. Don't you want to take out any books today?"

The girl shifted her weight from one foot to the other, chewed on one of her braids, and tried hard not to blush.

"If you don't want any books, you will have to move on."

"Excuse me, but I would like to turn in my library card," she whispered.

"Are your parents moving, Rachel?"

"No, Miss Schmidt."

"Then why do you want to turn in your card? You know how important it is for a student to read."

"Yes, Miss Schmidt, but I *have* to turn in my card."

"I never heard of such a thing. You do not have to turn in your card. I do not know why you waste my time with such foolishness."

Miss Schmidt turned to take care of the next person in line. Gathering all her courage, Rachel managed to blurt out loud and clear: "But

Miss Schmidt, they've passed a law—all Jews have to turn in their library cards—and I am Jewish."

Rachel then turned around and walked as fast as she could. All she wanted at that moment was to get out of the building before she burst into tears.

The Emigration of the Jews Out of Germany

Inge Heiman Karo
(*Written at age 11*)

For various reasons, the Jews are emigrating from Germany. They are all going, one after the other, unceasingly, every day, hundreds and thousands of them. Behind them stands sorrow. Unseen, it walks behind many of them, follows their every step into the new land, and never leaves their side.

And yet, we still have a faithful friend, a father who cares for us and will always care for us, our G-d! We will trust in Him and with His help will even be able to create a new life for ourselves in a strange country among strangers.

Our fate is like a huge hurricane; it blows us some place, lets us rest, and then, just when we want to put down roots, it pulls us out and drives us into another unknown part of the world. It was always so and will probably never change.

Our life is a gigantic thick book, in which fate always enters new words and rules that we have to learn. Theoretical knowledge is not enough; we have to show what we can do at once in a practical way. Fate will show no mercy to whoever does not keep up and lags behind and leave him stranded by the wayside. In this way, we all step into a different country. Not all of us into the same one. No, fate directs us into all of the countries of the world. It does not care where to.

Words that we did not know a few years ago have taken form and come to life, and they pursue us even in our dreams. Wherever one goes, one hears only: "Will you be called for a hearing soon?"; "My G-d, I have number 26,000"; "Will your child be sent away?"; "What are your American relatives doing?"; or "Do you have an affidavit?" Words such as sponsorship, children's transport, U.S.A., municipal office, Aid Society, passport, steamship ticket, export duty, suitcase, furniture, clothing, climate, etc. are the order of the day. Uruguay, Paraguay, Brazil, Dominican Republic, Cincinnati, Cleveland, Ohio, and many more have become familiar to us. Daily, this one and that one receives letters bearing all kinds of foreign stamps.

These are the inescapable consequences of emigration, and we have to bear them. I believe that we are gradually getting used to them.

George Scott

George Scott (originally Spiegel) was born in Hungary in 1930. His father died when he was only a year old, and his maternal grandparents raised him. After completing Grade 4, his grandparents placed him in the Budapest Jewish Orphanage, where there were about 120 boys, aged six to 18. He tried to run away from the orphanage when the Nazis invaded Hungary in 1944, but he was caught on the border of Slovakia and taken to Sarvar, a large concentration camp. In August of that year, he was transported to the Auschwitz-Birkenau camp in Poland. Although he survived the Holocaust, he lost five of his mother's six sisters and all of their children and husbands, as well as his grandparents.

The Canadian Jewish Congress, along with other agencies, assisted in bringing over 1,000 child survivors, including George, to Canada. George was 18 when his ship arrived in the summer of 1948. He stayed in Nova Scotia with several families who took him in, and he later moved to Toronto, Ontario. Having changed his last name to avoid prejudice during the Holocaust, he ended up settling on Scott. In 1954 he married Ruth Levstein, and they had three children.

For the last 30 years, George has enjoyed speaking to schoolchildren about the Holocaust. Ruth died suddenly in 1978. George is now in his third marriage with Harriet Brav-Baum, an artist, and also has two stepchildren.

Auschwitz 1944

George Scott

Not close enough for warmth
The lusty flames
In the crematorium's busy chimney
Rise and fall

Indifferent lies
The barbed wire's shadow
On the frozen ground

Very thin is the line
Between being and not being

The night is emptied

Rosh Hashanah 1944 in Birkenau

George Scott

(Read at a 2006 ceremony by the Canadian Society for Yad Vashem Holocaust Wall of Remembrance at Earl Bales Park in Toronto, Ontario)

Forever will you live, in our dreams and in our prayers,
in our imagination, and in the whisperings of hope!

Words, words, that is all we have
To bring out, to drag out, to talk about the dread
Words that erupt, feelings so basic they cannot wait to be pressed
Into words
Such is our deep and anguished cry for our Massacred Innocents

It is one week to the day many years ago
When the first "Selection" *inside* the Gypsy Camp took place
This diabolic act marked Birkenau's *Rosh Hashanah,*[1] 1944

Dislodged multitudes transfixed
Six o'clock *"Appell"*[2] in Birkenau's Gypsy Camp
Naked bodies, five deep in a row, stood waiting, hoping for reprieve
Breath suspended as if held by vacuum
Tall, chest out, the light faded from sunken eyes

---

[1] Jewish New Year.

[2] *Appell* is German for "roll call," when camp inmates were forced to stand at attention while they were counted.

To the back of us, on the other side of the tracks
Squat and rectangular behind a wooden fence, only the top half seen
The gas chamber's red brick chimney's insatiable flames
Between barbed wire, electrified geometric enclosures
Look-outs, "We see you" Guard Towers, built into the fence
The "Zwillings" or "Twins" on one side of us
On the other side, bald, shaven women, striped like us
Mothers, daughters, starved, faded, beyond reach
Rats the size of small dogs, most active at night

In one of our barracks, on the "odd number" side
One-hundred concrete holes, back to back, to sit on
Three circular wash basins, metal rings, eighteen inches off the ground
When stood on, chlorinated cold water poured
Spray that brought me back to life
The only place in here for us to drink
Entering, on the left, on wooden shelves, no shortage of soap
Stacked unwrapped, RIF stamped on them, in ample supply
They were pasty grey like death
No way, not "Pure Jewish Fat" we are now assured

Like echoes in an infernal cathedral
The sound of Mengele's[3] boots approach
They halt, closer they draw
The unstoppable beat of our numbed lives
Quickens in our chests
The dividing encounter
Eyes seeking eyes, light seeking light
Piercing steel grey eyes, a prodding look,
A tired face, a pair of steel grey eyes

---

[3]Josef Mengele was a German SS officer and a physician at the Auschwitz-Birkenau concentration camp. He supervised the selection of arriving transports of prisoners, determining who was to be killed and who was to become a forced labourer. He also performed medical experiments on camp inmates.

I scooped up my clothes and scurried
To the group where he motioned me to go
A fresh lungful of Silesian air housed my panic
Another shameful, ignoble day crowded into eternity

Panic and horror, pictures cannot describe
The sparks of G-d within us all
Prompt me to remember our voiceless outrage

I did not look a while, although I knew
Toronto's Yad Vashem stands here
Not merely a monument and warning
But the live hopes, our own parts
Innocent souls still demanding justice

Martyred beloved ones
Holy, Holy, Inextinguishable Lights
We shall remember you always
You continue showing us the way

As long as thought leads to thought
As long as spring follows spring
We shall remember you!
You are alive in our dreams and in our prayers
In the resolve of our better judgement
In flights of our imagination
In the sparkle of our children's eyes
In the whispering of hope

Rabbi Jacob G. Wiener

Courtesy of United States Holocaust Memorial Museum, Photograph by Arnold Kramer.

Rabbi Jacob G. Wiener, PhD, was born in Bremen, Germany, in 1917 and was the eldest of four children. Following high school, he began rabbinical studies in Frankfurt am Main and later attended the Jewish Teachers' Seminary in Würzburg, Bavaria. During *Kristallnacht* (Night of Broken Glass) in 1938, the Nazis arrested him and held him in jail for eight days. He returned home to discover that his mother had been murdered in their house and one of his brothers had been sent to the Sachsenhausen concentration camp. This led him to travel to Hamburg, where he found his father and a younger brother.

Although antisemitism was on the rise, in 1939 Jacob negotiated with the *Gestapo* (German Secret State Police) and set up a school for Jewish children. In May of that year he and his family managed to leave Germany and immigrated to Canada via Great Britain.

Jacob later moved to the United States, where he earned rabbinical ordination and worked at the Hebrew National Orphan Home in Yonkers, New York. He also obtained a PhD in Human Development and Social Relations and became a social worker for the New York City Human Resources Administration/Department of Social Services.

In 1948 Jacob married Trudel Farntrog, also a survivor. He now resides in Silver Spring, Maryland, and he is working on his autobiography and volunteers at the United States Holocaust Memorial Museum.

A Secret Trip to Berlin

Rabbi Jacob G. Wiener

When the Nazis came to power in Germany in 1933 they set up new laws under which anyone could be accused of being a "criminal" and sent to a concentration camp. To the rest of the world, being a "criminal" meant that someone had committed a crime, but to the Germans in the late 1930s it usually meant that someone was a Jew.

I was among the students taken into custody in Würzburg, Bavaria, in Germany, where I attended the Jewish Teachers' Seminary. After eight days of imprisonment, seven of us were set free, possibly because I was stateless, not a German citizen. I was ordered to return to my native city of Bremen and report to the local *Gestapo* (German Secret State Police).

I travelled all night in a train crowded with Nazis in their khaki brown uniforms, and I made myself as inconspicuous as possible by walking around from car to car. I was afraid to sit down and fall asleep lest they would notice that I was Jewish and beat or even kill me.

In 1939 the Nazis were still willing to let the Jews leave the country, but many other countries would not let us enter. Day after day I went to consulates of various nations to try to obtain visas, or even transit permits, for my family and others. The responses were always very disappointing. Many foreign officials demanded large sums of money, while failing to make a decision. Central and South American officials often gave us illegal visas, but usually Jews were refused entry at the border and turned back.

For the Jewish people, the world grew smaller and more restricted with every day. No longer were we permitted to be businessmen, doctors, lawyers, or landlords. Schools were limited, congregations supervised, precious metals and jewellery confiscated, and citizenships revoked.

One dark winter evening in January 1939, I was visiting the Gruenbergs, who lived near my parents. It was late, around 10:20 PM, when the bell rang and I received a telegram. On it were just three words: "Come here immediately." It was from Berlin, and it was signed by an old friend from the Agudath Israel youth group, to which we had both once belonged. I assumed I would meet him at the Agudath office in Berlin. Mr. and Mrs. Gruenberg urged me to take the early morning train.

The train arrived in Berlin a little after eight o'clock. I had not slept all night, except for some short naps. There were large signs in the city that read: "Jews forbidden to walk here under penalty of heavy fines." By acting natural and walking boldly, I avoided detection and followed my directions to the Agudath office.

"We knew you would not desert us," said the greeter.

"Why did you send for me?" I inquired.

"We must help as many Jews as possible to leave Germany," replied the Agudath representative. "We have arranged with the Baltic states—Lithuania, Estonia, and Latvia—to permit us to issue papers that will assign any Jew to *hachshara* (preparation for emigration to Israel) in those countries. The Nazis have given us until late tomorrow to submit the names of those for whom we can show letters of acceptance. They are only interested in making Germany *Judenrein* (clean of Jews) as soon as possible. Many of our members are still in concentration camps, so we need help to fill out as many forms as we can and get people freed."

I felt fortunate to be able to participate. In this way, we obtained the release of more than 200 Jews! While many of them were killed when the Nazis attacked the Baltic countries two years later, many others managed to escape and build new lives in Israel, the United States, and other countries.

Negotiating with the Gestapo

Rabbi Jacob G. Wiener

After *Kristallnacht*,[1] I returned to my hometown of Bremen in north-west Germany. A number of Jews had been released from concentration camps, and I had been set free after eight days of imprisonment. I was then in Würzburg, Bavaria, where I had gone to school. The Nazis called these arrests "protective custody." From whom did we need protection?

The few Jews who had come back to Bremen formed a small congregation to help with emigration and to establish a somewhat normal life again. The *Gestapo* (German Secret State Police) demanded information about the activities of our small community, because they wanted to increase their control over the Jews. They ordered us to send a contact person two or three times weekly to report on the status of our affairs. Being one of the younger ones—I was about 20 then—I was appointed to be that liaison.

I remember my first visit to the *Gestapo* office very clearly. The building was on the street called *Am Wall* ("at the rampart"). It was built along the medieval trench that surrounded the city. The building itself did not have a house number. There was a small bell at the top on the right-side main entrance door.

Cautiously, I pushed the button. The gate opened silently. Inside, I entered a large lobby with a big stairway leading up. In front of it was a big poster with a picture of a man holding two fingers upon his lips. Underneath was a German word written prominently: *Schweigen* (silence).

---

[1] *Kristallnacht,* also known as The Night of Broken Glass, took place on November 9 and 10, 1938. Nazis and members of the Hitler Youth violently attacked Jews and their homes, synagogues, and businesses throughout Germany and Austria.

A voice from upstairs called out, "*Komm rauf, Jude, zimmer 205* (Come up, Jew, to room 205)." That was the office of Mr. Parchmann, the Jew-hater in charge of Jewish Affairs. The office was cluttered with papers and chairs. He sat behind the desk, his feet on top of the table, smiling.

"*Setz dich, Jude* (Sit down, Jew)," he said, pointing to a chair and speaking in a degrading tone. It seemed to me that he enjoyed mocking me. Then he took out an envelope and emptied its contents. "Here are some of the items we found in your house."

Of course, I understood the irony behind his comments. Those were the items the murdering Nazis had pocketed after they killed my mother. The items were of no value to them. Among them was a small passport photo my mother had taken just a few days before, when she still had hope that we could all get out of Germany alive.

I reported to Mr. Parchmann on a regular basis. He would always ask me in a devilish manner how the Jews were getting along. I asked to obtain release of those Bremen Jews still in concentration camps, to hasten the process by which they could emigrate. He asked me how many Jews had already left or were about to leave Germany.

I have no idea why he forced the Jewish community to be in contact with him, other than to exhibit his power over Jewish life and death.

I usually stayed at Mr. Parchmann's office for only 10 or 15 minutes. I was sometimes able to obtain the release of a few Bremen Jews, especially youngsters. Besides this, my agenda was to ask his permission to set up a school for Jewish children. After *Kristallnacht,* all Jewish schools were closed and Jewish children were forbidden to be taught at all.

"Now that your government does not allow Jewish children to go to school anymore, our congregation plans to set up its own school for children," I told Mr. Parchmann one day. "We want to prepare the children for when they leave Germany."

Mr. Parchmann sneered at me. "You must be daydreaming," he snickered. "Do you think we will ever let you start a school where you will spread horror stories about our great nation and then tell them to the world? We are a law-abiding nation. We act according to the law, which has the stamp of our leader."

"We also act according to the law, our G-d given law, the *Torah* (Jewish Bible). That's what we will teach."

Mr. Parchmann enjoyed baiting me and revelled in the power he possessed. Meanwhile, the German population lived in fear of the threats, terror, and intimidation that characterized Nazi policies.

I continued to visit the *Gestapo* at the house on *Am Wall*. One sunny February morning, I entered the fortress-like building again, with pleas for the release of three youngsters from concentration camps. I prayed that G-d would soften the heart of Mr. Parchmann. Even Pharaoh's heart had eventually yielded to let the Jewish people leave Egypt.

I attempted to present myself in a self-assured but somewhat reserved way. I had learned that the threatening attitude of Mr. Parchmann was exacerbated if he viewed any person exhibiting self-pity or appealing to his emotions.

"Today I have had enough of you, Jewish swine!" shouted Mr. Parchmann. "You want those three pigs out? Out they shall go. I want all of you Jews out. It sickens the *Führer* (Leader, in this case Adolf Hitler) to have you Jews infect our pure nation."

"Fine," I retorted. "Our school will help us get out."

"You good-for-nothing . . . " he began.

I interrupted. "Would you want to feed someone unproductive? We will be preparing our children in order to be able to leave."

"Do what you want," Mr. Parchmann burst out. "Use the old rundown dilapidated gym building near the river at Dyke Street. Not in the mornings when German youth are taught—that would be race-mixing—but in the afternoon, after German school ends."

"We will use it," I said. "Sign us up for it."

"It's yours," he replied, "but see to it that you all scram out of Germany soon."

Suddenly, we had a schoolhouse to start educating our children again. This school was in existence until 1941, when the rest of the Jews still living in Bremen were transported to Minsk in Poland (Minsk is now part of Belarus). There, the Nazis killed and inflicted suffering upon the lot of the many millions subjected to their goal of making the world *Judenrein* (clean of Jews).

Fred M. B. Amram

Fred M. B. Amram is a retired professor of Communication and Creativity at the University of Minnesota in Minneapolis, United States. He spent his early years in Hanover, Germany, where he experienced *Kristallnacht* (Night of Broken Glass) and the aftermath. For a child survivor, his memories of events are surprisingly clear. The loss of uncles, aunts, a grandmother, and many other relatives motivated him to prepare a detailed family tree. The loss of his only cousin, who was murdered in Auschwitz-Birkenau at the age of three-and-a-half, continues to haunt him.

Although Fred found the transition to a new language and culture upon arrival in the U.S. difficult, he knew the alternative was much worse. Consequently, he and his parents discovered that this new continent was truly a land of opportunity where one could build a new life and become more than just a "survivor." He has relayed his Holocaust stories to his children and grandchildren, who share his commitment to "Never Again." Toward this end, he and his entire family are working to help put an end to genocide everywhere.

Fred M. B. Amram, formerly known as Manfred, lived at 25 Goethe Strasse in Hanover, Germany. Down the street was a small park called Goethe Platz, where Fred posed for this photograph a few weeks before *Kristallnacht* in 1938.

Fred is the author of several books and numerous book chapters, articles, and stories. He is currently working on a memoir and a novel and continues to improve his use of the English language thanks to the help of Ellen Weingart, who edits all his prose.

Kristallnacht:
The Night of Broken Glass

Fred M. B. Amram

I remember November 8, 1938 quite clearly. Any Jew living in Nazi Germany on that day will have clear memories of the Night of Broken Glass (*Kristallnacht*).

Even before *Kristallnacht,* Jewish men disappeared. Later, the *Gestapo* (German Secret State Police) came for the families. But in the early days they only came for the men. The soldiers would knock on doors and then take the Jewish men away. No one knew for sure in those early days where they were being taken, although there were stories. I think the kosher butcher disappeared first. Was his name *Mandelbaum?* A boy remembers names like *Herr Mandelbaum*, Mr. Almond Tree. Ironic that this man, whose apron was usually covered with blood, would be the first to go.

Whenever the tall uniformed men with their shiny boots and gruff tones knocked on *our* door, Papa wasn't home. He was "out on business." Because I was a youngster, no one trusted me with real information.

The truth, learned much later, was that he had "ways of knowing" and would disappear "downstairs." We lived on the fourth floor of an apartment building. I never found out how far "downstairs" he went to the apartment of some Christians where he was hidden under a bed. I can't shake the image of this tiny man fitting comfortably under a bed. I was never told the names of the righteous Christians who hid my Papa. Even when I questioned him directly, in his later and more comfortable years, he wouldn't reveal their names, their apartment number, or even the floor on which they lived. They were simply "downstairs."

Decades later, on a continent far away, Papa still protected these good people—not wanting to give them away.

And then came *Kristallnacht*. On November 9 and 10, Jewish shop windows were smashed. Some have described how men and women were humiliated and beaten on the streets. Others described how Jews were kicked while forced to clean streets with toothbrushes. However, for me, that night began in the evening of November 8, a Tuesday, as we stood on our balcony terrified by the sky's fiery glow. All of the synagogues in my city of Hanover were looted and burned. Watching the fires, we knew that *Kristallnacht* was not a good night to be out. Yet, Papa disappeared again. I was told that he was going out "on business," just as he did whenever the *Gestapo* came knocking.

Papa missed supper. When he finally came home, he reported that he had not been with the Christians "downstairs." He was carrying a huge bundle covered with large rags and blankets. Was it a body? When the wrappings were removed, I could see that they had sheltered a *Torah* (Jewish Bible) almost as big as my Papa. He had rescued the holy scroll from our local synagogue while the building was aflame.

Mutti, my mother, scolded him. "Why take the risk? One should take precautions. And why bring a *Torah* into an apartment where even radios are forbidden?"

Radios! I remember when the *Gestapo* came to all Jewish homes hunting for radios. The men in shiny, black boots searched every room. Radios were *verboten*. Contact with the outside world was forbidden.

I remember feeling like the man of the house while Papa was "away on business." I was, in fact, a frightened little boy. I don't know if I cried or not. But I did stand in front of my mother, not behind.

"Why bring a *Torah* into an apartment where even radios are forbidden?" Mutti asked again. A meaningful question! A full-sized *Torah* on the fourth floor of an apartment building would put all of the residents at risk. "Hero" was not a word that entered the evening's conversation. I didn't hear talk of "hero" until years later, when we were safely settled in the United States.

Papa had no plan for the *Torah*. The rabbi would know what to do. Wait until nightfall. Of course, no one told the young child, a bright five-year-old, where one would find a rabbi on *Kristallnacht*.

When I awoke the next morning, the *Torah* was gone. Apparently, the rabbi did know what to do. Papa was quite pleased with himself. I was only told that, again, Papa had been "out on business."

The Brownshirts Are Coming

Fred M. B. Amram

On Saturday evenings my family sometimes walked over to the neighbourhood cinema for a double feature and a few hours of relief
from the summer heat. Of course, our railroad tenement had no air con-
ditioning back in the summer of 1941. Windows at both ends of our flat
provided just a little circulation, thanks to a fan at the living room end.

The front door opened into the kitchen. We had a ritual for entering
that door into the dark apartment, and this Saturday night was no different. Mutti, my mother, unlocked the door with her key and stepped back.
Papa took off his right shoe and held it as if he would hammer a nail with
the heel. I hid behind Papa. We all took a deep breath in anticipation.

Then, Papa opened the door, reached around for the light switch, and
bam, wham, bam! He was pounding roaches. Thousands scurried for shelter in the baseboards and cupboards. They were on the walls, floor, and
ceiling—everywhere. Roaches fled from the table and the chairs. Skwoosh,
skwoosh, skwoosh was the sound as one after another was crushed by
Papa's heavy rubber heel. Sometimes Papa accidentally stepped on one or
two of the disoriented, frightened beasts with his stockinged foot. Brown,
stiff-backed, multi-legged, monster-faced roaches, who had been in total
control of the darkened apartment, were now trying to escape my father's
wrath. Fat bugs, some over two inches long, seemed to fly short distances,
or were they hopping? I was only seven years old, and I held onto Papa's
belt and hid my face in his back.

When no more live roaches could be seen, Papa cleaned up. On a
good night, Papa would kill more than 30. When each living roach had
found shelter from Papa's shoe and each dead roach had been dropped
into the garbage can, Mutti entered the room as if nothing had happened.

My heart raced. I was terrified. Surely these roaches were reproducing faster than Papa could kill them.

The cockroach chase filled my mind, even replacing the memories of the movie. Before undressing, I checked under my sheets and inside my pillowcase. I knew that once the lights were turned off for the night, our creepy tenants would reappear. I feared I would dream about the roaches—and I did. Was I dreaming that they walked on me during the night, or did they really?

In the morning, I checked my body and inside my pyjamas. I turned my slippers upside down and banged them individually and carefully against the bed frame. Too often, a roach fell to the floor and scampered away.

Concern about roach droppings became an obsession and prompted careful daily washing and inspection of my body. I welcomed my weekly bath, and I wiped all dishes before I allowed them to cradle my food.

There were cockroaches everywhere. I don't mean just everywhere in the room. I mean all over New York City. We had been living in the United States for about 16 months, escaping from Germany via Holland and Belgium, a step ahead of the Nazis. The next-door commercial bakery, where Papa worked, provided food for much of the big city and for the roaches. Poison around our baseboards did not have much of an impact. There were way too many millions of them to control. Surely, I imagined, there were at least 1,000 roaches for each of New York's seven million residents.

My dreams became ever more frightening, and as the weeks passed, the roaches seemed to grow larger. And they felt heavier when they walked on me. In one dream, they had hot feet and burned my skin as they wandered aimlessly on my chest and arms. When I awoke, Mutti was holding me. I had been screaming and had ripped the buttons from my pyjama top.

My friend Anna lived at the other end of our block in an apartment unit slightly more upscale than ours. Hers was a larger apartment with a separate entrance to her father's medical office. Anna was a special friend, almost a girlfriend, and I visited her apartment often. Anna's family had escaped Nazi Germany quite early and had learned to speak English while living in Manchester, England. They moved to New York when the European war seemed imminent. The family spoke German and a British version of English at home. They were able to help me develop command of the new language.

One evening, when Anna's mom had invited me to dinner, I regaled the family with one of my dreams. Mrs. Wertheimer's response—horror and disgust—encouraged me to elaborate in great detail, even identifying the number of legs each roach had and the fuzz on the legs.

Doctor Wertheimer could outdo me. He told us about another Jew who wrote stories in German. "Franz Kafka," he said, "wrote a story called *Die Verwandlung* (*The Metamorphosis*), in which a young man wakes up one morning to discover that he has been turned into a monstrous bug, perhaps a cockroach." He then proceeded to tell Kafka's story, simplified so that the two youngsters in his audience could understand.

In dismay, Mrs. Wertheimer left the room. Anna cried a little, and I tried hard not to. I skipped dessert.

That evening, as I lay in bed, I thought about Dr. Wertheimer's story. Would I dream about being turned into a roach? What if I really were? What if my family became disgusted by me and disowned me? Could I live with the Wertheimers? Could Dr. Wertheimer cure me?

I was *not* changed into a giant cockroach. I remained a small boy. However, giant roaches came to my bed. Giant roaches wearing shiny boots and brown uniforms. Hundreds marched in parade formation past my house. They wore pistols and carried large clubs like the SS officers I had seen in Germany. They marched four abreast, and as they passed my house, the last row peeled off and walked swiftly toward our front door. I heard the outside door slam and the boots in the hallway. They stopped at our apartment door, and one of them knocked. No, he pounded. Bang, bang, bang! Pause. Bang, bang, bang! Loud, determined knocks. Then, I heard a third series of three bangs. Another pause. The apartment door burst open and crashed to the floor. The four roach Brownshirts were in the room. Their armbands seemed familiar, but I couldn't quite place where I had seen them before.

"*Aufstehen*! (Stand up!)," commanded one of the soldiers. The Brownshirts were larger than Papa and Mutti. The shiny boots on their many legs confused and frightened me. In one motion, the lead soldier tore the blanket from my bed. Four large roaches and my bed were now squeezed into this tiny room. "*Aufstehen!*" they shouted, louder than before. Where should I stand? Sitting on the edge of the bed, I moved my bare feet to the floor. It now occurred to me that Papa and Mutti had not come to the rescue. Where were they? Still sleeping?

I looked down. Usually, when I stepped out of bed, I was careful not to crush a roach with my bare foot. Now, out of respect—no, out of fear of the roach soldiers—I certainly didn't want to crush a bug of any kind. I pictured the small roaches that dominated our tenement. Were they now all larger than me? But there was no time for speculation. The four soldier roaches moved apart, making a narrow path for me to walk out of the room. They marched me out of the cramped bedroom into the kitchen, past the broken front door, and into the dark hallway. "*Raus. Raus aus dem haus* (Out of the house)," they ordered.

They guided me outdoors onto a waiting truck. I climbed up and they locked the doors behind me. I stood in total darkness. Something touched me and I let out a huge scream. Scream after uncontrollable scream. I couldn't stop myself. Anna's voice reassured me: "I'm here." But I couldn't stop screaming. "*Ich bin hier, Freddy. Ich bin dein freund, Anna* (I'm here. I'm your friend, Anna)," she kept saying. She touched me again and we both allowed ourselves to cry.

After a short time, Anna began to report her thoughts. She noted that when the truck door was opened to let me in, she could see that there were no other humans with us. She had also observed that the roaches had boots on all their feet. They had no hands, only feet. That's why they pushed with their bodies. That was all we knew, other than the fact that we were locked in a large black box.

We sat in silent thought. Suddenly, I remembered that the roaches at our house scrambled about feeding in the dark. Were there roaches with us? Anna assured me that she had not seen any when I climbed aboard.

"No small ones and no giants?" I asked.

"None."

Anna had been first into the box. Apparently, the parade had passed Anna's building before it reached my end of the block. Four soldiers had peeled off the back of the parade to arrest her. I was second.

"Will there be others?" Anna wondered. Almost immediately, the truck door popped open, and another girl was pushed into the truck. Anna rushed toward the door and started talking very loudly so that the girl would know that we were in the truck, too. No more fearful screaming. The girl quickly crawled to Anna, who was ready with a hug. The frightened little girl cried for quite some time. Then, between sobs, she announced, "My name is Lisa, and I'm six years old." Her heavy accent hinted that she, like Anna and me, was not American.

After Anna calmed Lisa, we learned that she was Jewish and from Austria. Her father had been hauled away after the 1938 *Anschluss* (Nazi Germany's annexation of Austria). Lisa and her mother hid in the woods and secretly made their way across the Alps into Switzerland. She had arrived in the U.S. only a few weeks ago.

I blurted out the obvious: "They're rounding up the children." Something made me uncomfortable. The phrase "rounding up" troubled me. I had heard my parents use that phrase. Dr. Wertheimer used it. Why were the words so disturbing?

Lisa calmed down, and we waited. The three of us agreed that Anna would again talk to any newcomer, while Lisa would use the opportunity of light to study the inside of the truck. I was to see what I could learn from the outside world.

It was a long wait for the next child. Pincus was yelling at the roaches as they kicked and prodded him. He was fighting back. Several especially large roaches seemed to pick him up by biting his clothes. Others crawled beneath him, and a few butted him with their heads. Without hands, the roaches couldn't place Pincus into the truck. The roaches created a ladder by standing on one another and were able to eventually push and kick their victim into our box. Pincus' resistance gave each of us ample time to accomplish our tasks.

Anna introduced herself, Lisa, and me. Pincus told us that he was a 12-year-old Polish Jew who, with his older brother, had escaped from a concentration camp. An uncle had arranged his trip to the U.S., and he had just arrived a week earlier. That explained his bitter fight with the . . . Who were the roach soldiers?

"They're rounding up Jewish refugee children!" suggested Anna.

There was that phrase again: they were "rounding up." The image was horrible. Millions of giant roaches were rounding up Jewish children. Who were these monsters?

None of us knew what time it was, although we could tell it was still night. Pincus suggested that we set aside one corner of the truck box as a toilet. He had some experience with boxcars. We looked to Pincus for leadership. Anna took on the role of mother, providing comfort.

Yitzhak, Rachel, Sarah, Manny—we were soon 13 children clustered in this dark box. Not yet crowded. Pincus warned, "When we are too many for our space we will start fighting for territory. Then they will either move us in this truck or they will kill us all right here. Perhaps this truck is a mobile gas chamber."

"Will the roaches scatter when daylight appears?" I asked naively. I remembered how they scattered when Papa turned on the apartment lights. The very first rays of light were noticeable when the most recent child had been pushed into the truck.

Of course, no one could guess the answer.

"Who are these monsters?" asked Anna. "What are those marks on their armbands? They look so familiar."

"Don't you children know anything?" We couldn't see his face, but we could hear Pincus' frustration. "Those are the Brownshirts."

"What are Brownshirts?" asked Lisa.

"The Brownshirts came to get my father when we still lived in Germany," Sarah announced. "Those marks on their armbands are swastikas."

The picture was becoming clear for me. I had heard Mutti and Papa talking about the "rounding up of Jews" on *Kristallnacht*[1] in 1938.

Anna, realizing that we had to take action, asked, "Pincus, what shall we do?"

"If Freddie's thought about light is correct, then we will have to wait all day for them to come back at night," said Pincus.

Rachel, who was beginning to get the gist of the conversation about light, announced that she always slept with a flashlight and that it was still in the pocket of her pyjamas. With that, she provided a strong beam of light that reached the top of the truck.

"It is almost light outside," said Pincus. "If the roaches bring one more child before full daybreak, we can use the flashlight to frighten them and fight until the sun rescues us. If G-d helps us with the sun, we may be saved. I cannot see you. However, I'm guessing that I am the oldest and perhaps the strongest. If you like, I'll use the flashlight to frighten them, and all of you will have to fight for your lives. Beware. They bite."

---

[1] *Kristallnacht,* also known as The Night of Broken Glass, took place on November 9 and 10, 1938. Nazis and members of the Hitler Youth violently attacked Jews and their homes, synagogues, and businesses throughout Germany and Austria.

"What if they don't come before daybreak?" asked Anna.

Just as she finished her sentence, the door opened. Rachel handed the flashlight to Pincus, who was out like an angry tiger. We followed our leader, a gust of children leaping on the roaches. Clearly, we outnumbered the Brownshirts guarding the truck, although they were much larger than us.

I awoke to find myself pummeling my Papa, who was holding me on the bed with all his strength. I was wild! Fists swinging and legs kicking! Papa was shouting for me to calm down.

That evening, Mutti took me to meet with Dr. Wertheimer. She and the doctor spoke in German. He explained that dreams help us to cope with terror—real and imagined. The Holocaust has done that to many children and to millions of adults. Dr. Wertheimer told my mother that Anna also has nightmares. "As do I," he added. Mutti admitted that she also has bad dreams quite regularly.

"Those who have died and will die in the Holocaust pay the ultimate price," said Dr. Wertheimer in his most reassuring voice. "We survivors also pay a price—a price we are willing to pay to have our children alive and not in the gas chambers."

"But the cockroaches in our apartment are real," I said. Or was I asking a question?

"They are," assured Dr. Wertheimer. "They disappear when you turn on the light. I hope that you and Anna will enjoy the security of light and that one day you will no longer have to fear the darkness."

When we arrived at our home, Papa promised to buy me a flashlight of my own.

Anne Kind

Anne Kind (née Anneliese Rosenberg) was born in Berlin, Germany, in 1922. In 1934, a year after Hitler came into power in Germany, she fled to England with her parents. She went on to study nursing and later married a doctor. Over the years, she has also worked as an administrator for the Family Planning Association and as an administrator and fundraiser for the LOROS Leicestershire and Rutland Hospice. Her work earned her a place on the Order of the British Empire Queen's New Year's Honours List for services to the community of Leicestershire in 1990.

Anne is also an accomplished creative writer. Her poetry has appeared in such literary journals as *Stand Magazine, New Hope International, Staple, Iota,* and *North Words,* as well as in poetry anthologies, including *The Long Pale Corridor: Contemporary Poems of Bereavement* (BloodAxe Books Ltd., 1996) and *Beyond Lament: Poets of the World Bearing Witness to the Holocaust* (Northwestern University Press, 1998). In 1994 Volcano Press Ltd. published a biography she wrote on Leicestershire naturalist Jack Otter titled *Come and See This, Folks.*

Now widowed and residing in Leicester, Anne has two children, seven grandchildren, and four great-grandchildren.

Great-Aunt Mathilde

Anne Kind

I.

Was my great-aunt Mathilde
stoned to death in Berlin?
Was she killed
or did she die a natural death?

Gentle, dainty
darling of my childhood.
Fairytales, Anderson and Grimm,
did the horror come true for you?

We begged you to stay here
where it was safe,
but no, you would go back to Berlin
and your old age pension.
Didn't want to bother us,
left us full of guilt.

You with your white hair
piled high like a castle,
black silk dress,
white lace jabot,
high button boots,
smiling eyes,
darling of my childhood.

II.

Mathilde, I buried you today,
forty years late.
The letter told me
what they did to you.

"We regret
less than ten percent
came back from that camp."

Grosstante,
you were aged eighty-two,
you nursed me
through childhood days.

They dragged you into trains,
bundled you
with hundreds, thousands
into one category:
Jew.

III.

Mathilde
was killed in a camp,
first a prisoner at Terezin
and then sent to a death camp near Minsk.

Today I heard
her Viennese lilt,
asking for her pension
a day early
to save her weary feet.
I had to speak to the stranger,
knew our paths would meet.

ANNE KIND   **53**

"Please help me across the street.
I can no longer see so well, nor hear.
Come and visit me,
don't say you will
just to be polite."

I took her thin arm,
so well remembered,
held up my hand
to stop the traffic,
like Moses, parting the water.

IV.

Are you already forgotten
with your black-buttoned boots
on tiny feet?

Always dressed in black,
neck covered by white lace,
every bit of you covered,
except your lovely face.
Eyes half-closed
when you read us a story.

Years later,
my cousin's son said,
"Great-aunt who?"

Role Reversal

Anne Kind

Gisela,
you were a leader in the Hitler Youth.
You didn't see much wrong with him,
were told to hate, and meekly you obeyed.

But that was forty years ago.
You, dear, and I were children then.
Come, let us talk, you said.

Sit over here, *gemutlicher, nicht wahr?*
It's cosy in that corner, let's begin.
At that point, I recalled the poisoned showers.
You'd never heard of them.

Why did you leave the Fatherland, you asked.
Insensitive, I thought, shan't drop my mask.
The situation is grotesque;
if any of my kinsfolk saw me here,
they'd feel betrayed,
although you appear sincere.

Poor Gisela,
you wanted a response from me.
I cannot even hate you, dear.

Agi Geva

Courtesy of United States Holocaust Memorial Museum, Photograph by Arnold Kramer.

Agi Geva was born in Hungary in 1930. She was deported to the Auschwitz-Birkenau concentration camp in Poland in 1944 with her mother and sister. They all managed to survive and returned to Hungary after the liberation. Five years later, Agi immigrated to Israel, where she worked as an insurance broker.

Following a move to the United States in 2002, Agi began volunteering for the United States Holocaust Memorial Museum in Washington, D.C. Today she speaks throughout the U.S. about her Holocaust experiences, under the auspices of the museum's Speakers Bureau. She resides with her daughter's family in Rockville, Maryland. Her son and his family live in Tel Aviv, Israel.

Opera in Auschwitz

Agi Geva

One memorable Sunday afternoon in the Auschwitz concentration camp, I heard arias from *La Bohème, Tosca, Madame Butterfly,* and many more. Lili, a woman from my hometown of Miskolc, Hungary, sang them. How precious that music was to me. With each note that she sang, my spirits soared higher and higher over the gates of hell, lifted by the sheer beauty of the music and the sweetness of her voice.

Lili first sang to us on a particularly dismal day when everyone's hope seemed to have run out. We were all sitting outside, numb with despair, when she stood up and started to sing a beautiful aria. At first, her voice wavered from lack of use, but as she continued to sing, it became more confident and strong. It was hard to believe that such a beautiful and powerful voice could emerge from such a tiny, frail woman.

Our bodies had been pushed to their limits. We were all starving, our heads were shaved bald, and we were weak from exhaustion. Yet, when Lili sang, she seemed powerful, strong, and beautiful. Words cannot describe how deeply her simple act affected me. I was mesmerized by the music. It replenished my supply of hope, the most precious commodity one could have in Auschwitz.

From that point on, Lili sang every Sunday afternoon. Even the Nazi guards came to hear her sing. My looking forward to those Sunday afternoons helped me endure the rest of the week. In fact, my having something to look forward to helped make my life in the camp bearable.

I am not sure what prompted Lili to sing that day; perhaps she sang as a way to feel human again, or perhaps she sang for us. Regardless of her intention, the memory of that simple act still gives me goose bumps.

When I wrote this story, I had no clue what had happened to Lili after we were liberated from the camp and I returned to Hungary. Everyone went their separate ways and attempted to rebuild their lives. I thought about her often and finally decided to utilize the resources available to me at the United States Holocaust Memorial Museum to try to find out where she was, if she was still alive.

I cannot describe the emotions that overwhelmed me when I discovered that she was not only alive but also living in America, about a five-hour drive from me. Surely, fate had played a part in bringing us back together again.

The Selection

Agi Geva

I had never known what that word meant; I had never dreamt that my life would depend on it. I had never imagined that one day someone would have the power, just by looking at me, to decide whether I should live or die; just by the move of a hand pointing in the direction that I was supposed to move, my fate was decided upon.

On March 19, 1944 the German Army entered Hungary and occupied the country. On that same day my dad, Zoltan, passed away. He had already been very ill for a very long time. From that day on nothing made sense for me. Impossible, unexplainable, horrible, and unimaginable events started to take place, as if we had been taking part in a horror movie! Nevertheless, we had hope that it would eventually end. Every day was different, but with more bad surprises, restrictions, and humiliations.

My mother, Rosalia, my sister, Shosha, and I ended up being deported from our hometown, Miskolc, Hungary, to the Auschwitz concentration camp in Poland. After a few weeks we were transported to the Plaszow concentration camp. We were sure that we were getting to a better place: what could be worse than Auschwitz? There were no selections upon our arrival; that made it better already. And we had better bunks and more food.

At Plaszow, we were treated as though we had gone back thousands of years in time, as if we were the slaves in Egypt. There were many assignments of humiliating work that we were assigned, together with many other inmates. One of these assignments was to carry big rocks up a hill, put them down, and then the next day carry them back down to where we had originally picked them up. It was even more difficult to carry them downhill. Those of us who did not pick up a large enough rock were beaten. My sister, who had her 13th birthday in Plaszow, was one of those.

Our mother had repeatedly told us not to tell anyone our real ages. If we were asked, we had to say that we were 18 and 19 in order to be able to stay together. We were also warned not to refer to each other as mom or sister. My mother saw the way that families were separated when they had used the terms "Mom," "Grandma," or "Daughter!"

One day we heard cannon shots and our hopes soared. "The Russians are nearing; they are going to liberate us!" we thought. But that did not happen. The Germans wanted all of us to leave the camp. We were herded into the cattle wagons and left Plaszow. We always felt desperate when changes occurred: where to now? Our mother consoled us, "This time it could not be worse."

After a day's journey, the train stopped, and the doors were opened. Those who recognized the place started to cry, to despair . . . Mother had no consoling words this time. WE WERE BACK IN AUSCHWITZ!

We looked bad; we were very thin and our skin was badly burned from working in the sun for so many hours. Our mother had to make decisions. She saw the German officer selecting people. "I shall go first, Shosha will go second, and Agi will be last, since she looks the worst among us," she said. She had observed that workers had a better chance of staying alive and warned us that we had to keep working. But she told us to try to follow her to wherever she would be sent. She took the risk of all of us being killed together, instead of going through unknown suffering without her.

She was shaking when she faced the selection officer. He made a move with his hand, sending her to the right. Shosha was sent to the right, and I was sent to the left.

I did not move. I pleaded to be sent in the direction that my family had gone. I was so young, frail, and weak, standing opposite that huge SS officer, not knowing at the time that I was actually negotiating for my life. It suddenly seemed as if everything froze.

Then, as if in slow motion, the SS officer asked, "What? Why?"

"Because that is a work camp," I responded in German.

"You do not look as if you could still work," he said, surprised.

"Let me prove it."

At that point, he realized that we were speaking German. "This is a Hungarian transport. How can you speak German so well?" he asked.

"I had German nannies." But what I really wanted to say was, "Please let me go with my mother and sister." My mother's warnings to keep working and not mention that we were family were ringing in my head.

The officer looked me over and said, "Go."

When I started to go after my mother, she did not see me. She had already fainted. She was so sure that if one of us was taken away none of us could survive.

When I was later asked if I had been afraid to stand face to face with an SS selecting officer, I always said, "No. I was more afraid of not obeying my mom."

—m—

My mother later remarried and lived on a *kibbutz* (collective community) in Israel until she died at the age of 97. She had five grandchildren and 17 great-grandchildren.

Shosha still resides in the same *kibbutz* where my mother had lived. She has 13 grandchildren and seven great-grandchildren, all of whom live in Israel.

I lived in Israel for 52 years, in the beginning in Haifa and then for 10 years in Tel Aviv. I have a son and a daughter, four grandchildren, and one great-grandchild. Seven years ago, my daughter and son-in-law invited me to live with them in the United States. My son lives in Tel Aviv with his family.

Neither my mother nor Shosha wanted to talk about the Holocaust. Shosha only agreed to give her testimony to Yad Vashem: The Holocaust Martyrs' and Heroes' Remembrance Authority in Israel last year.

The SS selecting officer at Auschwitz was "The Angel of Death"—Dr. Josef Mengele.

Ruth Barnett

Ruth Barnett (née Michaelis) was born in Berlin, Germany. In 1939, at the age of four, she and her seven-year-old brother fled to England on a *Kindertransport* (Children's Transport). Together, they went through three foster homes and a hostel throughout the 10 years that they did not see their father, who had fled to Shanghai, or their mother, who survived in hiding in Germany.

In 1949, though she had been repatriated to Germany against her will, Ruth chose to live in England. She graduated from the University of Reading and then taught in secondary schools in London and served as a Chief Examiner in the area of Child Development. She wrote the first textbook for this school course, *People Making People: Child Development in Context* (Hutchinson, 1985).

Ruth left the education field in 1986 and worked as a psychotherapist, focusing increasingly on individuals and groups who had experienced the Holocaust. She crafted many articles about her work and delivered presentations at conferences and for other learning groups. After 30 years of practice, she retired from clinical work in order to devote more time to lecturing. Her poem "Mother" is featured in Iris Guske's book, *Trauma and Attachment in the Kindertransport Context: German-Jewish Child Refugees' Accounts of Displacement and Acculturation in Britain*, as well as in her own memoir, *Person of No Nationality* (David Paul Books, 2009).

Mother

Ruth Barnett

Majestic your hills roll on seaward,
Roughly caressed by the breeze;
Where the wind blows your tussock in ripples
And sighs through the gnarled yew trees.

Where many a time I rode horseback,
And the thunder of hooves on your turf,
And the silent hills soothed my heartache
With the comforting surge of the surf.

And the curving brow of the headland
Rises up clear in my mind
As I gallop again the wild stretches
And leave all my troubles behind.

Majestic your hills roll on seaward,
My green-robed mother of Earth;
Your scent fills the yawning absence
Of the mother that gave me birth.

Majestic your hills roll on seaward,
Gently caressed by the breeze;
Your bounteous bosom that lures me
Can always restore me to ease.

Why Didn't the Boat Sink?
How a Kindertransportee Kept Afloat

Ruth Barnett
*(First written in 1998 for the
second Reunion of Kindertransport)*

One of my earliest memories is of the enormous boat that took my mother, brother, and me to England in February 1939. I was just four years old and my brother seven. It was nightfall. Jostled by the crowd as we swarmed up a plank, I looked down into the dark water underneath and realized with horror and excitement that we were going up onto a huge boat. I was frightened, because the little boats in my bathtub always sank if you put too much in them. I saw how the boat deck was already piled high with suitcases and hundreds of people milling around.

In tears, I asked my mother, "Are we going to drown when the boat sinks?"

She tried to comfort me by saying, "Boats don't sink; they are made to carry people and things." I didn't believe her. I knew just how easily you could sink a boat in the bath.

Later, when we were back on land in England, I asked my brother, "Why didn't the boat sink?"

"You are much too young to understand; one day, you will know when you are bigger." Since my brother always had answers for me, even if I found out later that things were not quite as he said, I was satisfied for the time being. And, in this case, he proved to be right—I did later come to understand.

The boat that didn't sink was to become a very important symbol in our life in England after our mother returned to Germany. She had to, since she was an Aryan German on a holiday visa. Besides that, she needed to get back to Berlin, where our Jewish father was in hiding, wandering the woods to foil the *Gestapo* (German Secret State Police) until, at last, he got passage on a ship to Shanghai.

After she left, my brother took the place of "mother" and looked after me. He needed me to look after as much as I needed him to mother me. The last words of our parents to him were, "Look after your little sister." That meant he had an important job to do, and it kept him in touch with his parents in his mind. It also meant that neither of us sank into depression. Instead, we kept each other afloat.

Without my brother to look after me, my "boat" would almost certainly have "sunk." Our first foster family was harsh and cruel. He raided the larder to feed me at night so I would not starve. He pushed our foster mother aside and pulled me out of the bath when she pushed my head under water to drown me. He told the doctor, who came to give us vaccinations, that I was sleeping badly on my tummy because my back was raw with welts from being beaten for wetting my bed.

Later, when our foster father died of cancer, our foster mother would not have us anymore, and we were put in a hostel until another family was found to take us in. In the hostel, my brother became very ill with hepatitis. He thinks I saved his life as he might have given up if I had not been there to mop his brow and read stories to him. He believed that "an apple a day keeps the doctor away" and those apples would cure him. He was my big brother, and I believed everything he said; therefore, I sold my little doll to a lady with a baby for a few pennies to buy a bag of apples! That way we both kept afloat, and we continued to do so with the next two foster families, who had children and were much more caring.

The enormous weight of our loss during the war—of our parents, home, language, and friends—would have been enough to "sink the boat" if it had stayed in our minds. The only way to survive was to make the best of things as they were. In retrospect, we would surely have "sunk" if it had not been for one important factor, which, of course, we did not realize at the time: my brother and I were together, in close contact, during the 10 years that we were apart from our parents. We also got sporadic mail from our father from Shanghai, but nothing from our mother in Germany.

In 1949 my "boat" very nearly did "sink" without my brother to rescue me. My parents had me repatriated to Germany against my will and without him. He was on scholarship at Cambridge University. I went through the *Kindertransport* (Children's Transport) experience a second time, in reverse. Overnight, everything familiar had disappeared—home, parents, language, landscape—everything. I had imbibed British propaganda for 10 years, so I was terrified. I really believed that there were Nazis around every corner with guns ready to shoot. My brother would have told me that was absurd, but he wasn't there.

From a sheltered, well-behaved 14-year-old child, I suddenly became a teenage rebel, refusing to do anything anyone wanted of me. My parents had no idea how to handle me and I certainly couldn't handle myself. Being decent kindly people, they saw it was not going to work and let me go back to England, where I have remained to become a teacher and then a psychotherapist, and, most important of all, a wife and a mother of three lovely children.

It never occurred to me that I had been a member of the *Kindertransport* until 50 years later, when I attended Bertha Leverton's first Reunion of Kindertransport. For me, this was a very moving experience that opened up shadowy areas of my memory that had been closed off for half a century, while I had simply gotten on with my life. I was amazed to learn at this event that there had been almost 10,000 of us who came to England in the 10 months between *Kristallnacht*[1] and the outbreak of World War II.

Unthinking, I had presumed that my brother and I were totally alone as, indeed, we were when our mother left us with our first set of foster parents, who had no children and did not now how to look after children. There are still huge gaps in both our memories. For example, try as we often might, neither my brother nor I can remember how long our mother stayed with us in England or saying goodbye to her.

As a psychotherapist with former Kindertransportee clients, I came to understand three issues that made a big difference to how children were able to deal with the *Kindertransport* experience of separation and subsequent adjustment to a new and alien world: the amount of stability in the family prior to separation (and many families suffered horrendous persecution); the developmental stage of the children at the time; and, most importantly, whether they continued to have contact with someone who represented a link with the past, the old familiar world. My brother

---

[1] *Kristallnacht,* also known as The Night of Broken Glass, took place on November 9 and 10, 1938. Nazis and members of the Hitler Youth violently attacked Jews and their homes, synagogues, and businesses throughout Germany and Austria.

and I represented a lifeline for each other that precariously maintained our sanity and prevented us from fragmenting or "sinking."

My husband's love and tolerance enabled me to gradually unpack the "boxes" of unbearable experiences that I had relegated to the "dusty attic" of my mind. Later, when our children started asking probing questions about the past, I began the long slow process of reconnecting with my experiences. Nineteen years of teaching in five secondary schools, writing a textbook for teaching child development, and five years as a chief examiner in child development all played a part in this.

I later underwent training as a marriage counsellor and then as a psychotherapist, and I began to combine my two careers by giving talks and seminars on Holocaust education and understanding trauma and the transmission of trauma between generations. In the course of this work, I have written several papers for seminars, conferences, and journals in London and abroad.

Miriam Spiegel Raskin

*M*iriam Spiegel Raskin is a writer residing in St. Louis, Missouri. Her works often reflect her childhood experiences as a refugee from Nazi Germany and her subsequent reflections on the "War Against the Jews" that led to the Holocaust.

In 2008 Miriam published a book of her writings entitled *Remembering & Forgetting: A Memoir and Other Pieces of My Life.* In the book she describes her family's fortunate departure from Germany in March 1939 and their subsequent adaption to life in the United States.

Nevertheless, the Nazis murdered 22 of Miriam's family members, including three grandparents, at various execution sites. Her additional written works have been published in numerous periodicals, including the *St. Louis Jewish Light, St. Louis Post-Dispatch, Simcha Magazine, Sagarin Review, First Harvest: Jewish Writing in St. Louis,* and *Natural Bridge Literary Journal.*

Hilda Prays at Birkenau

Miriam Spiegel Raskin

I'd die a thousand deaths for you, dear G-d.

I am twenty and quite fair enough
to look at, but that's no help to me
while I am being thrashed.

They strap my fragile body to a chair;
my head hangs almost to the floor,
the cold and black cemented floor.

I'd die a thousand deaths for you, dear G-d.
I'd die a thousand deaths.

I hear the whooshing sound of the leather
belt before it hits my naked bony back
and coils itself against my skin.

Tight, tight, I grasp the chair's thin legs
and squeeze my nails into the wood.
Oh let the lashes come; I will not scream.

I'd die a thousand deaths for you, dear G-d.
I'd die a thousand deaths.

Thank G-d, there's no metal buckle
on the belt now swishing through the air;
far better if no buckle slices my skin.

I count black leather boots around the chair,
clench my teeth, and bite my tongue as lashes
slash and tear into my skin.

I'd die a thousand deaths for you, dear G-d.
I'd die a thousand deaths—but first give me
the strength to last this out.

My teeth are clenched. "Come, come, Jew whore,"
he shouts in rhythm with the blows.
"Let's see how smart your mouth is now."

"*Ja. Ja, Herr Kommandant.*"[1] I whisper it,
as respectfully as I can. I don't want him angry.
Just a few more lashes and he's done.

I'd die a thousand deaths for you, dear G-d.

I will not let him know my pain, dear G-d,
I will survive it.

"Get out of here, you scum,
before I kill you!" he shouts.

As I raise my racked, torn body
and weakly turn to take my leave, he asks,
"Where is your Jewish G-d now, *mein Fräulein?*"[2]

The fool doesn't see my G-d is with me, saving me again.
Blessed are you, G-d, who has allowed me to live,
although I would gladly die a thousand deaths for you.

[Hilda Lebedun, a friend of Miriam's, is the subject of this poem. She is a
participant in the Memory Project of the Holocaust Museum & Learning
Center in Creve Coeur, Missouri.]

---

[1]Yes. Yes, Mr. Commander.

[2]My young lady.

No Town to Call Home

Miriam Spiegel Raskin

I suppose there are people all over who have no town to call home, but nobody feels the lack more than those of us who were rejected by ours. It took me a long time before I realized that it might be best for me to allow those old ego wounds to heal and go back to the small town that had failed to protect my family many decades ago. Therefore, having recently accepted an invitation for an all-expenses-paid visit to Hamburg, Germany, I decided to make a quick ancillary trip to Bünde.

I had passed up an earlier chance to visit the town when, years ago, I travelled with my mother to Hamburg, the city of our births that we left behind in 1939, when imminent death or leaving were the only choices open to Jews. This time around, I didn't want to miss seeing the humble Westphalia, a village in which I learned to walk and talk and started my schooling. That schooling had abruptly ended, however, when education for Jewish children was no longer considered in the best interests of the State.

The barely remembered details of my personal history weren't the only forces drawing me to Bünde this time. There was also the fact that now I have friends there. I had become involved—during the prior four years, through various means of communication and, eventually, by personal meetings—in the activities of a special Bünde-based project with international impact. It began when Christina Whitelaw, a Scottish Christian, came to town to teach English at the local high school. An activist by nature, it didn't take her long to discover that there was no local consciousness of the town's Jewish past, no collective memory of there ever having been Jewish residents.

To correct that lack of awareness, Christina started an extracurricular research project in which students looked for evidence that Jews had lived in the town and then pursued the facts they found until they uncovered the life stories, and all too often, the death stories of the former Jewish residents. The work that Netzwerk Bünde undertook was not easy and did not garner the support of all of the current residents. Some of the uncovered facts were embarrassing for proud citizens to acknowledge.

Once caught in the web spun by the Netzwerk volunteers, I became fascinated by their dedication, selflessness, and the conspicuous fruits of their labour: regular public exhibits of pictures and biographies; annual commemorative services; and comprehensive annual reports documenting the personal histories of the former Bünde Jews. When, in June of 2006, about 20 of the Netzwerk group members travelled to Chicago and Denver to connect with survivors or their relatives who now live in the United States, I took the opportunity to meet them in Chicago. At a presentation there, the Netzwerk members described their projects and demonstrated how much they knew about Jewish life in Bünde. I was impressed, and I was charmed by the grace and spirit of the young people and their mentors.

So it wasn't a surprise when on that bright and shiny Sunday afternoon, a parade of balloon-waving Germans greeted my sister and me at the train station. Having arrived in Hamburg the day before after 18 hours of flying-cum-waiting-for-planes, we had found our way to the railroad station and embarked on what turned out to be a sentimental journey. We had to change trains in Osnabrück, and looking around that small station, we realized that the fateful trip our father had made the day after *Kristallnacht*[1] in 1938 was by means of this same train, on the same tracks, with the same view that we were now enjoying. He had taken the trip in full daylight from Bünde to Hamburg to be reunited with his little family, when he could have been apprehended by Nazis at any time but wasn't. Almost exactly 70 years later, we were retracing his path. The realization chilled us to our cores.

The atmosphere that greeted us when we disembarked in Bünde was far more cheerful. Barely outside the train, we saw—walking toward us— members of the Netzwerk group: four adults and as many young people, bright balloons in hand and wide smiles on their faces. There were hugs and kisses, laughter, and tears. They came determined to cheer us up,

---

[1] *Kristallnacht,* also known as The Night of Broken Glass, took place on November 9 and 10, 1938. Nazis and members of the Hitler Youth violently attacked Jews and their homes, synagogues, and businesses throughout Germany and Austria.

MARKING HUMANITY

presuming we needed that. The Netzwerkers all seem to have a finely honed sensitivity to the pain a so-called "homecoming" can evoke for returnees. Whether they have had evidence of such pain suffered by earlier visitors or simply intuit the pain as a necessary consequence of the events they know to have occurred is impossible to know.

The full two-day agenda started with a walking tour of my old neighbourhood. We walked down Eschstrasse, now an attractive pedestrian mall lined with small commercial establishments of the sort one would expect in an Alpine village. The pressure was on me to remember, and I tried to recognize something, anything. And then we came to No. 19, my former address. I knew from correspondence with a childhood friend who had lived in the same house that the front of the building had been torn down and rebuilt, but the back building, in which we had lived, was still standing. I slowly walked around toward the back to look at it.

Looking over this old building makes me very self-conscious. They are watching me, waiting for a reaction. Should I be feeling something? What do they want me to feel? I feel nothing, but I keep examining. The shape of the building looks familiar. The yard space is limited and landscaping spare. Where is the area that held our chickens and chicken coop? And the beautiful garden? The currant bushes? The lilies-of-the-valley? It's the right shape but barren now, like an inner city backyard that no one cares for. Even the grass is worn down, but I can see the spot where the sandbox stood—the sandbox in which I played with my friend Bärbel and where I once ripped my skin on a damaged sand bucket (there were no plastics in those days!).

In my mind's eye, I see it back there, in front of the back gate. It's the same gate, I think. The chain-link fence and the gate are equally dented and bent out of shape. They could easily be 70 years old or older. Yes, it's the gate that can be seen in the old photo showing me on my first day of school, wearing my pretty new dress and carrying the cornucopia filled with candy traditionally given to new students. It is the same photo that has now been enhanced by butterflies that my darling daughter added and stands on my piano. The building looks alien to me (it was never this colour) until I see in one small window toward the front the identifying iron bars. That clinches it. Iron bars did then my prison make.

It's ironic that it was the sight of iron bars that persuaded me that this was really my former hometown. It seemed almost real, but not quite. What was real was the warm affection we felt from all the locals that we met. They wined and dined us and generally treated us royally on the short visit.

On the second night, there was a festive gathering of all the good people we had encountered. We shared hugs and kisses, as well as stories and plans to visit the U.S. It was a perfect ending to our short visit, into which our new friends had packed so much activity and joy. Kids and adults all seemed in love with one another. We had fully dissolved all the barriers that might have existed between us. I felt so much real connection with every single person that I never once thought the inevitable Jew-to-German question: WHERE WERE YOU (or your father or grandfather) DURING THE WAR?

I am so naive. It was only months later that it even occurred to me to wonder. And the thought came, paradoxically, when I received a card from one of my hosts that said, "I hope that your visit to Bünde has altered your judgment of the German people for the better." I had thought my attitude toward the German people had been totally accepting. Suddenly, it hit me that the packed schedule for our quick visit was not the entire agenda and that I had not had the good sense to read between the lines. While I was trying to remember, my hosts were trying to get me to forget, to wipe the municipal slate clean of past transgressions.

I guess we need to talk. Because sometimes love is not enough.

Alfred Traum

Alfred Traum was born in Vienna, Austria, and had a happy childhood. Approximately 15 months after the 1938 *Anschluss* (Nazi Germany's annexation of Austria), his parents arranged for him and his sister to join the *Kindertransport* (Children's Transport) for a safe haven in England. The siblings stayed with a non-Jewish family throughout the war. In late 1946, after their guardian died, they

Alfred Traum at his wedding to Josiane Aizenberg aboard Israeli passenger liner the S.S. *Zion* while it was docked at New York Harbor in June 1958.

became part of a Jewish community in Manchester. A year later, when it became evident that their parents had not survived the Holocaust, the British government offered them British citizenship.

In 1948 Alfred volunteered to serve in the Israel Defense Forces. Two years later, he returned to England and entered the British Army for two years. Upon completion of his military service, he entered the Merchant Marine Academy in the United Kingdom and eventually received an appointment on the newly completed Israeli passenger liner the S.S. *Zion*. He married Josiane Aizenberg aboard the S.S. *Zion* when the ship was docked at New York Harbor in 1958.

Josiane and Alfred then returned to Israel, where Alfred worked for IBM in Haifa. Due to medical needs for their son, he and his wife were later advised to relocate to the United States. Alfred then worked in the States as a telecommunications engineer for Boeing. He is now retired and lives in Silver Spring, Maryland.

The Kiddush Cup

Alfred Traum

It was always the same. Ushering in the Sabbath,[1] my father, Elias, held the silver *Kiddush* cup in the flat palm of his hand. With his thumb resting against the brim of the cup, his head held high, and his eyes half closed, he recited the blessing over the wine. We all took a sip of wine from the *Kiddush* cup. This was carried out in the proper order along with all the other festive traditional activities.

Any bystander would have thought that this was just an ordinary Friday night in a Jewish home. So it would have seemed. But I am sure that both of our parents' hearts were breaking. My sister, Ruth, and I were leaving for England on the following Wednesday. This would be our last Sabbath dinner together. Although we thought that we would soon be reunited, our parents knew the difficulties that lay ahead. Indeed, it was the last Friday night meal that we shared.

Preparing for the Sabbath actually began on Thursdays, with my mother, Gita, preparing large, round batches of thinly rolled dough that would later be used to make noodles for soup. She busied herself in the kitchen all evening making a mouth-watering selection of cakes that would last through the week. We never bought any ready-made cakes. Everything was homemade.

That particular week, she would need more, since many friends and relatives would drop in, say their goodbyes, and wish me and Ruth well on our journey. On Friday morning, I would watch, as I had watched so many times in the past, as my mother platted the dough to make the *challahs* (special braided bread eaten on the Sabbath and other Jewish holidays) and then baste them with egg yolk and lightly sprinkle poppy seeds

---

[1]The Sabbath is a weekly Jewish holy day from sundown Friday until shortly after sundown Saturday that is meant to be treated as a day of rest from the regular activities of the week.

before placing them in the oven. The aroma from the baking and food preparation was a symphony for the nose. It was such a rare and wonderful smell that, even now, on the rare occasion that something comes close to it, I am whisked back in time. This was the routine in our home and similarly in many other Jewish homes in Vienna.

My father was physically disabled as a result of his service in the Austrian army during World War I. I never really knew what his exact diagnosis was, but he could only get around with the aid of two canes. He never complained about his handicap and was always cheerful and a pleasure to be around. When he was seated, though, there was nothing that he could not do. He had gifted hands that could work well on so many things.

He was fabulous at drawing, and he taught me so much, including how to use proportions and take perspectives into account when creating a drawing. Although he was never trained to be a tailor, he handled the sewing machine like a professional, making all kinds of clothes for us, even a new suit for me. He could also resole shoes, repair electric apparatuses, and even tinker with the radio when it went on the blink and somehow get it functioning again. Moreover, he was an amateur photographer and did his own developing and printing. We never went to a photography studio as a result, so we only have little snapshots that he produced himself.

I used to watch my father closely, picking up many cues that I would store away for use at some future time. I learned so much from him, but most of all, he taught me how to live with challenges and make the most of them.

At times such as when I was rebuilding an engine for the car or building an addition onto our home and friends would ask me, "Where did you learn how to do that?" I would simply shrug my shoulders. But in the back of my mind, I would imagine my father saying, "Go ahead, you can do it." Perhaps it sounds far-fetched, but he taught me so much without having to leave his chair.

On the Wednesday of our departure to England, the whole family went downstairs to the backyard, where my father set up the tripod and camera. He placed a black cloth over his head and had us all assemble for him to take a picture. He selected the delayed shutter so he could join in.

A short while later, it was time for us depart for the West Bahnhof, the railroad station for trains heading west. As we were about to leave, my dad said to me, "Go forward, don't look back. Just go forward." I was never quite sure what he meant, but I believe it was more philosophical than I realized as a small child. However, as the three of us proceeded along the sidewalk and were still only a short distance from our home, I did stop to turn around and look back. Just as I had expected, my father was at the bay window with tears in his eyes, attempting to

Alfred Traum at age 10 (bottom right) with his older sister, Ruth (left), his grandmother, Bina (standing in center), and his parents, Gita and Elias, posing for a photo on the afternoon prior to Alfred and Ruth's departure to England on the *Kindertransport*.

force a smile while watching my sister and me walk out of his life.

The platform at the train station was crowded with parents coming to see their children off on the *Kindertransport* (Children's Transport), heading to a new life in England. They were hoping the children would not forget their old lives and those who loved them. It was a specially scheduled train just for our group, probably a couple hundred kids, from toddlers to 17-year-olds. Ruth and I stood at an open window holding hands with our mother. She, too, was fighting back tears, trying to tell us that it would just be for a short while. In retrospect, I don't think she believed her own words, but what else could she say?

We were bravely looking at each other, not knowing what to say, when suddenly my classroom teacher, Professor Schwartzbard, appeared in front of us. He knew that I was leaving on the *Kindertransport* that day and had managed to have his young son accepted, too. He was holding his five-year-old son like a piece of luggage under his arm and passed him through the open window, asking if he could sit with us and that I would keep an eye out for him until we reached London, where someone would pick him up. Naturally, I agreed. I instantly felt all grown up, with newfound responsibilities dropped into my lap.

A whistle blew, and we kissed and hugged through the open window and reluctantly let go of each other as the train began to pull away. My mother tried running along with the train, holding onto our hands, but not for long. Soon, her lonely figure diminished as we snaked our way out of the station. She had just passed the most difficult test that could befall any parent.

Our belongings consisted of two large backpacks stuffed to the brim with clothing and lots of sweets that friends and relatives had given us. My parents sent along a very nice box of chocolates for the Griggs family, who had agreed to take us into their home. We were not permitted to bring any valuables—jewellery or money. If found, they would be confiscated or bring us even more trouble. I hid the watch that my parents had given me for my 10th birthday and didn't remove it from its hiding place until we reached Holland.

When the photograph that my father took on our last day together had been developed, he sent us a copy to England. The photo captured all of our feelings. It is the saddest picture I have ever seen; nevertheless, it is a treasured memento of that day. On one of the negatives, my father had written, in German, *Der Abschied* (The Farewell).

This story is not about our time in England, but rather about two significant dates: June 20, 1939, our departure from Vienna; and June 24, 1958, the day of my wedding to Josiane Aizenberg aboard the S.S. *Zion* ship as it was anchored at New York Harbor. Ruth had come from Israel to be at our wedding. She had a very special gift for me, one that she had been saving for such an occasion. It was my father's *Kiddush* cup, the same cup that I had seen on so many Friday nights. My father had taken an enormous risk and stuffed the cup amongst my sister's clothing. He did not tell her so as not to frighten her, but he knew that she was mature enough and would know what to do with it and, when the moment was right, to pass it on to me. More importantly, in parting with the cup, which my father probably received on some special occasion, he must have been acutely aware of the severity of the situation and the doubtfulness of his and my mother's survival.

The cup is my most prized possession. Every Friday evening as my family ushers in the Sabbath it graces our table. Perhaps I don't hold it in the same manner as my father did; however, I recite the same blessing, and I look around at my family and count my blessings, thinking, "How fortunate I am to have had such parents."

Gerda Krebs Seifer

Gerda Krebs Seifer was born in Przemysl, Poland. In the spring of 1940 she and her parents moved to Lwów. Her father, Henryk, owned a fabrics business, while her mother, Edyta, was a homemaker and sometimes helped with the store. Her parents were educated, middle class citizens, and the family only spoke Polish at home.

Gerda survived the Holocaust in hiding, living on false papers with a Catholic family. However, her entire family of 38 people were murdered, except for one cousin, Zygmunt Schwarzer, who survived the Auschwitz-Birkenau camp.

In March 1946 Gerda left Poland on a transport of war orphans to England led by British Rabbi Solomon Shonfeld. There, she

Gerda Krebs Seifer at age six with her mother, Edyta Goliger-Krebs, and her cousin, Zygmunt Schwarzer, in Szczawnica, Poland.

learned English and enrolled in a nurse training program at St. James' University Hospital in Leeds. She became a registered nurse in 1950.

In 1951 Gerda moved to the United States, and she worked in hospitals in New York. She met Harold W. Seifer at Mount Sinai Hospital, and they were married in 1955. They now have three children and four grandchildren, all living in Los Angeles. Gerda has also been involved with the Jewish Federation and worked for various Israeli causes. For over 40 years, she has been providing lectures to students at schools about her experiences during the Holocaust. She and Harold now reside in Long Beach, California.

Acquiring a New Name and a New Family

Gerda Krebs Seifer

We had been living in the Lwów ghetto since the early spring of 1942. A high wall with barbed wire and broken glass on the top surrounded the ghetto. The apartment buildings were crammed with several people living in one room.

After spending days seeking shelter, we came upon a greenhouse (all glass and with dirt floors), where 18 families were living. We found a few extra square feet of space there and decided that would have to serve as our new living quarters. The weather was warming up, so we had one less thing to worry about. Our new lodging consisted of two iron beds, a folding table, a gas burner, a stool, four chairs, linens, clothing, and dishes, which were all kept in suitcases that we managed to bring with us to the ghetto.

My family included my parents and a younger cousin, Richard, whose mother had disappeared while waiting in line to buy bread. Rounding up Jews from the streets was a common practice. No one was told why they were caught or where they were going, but in most cases they never returned. An army truck was usually waiting on the street, and a few German soldiers would grab Jews and get them on board. When the truck was full, they would drive off.

We had no rights, and the Nazis considered us "subhuman." In Lwów, all Jews above the age of 12 had to wear white armbands with a Star of David embroidered in blue. That order was enacted during the first few days of the German occupation in July 1941.

My father worked in a factory, where fabrics were woven for army uniforms. His job was necessary for the war effort; therefore, he was a "useful" Jew. My mother, Richard, and I did not have jobs, so we passed our time in the ghetto trying to be inconspicuous. We tried to stay in the greenhouse, because if we were on the street we were picked out by the militia to perform labour such as cleaning the streets, removing the trash, or helping to lift dead bodies and load them on carts to be buried.

Homeless Jews, old and sick, and orphaned children lived on the ghetto streets, leaning against buildings and begging for scraps of food. The weak ones died at night, and we had to remove the bodies to prevent the spread of disease.

One day, my father returned from "outside" with frightening news: there was going to be a big *Aktion* (Nazi operation involving mass murder and deportation). Such stories constantly circulated, and we never knew whether they were gossip or the truth. An *Aktion* meant that Nazis, armed with machine guns and vicious dogs, surrounded the ghetto. The German police and Ukrainian militia entered the ghetto and ordered people to come out. Shooting and screaming they ran up and down the buildings searching for hidden children, dragging old and sick people out of beds, tossing babies through the windows into the streets, and causing panic. They tore out floors and walls and broke cabinets in search of hidden victims.

My father knew that since my mother, Richard, and I did not have *Ausweise* (ID cards), none of us would be spared. He told me to pack a change of clothing and go out to the exit gate, where an old Polish neighbour of ours was to meet me and take me to her apartment. My father paid her for hiding me in her cellar throughout the duration of the *Aktion*. There was little time to get ready, and on the way out I held and kissed my mother. My last words to her were, "Mommy, please hide." She said she would.

The Polish woman showed me her 6-by-4-foot cellar, gave me a wooden box to sit on, and told me to be very quiet, moving as little as possible. Although she gave me a candle and matches, I was told to use them only in case of emergency. She'd come once a day with food and to empty the chamber pot.

Each apartment had a small cellar, one adjoining the other, divided by walls made of boards. If a candle was lit in one cellar, you could see a thin glimmer of light coming through the boards to the other cellar.

There I was, lonely, sad, and fearful that at any moment someone might hear me move or a Nazi search party might come into the building looking for hidden Jews. Some Poles were determined to not so much aid the Nazis but to eliminate one more Jew. They looked for Jews to report to the Germans. Often, it meant one human being in exchange for a loaf of bread or a bottle of vodka. Those who hid Jews—whether for money or not—would also face death. The Nazis wielded power and expected total obedience by creating fear.

At first, I thought of my family and friends, books I read, songs I knew, vacations I took, and the wonderful dishes my mother cooked and the torts and cakes she baked. She was an amazing cook and baker. I would sit and stretch, and then sit again. I couldn't sleep all the time, especially because I was a teenager, full of energy. I dreamt of being able to run barefoot on a grassy field, feeling the blades of grass between my toes and the wind blowing through my hair. How I wanted to be free and bask in the sun!

But that was not to be. I was a prisoner in that pitch black cellar, with only an occasional mouse running along the wall, afraid of me as much as I was afraid of it. After three or four weeks, one gets lost in time and days seem to last forever. I couldn't tolerate this loneliness any longer. One moment, I was in my prison, and the next moment, I was out standing in the middle of the street, blinking at the bright shining sun.

Luckily for me, no one was around. The street was empty, and the only person who saw me was the woman who hid me. She ran out of her apartment, looked both ways to make sure that no one saw her, grabbed me by my arm, and dragged me inside. "What do you think you are doing?" she shouted. "Do you want both of us killed?"

"I don't care," I kept repeating. "I can't take it anymore!" She took me into her kitchen, gave me some tea, and convinced me to go back and hide in the cellar.

After six weeks, which seemed like an eternity, I was told it was safe to go back to the ghetto. My knees were buckling under me as we walked toward the ghetto that evening. I kept asking the Polish woman over and over again how my mother was, and each time she replied, "Fine." But somehow I was not convinced by her answer.

Back in the ghetto I ran into my father's arms and then looked around for my mother, but she wasn't there. "Daddy, where is mom?"

He put his arms around me as we sat on the bed and told me what I dreaded to hear. Richard was sent into hiding like I was, but he was afraid to stay there and ran back to the ghetto. My mother could hide alone, but she could not take Richard with her. She bravely opted to stay with him in the ghetto. The Nazis came, checked all the ID's, and took my dearest mother and Richard to the Janowska concentration camp. From there, all victims were transported to Belzec, the infamous extermination camp. No one could survive that camp. All of the people in each transport were immediately unloaded, stripped of their clothing, and marched directly to be gassed.

Learning of my mother's fate was the worst day in my life. Only years later, I realized that I went into shock, because for the next several months I couldn't recall anything that happened after I heard this news. My MOTHER was my dearest friend, someone I greatly admired, respected, and loved. She was a marvelous human being, very generous, bright, intelligent, educated, and one of the most elegant ladies I knew. She was everything I wanted to be. I NEVER HAD A CHANCE TO SAY "I LOVE YOU."

Following my mother's death, my father desperately tried to save me, since he knew that I had no chance of surviving without any work. The Nazis were in a hurry to make the large Lwów ghetto *Judenrein* (clean of Jews). There was little chance to escape extermination.

My father found a Polish woman, who, with four children, was starving and unable to work and take care of a newborn baby. He arranged to pay her for keeping me.

In October 1942 I left the ghetto for good and joined the Polish family. I used the woman's dead child's birth certificate and moved in with her as her eldest child. My new family consisted of two teenage boys, a four-year-old girl, and a newborn baby boy, also illegitimate. The woman's husband was in Germany as a prisoner of war. The family, including myself, moved to a new apartment in a section of town where no one knew us. We moved in there as a one whole family and occupied an apartment near the ghetto that a Jewish family had recently vacated. As Jews were "resettled" from the ghetto and its borders shrank, more apartments became available for the Poles.

During that time I took care of the entire household, the three children, and a newborn baby. I cooked, cleaned, washed the laundry and diapers, and performed many unpleasant duties. My life depended on that woman. I had to carry buckets of water up three flights of stairs. There were great shortages of basic necessities, so anything and everything that had to be done was made from scratch with a few staples and great difficulty. I quickly learned to avoid the wrath of my "mother." I was constantly criticized and screamed at, and she demanded better performance. I was called stupid, no good, dumb, and worse.

"How come," I sometimes wondered, "I was never considered stupid or called names before I came to live with this woman?" I was not able to realize that I was being brainwashed by my "mother" to lose any confidence in myself and completely depend upon her.

I tried to stay home most of the time, while my "mother" worked. This way I avoided the curious and suspicious looks of the neighbours and prevented any incidents on the streets that could arise if someone recognized me from the pre-war era.

My life was difficult and dangerous, but I didn't really mind the work, living in misery, or being a slave to the woman of the house. What I minded most was the sudden loss of my mother, and not being able to grieve her loss or have anyone to confide in about my sadness and pain. There was no one that I could trust, no one I felt close to, and I still had to act like a happy Polish teenager.

I studied Catholic prayers, hymns, holidays, and saints. I knew how to recite a rosary and felt confident in answering questions connected with Catechism. Once in a while, I'd take the baby in my arms and go to church, making sure that our neighbours saw me go out. Holding the baby was a safety measure so I could hide my face behind him if I happened to see someone who might know me and report me to the police.

Looking back at those years, I was willing to put up with abuse, hunger, and lack of basic comforts, as long as I'd survive the war and finally reunite with my wonderful father. Living near the ghetto, I constantly watched through a drawn curtain. Jews in open trucks were transported to Janowska or to the Piaski transit camp. My blood froze as I thought about my mother and thousands of other helpless victims.

Living among Poles meant being constantly aware of the possibility that someone (even a total stranger) might be suspicious of my looks or my "non-Polish" behaviour. One had to be cautious and wary every waking moment. It didn't take much to fall into a trap. Even the neighbours in the apartment building commented to my "mother" that I didn't look like her. When they watched me do the washing, one woman said that I wrung the laundry like a Jew.

My father planned to go to Germany on false papers as a *Volksdeutsche* (a historical term used to describe ethnic Germans living outside of the German empire). He spoke fluent German and did not look Semitic. At our last meeting, he warned me not to expect any letters or news from him, because this would have been very dangerous. He then showed me a tiny white pill, hidden in his belt buckle. It was cyanide, a very quick acting, powerful poison, which he said he'd take if he was caught by the Nazis.

When the war ended in 1945, I was overjoyed with the prospect of freedom and looked forward to seeing my father. However, my happiness was short lived. I learned from a young man, who recognized me on the street but whose name I never learned, that my father secured a room on the "outside," paid rent for it, and planned to remain in that room when the ghetto was liquidated. He hoped to stay there for a short while and then, dressed in lederhosen and a Tyrolean hat and carrying false papers, head to the railroad station, buy a ticket for Germany, and leave Poland. He felt he had a better chance of survival in Germany than in Poland. How right he was!

The plan was solid. However, as he was leaving the ghetto, several men begged him to take them with him to his little hiding room and save their lives. My father was a generous and brave man. He always helped others, and he agreed to take them with him. Because, I suppose, he was the only one who did not look Semitic, it was up to him to go out and find food for all of them.

One day, a man recognized my father on the street and pointed a finger at him. Whether he was shot on the spot, taken to jail, or sent to a concentration camp, I do not know. What happened to my father will always remain a mystery. All I know is that my daddy was a victim of hatred and antisemitism.

Out of my 40 family members, there were only two survivors: a cousin (my mother's sister's son) and myself. My cousin, Zygmunt Schwarzer, was sent to Auschwitz-Birkenau and Buchenwald, and we found each other via the Red Cross after the war.

Eventually, I managed to escape from the claws of the Polish woman I had lived with. The "mother" wanted me to stay with her forever and remain her slave. It took a great deal of courage and determination on my part to leave this dreadful life. My future with her was bleak and depressing. I even considered committing suicide rather than continuing to live with her. She was a greedy, mean woman, not just to me, but also to her own children. Still, she needed me almost as much as I needed her during the German occupation. She did save my life, and for that I was forever grateful.

Without my other family members, I was all alone. I did not know what to do or where to go. When I left Poland, I stayed in touch with the "mother" and helped her as much as I could, although I had little means of support.

—⚋—

Throughout my life, I couldn't bring myself to imagine the last moments of my birth mother's life. It was too painful to think about.

About six years ago, my husband and I took a trip to Belzec. I had to get some kind of closure. What remained of the Belzec camp was a huge, empty, sad, and neglected field. A broken, small monument stood lonely in that huge empty field, and if you listened carefully, you could almost hear the cries of the victims. At one end, there were grassy mounds, where the bodies were buried, because the Nazis had no time to build crematoria. By then, they were deep into Russia, losing the war, and they had to concentrate on the Eastern Front. Despite being in the throes of losing the war and suffering from food and ammunition shortages, the Nazis were still fixated on killing every Jew. Cattle trains for Jews to be driven to the concentration camps were more important to the Germans than sending soldiers and supplies to the front lines.

Three years later, we visited Belzec again. We wanted to see the new monument that was completed on the 60th anniversary of the end of the Holocaust. It is a magnificent memorial to the victims of the Nazi murderers. It spans the whole length of the camp, and it portrays the enormity of the bestiality that human beings were able to commit against others.

We must never forget this tragedy, and we must never allow such bestiality to happen. *Am Israel Chai* (the nation of Israel lives).

George Liebermann

George Liebermann was born in Bihor, Transylvania, in Romania in June 1925. By the summer of 1944 the Nazis had deported many of Bihor's Jews to the Auschwitz-Birkenau extermination camp. George, along with 500 Hungarian-Jewish so-called "locksmiths," ended up in a V1 Factory in Thil/Longwy, France. As the Allies advanced so did he, moving from west to east: Kochendorf, Dachau, Allach/Karlsfeld, and then on a hostage train destined to save high ranked SS officers and deliver them to Tirol, Italy, and then South America. However, an American Sherman tank unit captured the hostage train and made them prisoners. George and 3,000 others were liberated in Staltach, Germany, in April 1945.

George Liebermann at age 19 in 1944.

A few months later, George returned to Transylvania. He went on to graduate from medical school and get married. In 1965 he and his wife left for Austria, where they worked as doctors for 11 months. Although they had French passports, they ended up in the United States against their will. They stayed in Dallas, Texas, where George specialized in neuropsychiatry. The couple later moved to California.

Over the years, George enjoyed carving wood and travelling, as well as writing poems, short stories, and novels such as *Twisted Avenues*. He was divorced, remarried, and then divorced again. He has two children and three grandchildren.

The Only Survivor

George Liebermann

Maybe Peter will make it.

At first, white circles designed themselves onto the sky. Explosions echoed throughout the airplane factory. The men were ordered to hide under a row of pine trees. Peter did not budge, and it took him by surprise when his eyes caught a guard nearby. The guard looked at Peter with a gnomic smile.

"It will not last long," said the guard. Peter thought that he meant the air raid, but he shook his head and added, "The war."

The men had a lunch break, but there was nothing to eat. His stomach gurgled in pain, but he forgot about that when he saw the guard share his lunch with his dog. He never paid attention to the houses nearby and was taken by surprise when he saw a woman carry a pot and head toward them. She looked around and then handed them a potato, one by one, and then one more. She then caught the eyes of the hungry guard and offered him one, but he shook his head and only said, "*Danke shön* (thank you)." She split the last two potatoes between the four of them.

The warm breath of the dog on the back of his hand startled him. Two hungry eyes focused on the half potato in his left hand. He let the dog kick it and then gave it to him. The German Shepherd licked his face.

Peter knew that he would never forget that motherly face and followed her as she dragged her emaciated body to a yellow house on the left side of the street, until an opening swallowed her. "She could have a son who was taken by the war," he thought.

No more than two weeks later, 3,000 prisoners had been taken to the Karlsfeld railroad station as hostages of the SS High Command. *Obersturmführer* Kurz directed the ant-march, a submachine gun in his right hand, with his hawk-eyes turned 180 degrees to catch any deserter.

Peter lagged behind, slowing down with each step closer to the end of the line, but Kurz caught him.

"*Du schweinehund, bewegung, schnell!* (You swinehound, move quickly!)" demanded Kurz.

Peter memorized the famous blue scar on Kurz's forehead that a prisoner inflicted on him. "He read my mind," he thought. One of the guards, eager to assist Kurz, hit him between the shoulders with the butt of his rifle.

The sky was crowded with lead-grey clouds, which slowly advanced above the thick, grey fog. Peter scouted his surroundings. Guards were scanty compared with 3,000 prisoners. Kurz was far to the right. Peter saw no guard nearby. With the threatening shouts of the guards, his fellow prisoners squeezed him where he wanted to be, against the wheel of a boxcar. He sneaked under the car, hid behind the wheel, and then waited until the entire armada climbed onto the train.

When the last sliding door had been shut with a bang, he crawled across to the railway building. For a while, the area was clear. He dashed onto a street, lay low, and slowly crawled toward the yellow house.

Suddenly, he knew he had company. His freedom was short-lived. They would either hang or shoot him if he was lucky, but they might also beat him to death. He peeped from behind the corner but saw no one.

When Peter felt the dog lick his hand, he sighed in relief, sat down next to him, and pulled his big, warm head into his lap. He saw the woman look at him from behind the curtain. He worried about her reaction to the dog. She opened the door wide enough to make room for the both of them.

Peter slept in the attic of her home, where he felt safer. He called his companion Angel, because he did not know his name. Within a week, the Nazis ran out of Germany.

[Peter represents the author, and this story is based on true events that he experienced shortly before the liberation.]

Marietta Elliott-Kleerkoper

*M*arietta Elliott-Kleerkoper was born in Amsterdam in 1937. In 1942 she and her sister went into hiding with separate Christian families, under an assumed name, in the countryside. After liberation, they were reunited with their mother, who had survived by working with a resistance group underground in Amsterdam. Their father, who had been trapped in England by the outbreak of the war and had joined the Dutch army abroad, was released in 1946.

In 1949 the family moved to Australia. Marietta completed a modern languages degree and a diploma in education at the University of Melbourne and went on to teach at secondary schools and English language centres before completing a Doctorate and lecturing at universities. Also involved in the local poetry scene, she was President of the Melbourne Poets Union from 2002 to 2004. In 2006 Hybrid Publishers released her Dutch-English poetry collection, *Island of Wakefulness.* She currently works as a freelance editor.

Marietta married her husband Ian in 1961, and they had a daughter and a son. The couple divorced in 1977. She now has four grandchildren, including twin girls. Although she was diagnosed with breast cancer in 2003, she underwent aggressive treatment and is currently in remission.

Cellar

Marietta Elliott-Kleerkoper

Since I was five
I have been writing the cellar

How the light beam
from the grille at street level

struck the dust motes
the way they danced

How the shadow of the grille
created a pattern on the stone floor

How the intensity of light
made the darkness darker

How if I stood in the light
it illuminated my hand

and darkness became an absence

Lost

Marietta Elliott-Kleerkoper

My name is lost.
Yesterday I still had it.

Mother gave me a new one.
"What's your new name?" she said

and I had to repeat it
until I could say it

without mistakes, until
she was satisfied: *Klinkhamer.*

Nice name. A hammer
belting things, making noise.

Not a *Kleerkoper,* walking the streets
with old *shmattes.*[1]

And then the officer asks me:
"What's your name?" And I say

proudly: "My new name is . . . "
"New? New? What was it before?

Are you a Jew?" Jew—Jew?
What's that—am I one?

---

[1]Old or ragged garments.

I burst into tears. Now my old name
lost as well, clear out of my head.

He hesitates. Such a little girl
with her blonde curls.

What if he let her go . . .

Andy Réti

ndy Réti is a child Holo-
caust survivor who was
born in Budapest, Hungary,
in 1942. He came to Canada
with his widowed mother after
Hungary's October Revolution
of 1956. In 1958 his mother
married Emil Grossman, who
was also a survivor. In 1990 Ibi
Grossman published her memoir, *An Ordinary Woman in
Extraordinary Times*. Then, in
2002, Andy released his memoir, *The Son of an Extraordinary
Woman*, published by AMA Graphics.

Andy Réti and his mother, Ibi Grossman, in February 2005. Andy and Ibi are wearing the B.A.D (Bikers Against Despair) T-shirts representing the Yidden on Wheels Motorcycle Touring Club of Toronto.

Andy is a retired taxicab owner. He has been writing for over 40 years and has had articles featured in the *Jewish Tribune, Cab Connection, Taxi News, Good News Toronto,* and his B'nai Brith lodge bulletin, *The Observer.* Since 1998, he has served as a docent (museum guide) at the Holocaust Centre of Toronto. He and Ibi were the only mother and son team at the centre who were both survivors.

Ibi passed away in 2005, and Andy has since become a full-time speaker during Holocaust Education Week. His latest presentation was titled "Motorcycles and the Holocaust." He is also a member of the Yid-den on Wheels Motorcycle Touring Club of Toronto, the largest Jewish motorcycle club in Canada.

The Ring of Love

Andy Réti

I became a biker because of my mother—I don't think too many people can make that claim. Life was just beginning to get back to normal after the Holocaust, which my mother, Ibi, and I had survived, though my father had not. It was 1948 in Budapest, Hungary, and I was six years old. My mother took me to an amusement park for the first time in my life.

One of the attractions was a motorcycle ride around a small dirt track. When the carnival worker saw that I was begging my mother to let me go on it, he promised her that he would put me in the saddle and catch me after I went around the track three times. It was a full size adult bike, and my legs did not reach the ground. All I had to do was hang on and press the brakes when he gave me the signal. My mother was way ahead of her time in child rearing and gave me permission. Needless to say, I was hooked for life.

For almost 20 years, my mother was a Survivor Speaker at the Holocaust Centre in Toronto. Thousands of students heard her story and read her book, *An Ordinary Woman in Extraordinary Times*, which was used as text material at York University for nine years. In 1998 I also became a volunteer as a docent (museum guide), but it took four years before she allowed me to work with her.

The story begins when we worked together for the first time. During her presentation, she mentioned her baby, who she had been trying to save from starvation. She also related an incident when she hid her wedding band in the baby's diaper. The students were all in Grade 6, and there was a little girl in the front row listening with rapt attention.

At the end of the presentation, this girl was the first to ask a question. "Where is your baby now?"

I was standing at the back of the room, and without hesitation, my mother pointed at me and said, "You see that middle aged man? That is my baby."

The next question was the turning point. The student wanted to know about her wedding band that she had hidden inside the diaper. The ring in question was the wedding ring that my father—the man I never knew— had given her. My mother was so in love with my father and so determined to save that ring that she took the exceptional step of hiding it, at the risk of our lives, rather than handing it over to her captors.

Unbeknownst to me, my mother hadn't allowed me to be her docent because she was afraid that I would criticize her. Using the opportunity the little girl gave me, I later told my mother that I would only make suggestions. By this time, she was married to my wonderful stepfather, Emil, and, naturally, she was wearing the ring that he had given her.

After the presentation, we went to lunch and discussed the event. I suggested that she put the original ring on her necklace and show it to the students in all future presentations. That is exactly what she did.

My extraordinary mother passed away on February 26, 2005. When I had the horrible task of clearing out her apartment, I came across the wedding ring that my father had given her. I decided to make the ring into a showpiece, which I would wear only when I was at the Holocaust Centre and on special occasions. The ring was ready in April of that year, and the first special occasion was on May 5.

Did I mention that I became a YOWie? For my 60th birthday, I bought a motorcycle and joined the Yidden on Wheels Motorcycle Touring Club of Toronto. Our club was part of the first ever Ride to Remember in 2005, to commemorate the 60th anniversary of the end of the Holocaust. We rode to Washington, D.C., where we met 250 other bikers and visited the United States Holocaust Memorial Museum.

When you ride a bike, you take as many scenic routes as you can, and Pennsylvania has some of the best. Since the ring was too big to wear under my riding glove, I kept it inside my breast pocket—close to my heart. One particular scenic curve held my attention longer than the law of physics would allow. When you crash a motorcycle going 40 miles per hour, you usually get something banged up, either the bike or yourself.

Not this time—I was riding with the "Ring of Love" next to my heart.

Louise Lawrence-Israels

*L*ouise Lawrence-Israels was born in Haarlem, The Netherlands, in July 1942. At six months of age, she went into hiding in Amsterdam with her parents and older brother. When the war ended in 1945, her family moved to Sweden. Three years later, they returned to Holland, where Louise completed her education and earned a degree in physical therapy. While in Holland, she also met her husband, and they were married in 1965.

In 1967 Louise and her husband immigrated to the United States. Louise volunteers at and works as a translator for the United States Holocaust Memorial Museum in Washington, D.C. She has relayed her war experiences to various groups. She lives in Bethesda, Maryland, and has three daughters and six grandchildren.

Courtesy of United States Holocaust Memorial Museum. Photograph by Arnold Kramer.

The Table

Louise Lawrence-Israels

The old family table now stands in the dining area of our house in Bethesda, Maryland. The table was made when my grandparents got married in Holland in 1907. It was made from solid mahogany wood, and it was our custom to gather around it for big meals at birthdays, holidays, and other occasions spent with family and friends. The table was made to seat 24. When it is closed, it seats eight; however, you can pull it open, and for each board you insert, another set of legs pops out from the bottom.

My grandmother loved to cook and bake, and she prepared many dinners. Her cooking tasted so good; her recipes called for pounds of butter, many eggs, and always cream instead of milk. There were not many Friday nights when the table was not surrounded by people who had a very good time during *Shabbat*[1] dinner.

This routine was abruptly halted when the Nazis invaded Holland. German officers confiscated the house, and my grandparents went into hiding. What happened to the table? I wish the table could tell its story.

The house was quite comfortable and had many rooms filled with beautiful furnishings. Did these Nazi officers have nice banquets? Did they enjoy sitting at such a beautiful table? What did they discuss? Did they talk about their strategies to murder Jews? Did they realize that many *Shabbat* dinners were enjoyed at the same table they were using for meetings to plot the removal of all Jews from Holland? They must have had very good food, while we were always hungry in hiding.

After we were liberated, it took a while before my grandparents returned to their home; they were afraid of what they would find. But

---

[1] The Sabbath, a weekly Jewish holy day from sundown Friday until shortly after sundown Saturday that is meant to be treated as a day of rest from the regular activities of the week.

they were very surprised. The house seemed well cared for, and most of their furnishings were still there, including the table. Of course, a lot of the artefacts were missing. Before they went into hiding, my grandparents tried to safeguard many beautiful things.

My grandmother was so happy to see her table still standing. She realized, though, that many of her friends and family members would no longer enjoy her cooking, sing *Shabbat* songs, or help her celebrate birthdays. They were dead; they had been put on transports and brutally murdered.

My grandmother was a strong person, and she made up her mind to continue with her gatherings. It was not easy. For many years, food was rationed, and it was difficult to get the right ingredients for her recipes.

The first party that I remember was my grandfather's 70th birthday in 1949. The table was so pretty; there were flowers, and everything was shining. I think there were about 14 people in attendance. Dinner was delicious.

My grandmother passed away eight years later, and the table remained in her house. Yet, it was not used for the next two years while my grandfather lived alone. Then my dad needed a table in his office, and it was moved to Amsterdam after my grandfather passed away. My dad used it as a desk and for meetings for the next 14 years.

When he retired, we had one more gathering in his office. We celebrated my dad's retirement, seated at the table with wine and cheese. I was living in Italy, but I did not want to miss the event. I did not tell my parents that I would try to come. At the time that the party was supposed to start, I rang the doorbell at the office. It was dusk, and when my father opened the door, he did not recognize me right away. Then a big smile spread across his face.

The table remained in the same building for a few more years. Meanwhile, my family moved to Belgium.

One day, my parents asked me and my husband if we had an interest in the table. We immediately said, "Yes." A few weeks later, we borrowed a friend's van and went to Holland to pick it up, along with all of the boards to extend it.

When my grandmother had the table made, she also had beautiful linens made for it. My mom gave me the largest tablecloths and napkins, and the smaller ones went to my sister. I made a promise with my sister that we would lend the tablecloths to one another, since some of them were matching.

My family did a lot of entertaining while we lived in Belgium, and the table was used a lot. Our eldest daughter had her *Bat Mitzvah*[2] in 1980, and many of our relatives came to celebrate with us. I went to France to buy special croissants, and my mother-in-law brought many pounds of smoked salmon from the States. The day after the *Bat Mitzvah,* we had a family breakfast. We opened the table with all the extensions and had a breakfast for 24. I borrowed the extra tablecloths from my sister.

The table was extended again to all its glory when we did the same thing for our other two daughters. After our assignment in Belgium was over, we moved back to the U.S. The army sent movers, who carefully packed the table so it would safely make its way to our new house.

The next big event was our eldest daughter's wedding in 1989. The table was used for dinners with family and friends, and we sometimes had to add another table so we could seat everybody. This time, my sister brought her tablecloth and napkins all the way from Holland.

Cooking and setting the table always kept me busy. We celebrated all the holidays and birthdays at the table. When my husband retired from the army, we brought the table to our house in Maryland. Now we sit for dinner at the table with our own children and grandchildren. There are 14 of us. Our youngest granddaughter danced on the table, and it is as strong as ever.

---

[2] A *Bat Mitzvah* marks the occasion when a Jewish girl comes of age at 12 years old. According to Jewish Law, she is then obligated to observe the Commandments. For boys, a *Bar Mitzvah* takes place when they turn 13.

Fruma Gulkowich Berger

*F*ruma Gulkowich Berger was born in 1918 and raised as one of five children in Korelitz, Poland. As a teenager, she was a member of a drama group and active in various Zionist youth groups, where she first began writing prose and poetry. Driven into the Novogrudek ghetto after the Nazi occupation of the town, she survived a major *Aktion* (Nazi operation involving mass murder and deportation) by hiding in a cesspool with her sister-in-law, Judy Gulkowich, for six days.

After being rescued by her brother, Ben Zion Gulkowich, and fleeing into the surrounding forests, Fruma became a fighter in the Bielski Brigade and was the first woman in the Brigade to be issued a weapon. During this time, she met her future husband, Murray Berger, who was also a fighter and one of the Brigade's original members.

Fruma and Murray Berger in Rome, Italy, in 1947, shortly after they were married and before they moved to the United States in April of that year.

Following the liberation in 1944, Fruma and Murray, along with other former Bielski partisans, made their way across Europe, living in Displaced Persons camps in Romania and Italy. They were married in Rome in February 1947 and immigrated to the United States in April of that year. Settling in Brooklyn, New York, they went on to have two sons and later two grandchildren. Fruma became well-known in Yiddish speaking circles for her poetry about life during the Holocaust and being a partisan. She passed away in 1995.

Jewish Partisans

Fruma Gulkowich Berger
(Translated by Professor Percy Matenko)

I.

At the very time of black despair's grim chance
A brilliant thought shone forth: resistance!
The dense forests into barracks changed will be,
And to the lofty trees we'll swear our loyalty.

The gloomy night will our protector be,
Far from strife of equal partners shall we see,
Not warriors here shall our power mete,
But death with dignity is also triumph great!

The heart is sad, but the body is with comfort filled,
For 'tis the day when vengeance's hour will be fulfilled.
Also the hour of fate, uncertain I must say,
Whither the angry storm our lives will bear away.

And if this is our fate, since the world has us betrayed,
With courage shall we fight, with gun and with grenade!
The bright days pass, before me dark shadows rise,
My comrade fell today, gloom grips me in its vice.

For it is not a struggle of equals, justice fair,
But against the slaughterer, a lamb's struggle in despair,
Yet suddenly lamb as lion transformed we see
Fight with pistol in its hands for a better morning, free!

II.

The hour has struck, 'tis time to take a stand.
A call to battle! Quickly take the gun in hand!
The ash of murdered ones the wind has blown,
With blood of millions is my courage sown.

I stand here on guard—a shot rends the air,
For vengeance it calls! For the mission I bear.
My struggle is just, this in my soul I feel,
The enemy to destroy—that is my goal.

The camp is aroused, to their arms they go,
The bullets are flying to and fro,
With earnest piety, sacred as prayer,
To strife called "guerrilla" into battle we dare.

The night is descending, take stock of the dead,
Death stalks our path, but for this we're prepared!
Over dense forests now onward I bend,
With gun at my shoulder, pistol in hand.

III.

I stand like a guard at the hour I'm free,
At my sigh the trees seem to mourn with me,
Lines of misfortune still etched in my face,
Stone and victim cry out, the loss to replace!

I can still feel the tremor, the horror, the rage
Through blood-soaked whips of my Holocaust-age,
From mountains of corpses goes my wandering soul,
With gun on my shoulder through dense forests I roam.

FRUMA GULKOWICH BERGER

Sole survivor am I, no place need I hasten,
For miles and miles death its grim toll has taken. . . .
Victory . . . how can I with triumphant tread
Join the nations that march, while I mourn for these dead?

Many an image appears before my eyes,
Time like an arrow from its bow can fly,
But forget shall I never that season's black day
Of blood and of flame that has shadowed my way.

The Young Mother

Fruma Gulkowich Berger
(Translated by Zelik Bedell)

Like a misty wind on a summer's night
The mother takes the dead child to the dark forest.
She shakes a little and hardly manages to rest on something
And what she rests on, a tree, she does not care.

The night, a black one,
Covers everything,
But the sparks of madness in her look
Move her feet.

The mother walks from far away, mile after mile,
Since her mind was emptied
Her body, her heart, her child, a little one
Today had tasted the first spoonful of tea.

She hugs the little body, she searches,
She touches where it is sore,
And why is the diaper not wet?
Suddenly the mother's madness imagines
Everything about her is crying
And she batters her head against the tree.

She saw it, everything in front of her eyes
Her house . . . it burns!
A German runs to her,
He grabs her child and throws her down,
And it scorches her very being.

And further, further, the head could not take it anymore
Who is crying, the child?
It wants to eat?
Wait! She bends down quickly—the milk in the full breast is
Painful.

She bares her breast. Here, suck, she begs.
The breast remains bare, and the wind cools and fondles it.
The mother thinks it is the mouth,
The little hands of her child.

The skies light up, a ray shines
And partisans arrive and gaze at the scene:
The dead child, the young woman,
The breasts in the blue hands of the child.
With pain and tears, they recognize a friend.

Leon Krym

*L*eon Krym was born in 1923 in Warsaw, Poland, and was the second eldest of four children. Like many others, he and his family were forced to leave their home and relocate to the Warsaw ghetto. He last saw his family in 1942 as they were taken away to be transported to the Treblinka extermination camp.

After the war ended, having lost all 65 members of his family, Leon left Poland and spent some time in Paris. He then sailed to Israel on the ship *Negba* and arrived in Haifa in 1949. For the next four years he served in the Israel Defense Forces, and then he immigrated to Toronto, Canada. He earned a diploma from the Jewish Teachers' Seminary and taught Hebrew in Ontario, first in Kirkland Lake and then in Oakville. He also volunteered with a number of community organizations.

In 1964 Leon was married, and he and his wife, Sylvia, had two children. Leon and Sylvia opened a shoe store in Toronto, which they operated for 27 years. Since Leon's retirement, feeling a connection to his history, he has focused on recording the experiences of his youth and the memories of his dear lost family in short stories and poems, some of which have appeared in the *Canadian Jewish News* and the *Jewish Tribune*.

The Great Action, 1942

Leon Krym

In July 1942, on a bright summer day in the Warsaw ghetto, my mother was peeling potatoes for our one and only meal of the day. Suddenly, we heard unusual noises and voices coming from the courtyard. Scared and confused, tenants ran up and down the stairs. As I looked out the front window facing the street, I could see that our building was surrounded by Nazi troops and military trucks.

Soon, German soldiers and officers marched into the courtyard of our building on Swientojerska Street No. 30. From the third floor, we could hear voices of Jewish policemen translating German orders into Polish, calling on the tenants to get down to the courtyard immediately with no luggage in hand. Anyone caught in the building would be shot.

Luckily, my older brother, Abraham, wasn't home at the time. However, my parents, my younger brother, Jacob, my sister, Luba, and I went downstairs and joined the hundreds of tenants now standing in line. One of our tenants, Mr. Lot, jumped from the rooftop to the pavement below, preferring to die in his own way and time. Mothers were clutching their babies in their arms, covered by their garments, while terrified children held onto their parents in desperation.

In the afternoon, the courtyard was crowded with about 400 tenants. As the first column of people started to walk out toward the military trucks parked on the street, my father turned to me and said, "Laibale, get out of the line and show your working permit to the German officer. Maybe you will survive."

I hesitated, not wanting to be separated from my dear family, for better or worse. However, my father insisted and gently pushed me out of the line. With my working permit in hand, I approached the German officer who happened to be standing in front of our line. He briefly stared at me and without paying attention to my permit pointed his finger toward the resident's entrance, motioning me to go back inside the building. With mixed feelings, I took the stairs back to our apartment unit.

As soon as I reached our third floor apartment, I was struck by the sight of the peeled potatoes left on the stove uncooked. I cried bitterly, knowing very well that I would never see my mother or the others again. I never did.

Toward the evening, several hundred tenants of the building were hurled onto military trucks and driven to the Warsaw train station, the "Umschlagplatz." There, they were packed and pressed into a cattle train and shipped to the Treblinka death camp.

That night I cried all alone. My heart was breaking and my head spinning. As I tried to get some sleep, I could hear a door slamming and the window curtain fluttering in the summer breeze.

The next morning, after arriving for work at the factory, I choked back tears while operating the toothbrush machine. "I must not cry," I told myself. "I must be strong, and the world shall know. I must still produce the daily quota of toothbrushes, as if nothing has happened."

Several days later, as I was sitting in my room and grieving for my dear family, I heard a faint knock at the door. At first I thought that I was dreaming; yet, when I heard another knock I jumped to my feet and ran to the door. "Abraham?" I asked.

"Yes, I'm your brother Abraham," he whispered.

I quickly opened the door, and Abraham, with his longtime girlfriend, Hanka, rushed into the room. I locked the door behind them. They heard about our tragedy and had stayed away from the building for several days for their own safety. We hugged and kissed, tears flowing down our faces.

I knew of my brother's Zionist activities and understood that they belonged to youth group Betar but didn't talk about it. Hanka had a beautiful face and black eyes. Her hair was combed tightly to the back and rested on her shoulders. A dimly lit candle was on the center of the table, illuminating their young and beautiful faces that were filled with love. I went back to my bed, buried my head in the pillow, and grieved for my dear family that I lost only days ago.

When I woke up the next morning, they were already gone. They had slipped out at night so as not to be detected by German soldiers patrolling the ghetto. As usual, I left the apartment for work at the toothbrush factory, where we received our daily meager food rations.

After a day's work, the shop was closed. All of the Jewish workers, including me, boarded military trucks and were transported to a transit camp.

One day, as if out of nowhere I noticed Abraham a short distance from the camp fence. We exchanged glances. With tears in my eyes, I watched him wave goodbye and disappear within the lifeless walls of the Warsaw ghetto.

Every day I looked out and around the fence, hoping to see him once more. He never came back, and I never saw him again.

Pictured from left to right: Leon's parents, Mordechai Mair Krym and Sarah Krym, his older brother, Abraham, and his younger brother, Jacob.

The Holocaust Inferno

Leon Krym

A rose garden I didn't walk,
of children's thrills I knew not.

A boyhood I lived, happiness I sought,
getting through the day was my only thought.

I walked a road burning beneath my feet,
slumped in a pit, Warsaw ghetto retreat.

When the night came to a close,
I dreaded the coming morning.

I feared my shadow, my foe in waiting,
eager to forsake me and give me away.

Treblinka, Auschwitz, there stops the train.
Lives extinguished; no more pain.

Smoke and ashes blowing in the wind,
eclipse the sun, stain the moon.

Silenced forever, a child's cry, a mother's plea
echo in the valley, resounding eternally.

Nothing but a miracle can save my day.
Postpone my demise, come what may.

Amid the horrors of the Holocaust
as the world kept silent and hope was lost

On the shores far away, the beaches of Normandy,
the sun's peeking, shattered hearts again smiling.

A new life emerging out of ruins and pain.
Six million perish, just memories remain.

From the Nazi Inferno to the Land of the Free
I salute thee Canada, my impossible dream.

Pete Philipps

Pete Philipps was born in Essen, Germany. Three years after Hitler's rise to power, together with his parents and two younger brothers, Pete fled to Prague, Czechoslovakia. Following the Nazi takeover of Czechoslovakia in 1939, the family moved to Genoa, Italy. Half a year later, they again relocated, this time to Quito, Ecuador.

In 1941 they arrived in the United States and settled in New York. After graduating from the City College of New York, Pete served with the United States Army in Germany for two years. He then went on to become an award-winning writer and editor for *The New York Times* and *BusinessWeek*. He also spent nine years as a volunteer at the United States Holocaust Memorial Museum. He currently resides in Bethesda, Maryland.

In Memoriam

Pete Philipps

Benno turned up his collar and cursed the rain, convinced after the third limousine dropped off its passengers at the opposite end of the soggy field from where he stood waiting that something had gone wrong. He'd been given a plum assignment—to greet members of the diplomatic corps and other foreign dignitaries and escort them to their seats. Now there was nothing to do but to swallow his disappointment and look for a seat of his own.

The seats in front of the dais were already taken by Holocaust survivors, many of whom looked as though they had been huddling under their blankets and umbrellas all night. Looking out across the crowd brought to mind another cold, drizzly April day when he had stood, almost alone, watching his father's coffin being lowered into the ground.

His reverie was interrupted by a Park Police bus that quietly coasted past and came to a stop nearby. An officer emerged, nodded in his general direction, and disappeared in the crowd. A few moments passed; then a gradual trickle of people with credentials identical to his hanging from their necks climbed aboard, presumably to warm up. He decided to follow them, absently choosing a seat next to young woman with a profusion of curly bronze-coloured hair.

The woman looked up, smiling. "The driver said we'll have to get off when the lieutenant returns," she said. She was pretty, with a high forehead, untroubled blue-green eyes, and a flawless complexion.

"I just want to thaw out."

"Me, too," she said. "I was handing out programs until my fingers got so numb that I could barely move them."

They compared hands to see whose were bluer, and their fingertips came within a millimetre of touching.

"Maybe we should introduce ourselves," he said when they stopped laughing. "I'm Benno Perlman, a volunteer."

"I'm Nicole Smith from Visitor Services, but I go by Niki." She paused. "May I ask what made you want to become a volunteer?"

"My father spent three years in Auschwitz-Birkenau."

"And survived?"

Benno nodded. "Unfortunately, he died almost exactly a year ago. In fact, this used to be his coat. It was his first big purchase in America. He was so looking forward to the opening of the museum. He wanted to show kids around and talk about his experience."

"And your mom?"

"Her family lived out the war in England. She now lives in Florida. I'm sure she'll be watching on television."

Niki looked at him thoughtfully. "This must be an auspicious day for you," she said.

"It is," replied Benno. "I only wish I had paid more attention and been more inquisitive when my parents wanted to talk about their experience, especially my father."

"I know what you mean." Niki turned slightly, and her green and black skirt inched up a bit more above her knees. "As kids, we don't want to hear about the old days," she said, making quotation marks in the air.

Benno looked at her—professor to student—and wondered how many hearts she had already broken.

"I hope they don't fire me for abandoning my post," said Niki.

"I wouldn't worry," said Benno, and then proceeded to tell her about the mix-up with his assignment. "I'm sorry my father didn't live to be here today. He often said that when the survivors are all gone, there will be no one left to tell their story." He stopped to look out the window. "Speaking of stories, you haven't told me what brings you here."

"Pure serendipity," replied Niki. She told him a bit about her background, how after earning a degree in art history she had come to Washington and looked in vain for a museum job. In desperation, she had finally applied to the United States Holocaust Memorial Museum, a few months before the museum's opening, hoping that it might be a stepping-stone. "I was also running out of money." She laughed. "Anyway, by the time I'd gone through the training program, I was so fascinated with the Holocaust that I put my original plans on hold."

"So this may not be a temporary job," said Benno.

"It's too early to tell, but I very strongly believe in the museum's mission," replied Niki.

"In other words, you don't have to be Jewish to feel a commitment."

"In the little town of Mississippi where I grew up, there were no Jews. I don't remember ever hearing anything about the Holocaust. Being here has given me a whole new perspective."

"How so?" asked Benno.

Niki took a long pause before responding. "What happened then affected everyone. And it does to this day. It's horrifying to think that so much human cruelty and depravity occurred in the lifetime of my parents."

Benno was still trying to come up with a fitting response when the driver called out, "Sorry folks, I see the lieutenant. You all need to get off now."

"Too bad," said Niki. "I was just getting warm."

"Are you going back to giving out programs?"

"Too late now."

"In that case, why don't we look for seats together?"

"That would be nice," said Niki, accepting Benno's hand while alighting.

The rain let up, and the United States Army band began to play. Benno and Niki eventually found two empty chairs toward the rear of the field. Benno took off his raincoat and draped it across both seats.

"Your poor coat," said Niki.

"Believe me, it doesn't owe me a thing," said Benno. "It's just that I haven't found the heart to give it away. It isn't even waterproof anymore."

"All the same, it's lovely that you've held on to it."

As the ceremony got underway, Benno occasionally turned his head toward Niki, giving her appraising little glances. The second or third time he stole a look at her, their eyes met and he laughed. Then they were both laughing. He could easily imagine his mother's reaction if he were to tell her about the young colleague sitting beside him. *What business does a shiksa* (young non-Jewish woman) *have working in the Holocaust Museum? How can she understand? How can she possibly feel anything of what we went through?* He quickly brushed the image aside; he had long since given up trying to change his mother's narrow mindset.

"Are you all right?" he heard Niki ask.

"Sorry, I was lost in thought."

Suddenly, a group of protestors from somewhere behind the chain-link enclosure began a rhythmic chant: "We don't buy / the Holocaust lie."

"They should be locked up," whispered Niki. "Goes to show that the Adolfs are alive in spirit." Seeing Benno's puzzled look, she added, "Hitler and Eichmann."[1]

"You're so right," said Benno. "But try to ignore them. They're just a fringe bunch of antisemitic rabble rousers."

They chatted for some time and now and then exchanged comments on the succession of speakers. When it was Elie Wiesel's turn to speak, the sun, as though on cue, broke through a hole in the pewter clouds and bathed the dais in a halo of light.

"How is it," asked Wiesel at one point, "that man's silence was matched by G-d's?"

"That's what I'd like to know," said Benno under his breath.

Niki gave him a searching look and said, "Me, too."

As soon as Wiesel returned to his seat, the hole in the cloud closed again.

"He has such a haunted expression," said Niki.

"The expression of someone with a heavy heart," said Benno. "Somehow, he seems to give the Holocaust a human dimension, don't you think?"

Niki nodded and pointed to Bill Clinton, who was then approaching the lectern. His hair flattened by the wet wind, the U.S. President noted that the dedication of the museum coincided with the 50th anniversary of the Warsaw ghetto uprising. He prophesied that it would "bind one of the darkest lessons in history to the hopeful soul of America."

The rest of the ceremony passed Benno by in a pleasant blur, and then it came to a close with the lighting of the commemoratory flame and Jessye Norman singing "America the Beautiful."

It was going to rain again, but there seemed to be no rush for the exits. Particularly slow to leave were the survivors, many of whom gathered in small, animated groups that gave the scene the feel of a college reunion.

---

[1] Adolf Eichmann was an SS Lieutenant-Colonel who managed the logistics of mass deportations of Jews to ghettos and extermination camps during the Holocaust.

"They're the last of the witnesses," said Niki, pointing to a handful of grey-haired figures clustered under a large umbrella.

Benno was about to suggest going for coffee, but something held him back. Instead, he said that he hoped their schedules would occasionally overlap. They were standing on Raoul Wallenberg Place by now, a few feet from the steps leading to the museum.

"I hope so, too," said Niki. "Tomorrow, the public gets its first look. Keep your fingers crossed. Meanwhile, it was nice to meet you, Benno." She accepted his outstretched hand. "I enjoyed talking to you."

Had Niki held his hand a fraction of a second longer than necessary, or did he only imagine it? Having already decided to take the rest of the day off, he waited until she entered the museum by a revolving door before starting down the two long blocks to the Smithsonian Metro station.

Not until he had stepped off the escalator did he realize that he had forgotten his coat. He debated whether to go back. Just then, a train rumbled into the station. Figuring that someone might have walked off with the coat by now, he sprinted down the platform in time to thrust himself into the last car before the doors slid shut.

This story is fictional, except for the main events of the dedication ceremony for the United States Holocaust Memorial Museum that took place in April 1993.

The Invitation

Pete Philipps

It was another uneventful afternoon fielding routine questions at the information desk in the United States Holocaust Memorial Museum. Or so I thought, when from behind me came a sound quite unlike anything I'd ever heard before. Spinning around, I found myself standing face to face with a burly, red-faced man who appeared to be having a convulsion. An epileptic seizure, I thought, and immediately realized that the potential for such an occurrence never came up in the course of my training as a Visitor Services volunteer.

Helpless, I remained rooted to the spot until my ear caught a few words of guttural German. Shaken from my stupor, I asked the visitor in German if I could be of any assistance. Astonished to be so addressed, the visitor gradually calmed down. He assured me that he was not in any physical distress and introduced himself as Rudi, a retired stonemason from a small village near Cologne, Germany. He had come to Washington with a touring men's chorus and had just come from the permanent exhibition.

"Where are your friends?" I asked, surprised that his colleagues weren't looking for him.

Rudi pulled out his handkerchief and dabbed at his eyes. Had I said something wrong? "They had absolutely no interest in coming here," he said. "They went sightseeing. I came alone."

Nothing has changed, I wanted to say, but then checked myself. Instead, I asked Rudi what had drawn *him* to the museum.

With the crimson colouration gone from his face, he began with an apology for having lost his composure. After a long pause, he said that he had just relived the worst experience of his life. He went on to share the story of a man still tormented by the memory of an ordeal that occurred nearly 50 years earlier—one that I will never forget either.

First, though, Rudi wanted to know where I had learned to speak flawless German. In the interest of time, I kept my answer brief. "I'm a survivor of Nazi Germany," I said.

Rudi's face lit up and he began his story. Weeks before the war ended, the Nazis began the infamous death marches of concentration camp inmates westward ahead of the advancing Russians. One day, a group of skeletal women was force-marched through his little village. Moved by the spectacle of the emaciated prisoners shuffling down his street, Rudi's mother and several other townspeople tried to throw scraps of food to them. Rudi emphasized that by food he meant "slops that we ordinarily fed to the pigs." The instant the guards saw what was happening, they ordered the villagers to stop. Anyone caught giving aid to the prisoners would join their ranks and face the same fate. "We weren't even allowed to give those half-dead women a little water to drink," he added and began to weep all over again.

It took him a while before he continued. "Then one of the guards just knocked my mother into the mud with the butt of his rifle." For a moment I was afraid Rudi would collapse. But he caught his breath and said, "I was just a boy of 13."

To this day, I cannot begin to imagine how I would have felt if I had been in Rudi's place. He had other, equally horrific anecdotes; each brought on fresh tears. As it was time for me to rotate from the information desk to my next assignment, he and I hurriedly exchanged addresses and promised to stay in touch.

"I am a simple labourer," he reminded me, "and not a good correspondent," but I assured him we would manage. The last thing he said before we went our different ways was, "Come visit me. You can have your own room and bath and a television with American programs." We shook hands, and I hurried off.

I had little expectation of hearing from Rudi, much less of ever seeing him again. But I was wrong—on both counts. A few weeks later, I received a hand-written letter in which he repeated his invitation to pay him a visit. He even enclosed photographs of his house.

So began an irregular correspondence that continues to this day. It did not take long before I came to the conclusion that what Rudi lacked in formal education he more than made up for with his warmth and understanding. Especially touching were his oft-repeated laments about man's inhumanity to his fellow man and, in particular, "the suffering of the Jewish people over the centuries."

Two years later, the city of Essen, where I was born in Germany, invited me and my American-born wife, Evelyn, for an all-expenses-paid weeklong visit. This was a gesture of contrition to former Jewish residents who were forced to flee. Despite Evelyn's reluctance to travel to Germany, the opportunity was too good to turn down, especially since it held the prospect of a side trip to Cologne to visit Rudi.

Four decades had passed since I had last set foot on German soil as a member of the United States Army of Occupation. I had the eerie feeling of having emerged from a time capsule. But all the emotional baggage was quickly pushed aside by the welcome we received from Rudi and his wife, Maria. A bystander seeing us as we arrived at Cologne's main railroad station would have thought we were old friends celebrating a reunion. The four of us established an instant rapport, and, within minutes, we were off to lunch and to see the city sights.

High on Rudi's to-do list was a visit to the imposing synagogue on Roonstrasse. Destroyed on *Kristallnacht*,[1] it was meticulously rebuilt after the war and rededicated in 1959.

"Just wait," said Rudi with the enthusiasm of a three-year-old about to enter a toy store. "It's so beautiful."

Alas, when we got there the gates were shut. "It's *Shabbat*,"[2] a disembodied voice reminded us over an intercom when we rang the bell. Crestfallen, Rudi led the way to the next attraction on his list. Altogether, we managed to cram quite a bit into our day.

Our final stop was Cologne's famous gothic cathedral. Begun in the Middle Ages, its twin 525-foot towers make it the defining symbol of the city's skyline. Despite some still-visible damage from Allied bombs, the massive, ornately carved exterior is nothing short of breathtaking. Equally awe-inspiring is the interior, with its elaborate woodcarvings and gilded

---

[1] *Kristallnacht,* also known as The Night of Broken Glass, took place on November 9 and 10, 1938. Nazis and members of the Hitler Youth violently attacked Jews and their homes, synagogues, and businesses throughout Germany and Austria.

[2] The Sabbath, a weekly Jewish holy day from sundown Friday until shortly after sundown Saturday that is meant to be treated as a day of rest from the regular activities of the week.

altars. Here and there, small groups of people were silently praying, seemingly in a world of their own. Soon, I, too, felt enveloped in a spiritual embrace.

Rudi, not one to linger over artistic or historical details, soon had us follow him to a bank of votive candles in front of the main altar. "Here," he said, insistently handing me a candle while he dropped some coins into the collection box. "Light it and say a prayer for all the members of your family who were murdered."

I, who had never been inside a church except as a tourist, did as he told me, without feeling the least bit uncomfortable or self-conscious. If anything, I walked into the open air again with a wholeness of spirit—and renewed hope.

Two years later, Rudi and Maria came to the U.S. as members of a tour that included a two-day stop in Washington, D.C. Naturally, Evelyn and I prepared to show them around. To our surprise, almost the first thing they said when we picked them up at their hotel was that they were only interested in seeing us. No touring of the capital's historic sights and museums for them. I saw little point in arguing with Rudi, and we drove straight to our house for lunch.

It was a beautiful day in May, and as we showed them to the deck in our backyard, Rudi began to tug at a bulge in his pants pocket. Out came a small harmonica. Without saying a word, but with the look of a conductor about to give the downbeat to a large symphony orchestra, he launched into "God Bless America."

John H. Adler

John H. Adler was born to Jewish parents in Germany in 1923. He was an only child. When he was 13 years old, he was forced to quit school, since Jews were no longer permitted to attend German schools.

In February 1939 John's parents fled to Shanghai, China. In August of that year, three days before the Germans invaded Poland, John immigrated to Palestine (now Israel), where he lived in a *kibbutz* (collective community) for the next 18 months.

In 1941 John left the *kibbutz* to join the Palestine Police. Being 18, he volunteered for the British Armed Forces, serving in the 8th Army in the Sahara Desert and in the Italian Campaign. Following his service, in 1946 he moved to Rome, Italy, where he lived and worked for an American Jewish organization engaged in assisting Holocaust survivors. He reconnected with his parents, who had survived the war in a Shanghai refugee camp, and they immigrated to the United States in the spring of 1948. He followed them that fall.

A year later, John was married. He and his wife had a daughter. John went on to work in the food industry for 43 years and retired in 1991. It was at this time that he began to write. He has now written seven books, three of which have been published.

Through a Child's Eyes

John H. Adler

Henry LaVine had a bad night. He could not sleep thinking of the letter he had received in yesterday's mail. He rose from bed, showered, and dressed. He would go to the office and try to get the news out of his mind. Kissing his wife and children goodbye, he left home skipping breakfast.

The commuter train took him to the city, and he walked five blocks to the high-rise building housing his office. Sitting behind his desk, he buried his face in his hands.

"Hold all my calls!" he instructed his secretary.

Henry, a respected member of a large commercial bank, was a tall, broad-shouldered man. Hard work and a competitive nature enabled him to quickly rise through the ranks of the bank's organization. Joining the bank upon his return from Vietnam, where he was a captain, he specialized in foreign currency transactions and eventually became the head of the department. A devoted family man, he was well-liked and respected by most people in business as well as in private life.

Henry was a deeply troubled man. Thoughts of his childhood flooded his mind as he recalled being a small boy, aged five, sitting in the back room of a police station in the port city of Oporto in Northern Portugal.

The year was 1938, when Kurt and Edith Berger were medical interns at the General Hospital in Göttingen, Germany. They were part of a group of 12 young doctors serving their internships. Most of them, graduates of the same medical school, had been together for several years. It was a good life, and, in spite of growing antisemitism, the young couple socialized with the other interns and enjoyed a good relationship with gentiles. Some of the teaching physicians were Jewish, and the atmosphere at the hospital was cordial, in total disregard of anti-Jewish Nazi propaganda.

Kurt and Edith were married while still in medical school and were, by now, parents of two lovely children. The eldest, Heinz, was not quite four years old, and Eva, the baby, was two.

That year, during and following *Kristallnacht*,[1] all German Jewish men in Göttingen were arrested. The Bergers, tipped off anonymously, escaped the fate of their fellow Jewish interns by fleeing to Portugal. That is why in 1939 they lived in a one-bedroom apartment in a low-class neighbourhood of Oporto. Fourteen months had passed since they arrived in this city after hurriedly leaving their hometown.

For Heinz, it was a great adventure. His little sister, Eva, was too young to be affected by the events. The Bergers had been very lucky to obtain Portuguese transit visas good for three months. Kurt's uncle, who lived in the United States since 1933, was the head of oncology at a prominent New York hospital. He posted an affidavit for the Bergers, enabling them to obtain visas for the States. However, due to their hurried departure from Germany, the documents arrived too late. When the family could not be found at their given address in Göttingen, the affidavit was sent to the U.S. Consulate in Berlin. Since the applicants did not show up to claim their visas within three months, all documents were returned to America.

Fourteen months passed, and the documents had not yet been forwarded to their present address. Kurt telephoned the U.S. Consulate in Berlin and was told that they would have to wait. The American clerk promised to forward the papers to Oporto as soon as they arrived. He was aware of the urgency but asked them not to worry. The telegram that Kurt sent to his uncle in the U.S. remained unanswered. They were in limbo not knowing what to do next.

At the end of 1939, the Portuguese Government, under pressure from the German Nazi regime, decreed the expulsion of all foreigners residing in their country without proper visas. It was a Nazi ploy to force all Jews out of Europe. At the time, almost no country in the world accepted Jews, and the Bergers, along with many others, faced the return to Germany and a bitter fate.

---

[1] *Kristallnacht,* also known as The Night of Broken Glass, took place on November 9 and 10, 1938. Nazis and members of the Hitler Youth violently attacked Jews and their homes, synagogues, and businesses throughout Germany and Austria.

There was also a money problem. Fleeing in the middle of the night, the Bergers did not have enough time to visit their bank, and their written requests for their funds were ignored. They assumed correctly that their accounts had been frozen by the German government

Kurt and Edith were realists, feeling sure that their forced return to Germany would result in their eventual death. They agonized over what to do with the children. Approaching the Jewish community in Lisbon, they obtained the address of a childless Jewish family in Oporto. Contacting them, they were able to make arrangements for the boy, but not for the little girl.

Now, at age five, little Heinz sat in the back room of the Oporto police station playing with a toy automobile. Through a glass panel in the door, he could see his parents arguing with a police official. His mother did most of the talking, while his father cradled Eva in his arms. She had fallen asleep; her face snuggled up against her father's unshaven cheek.

The door to the back room opened, and a strange woman with a kindly face looked at Heinz, smiled, and left. Following her with his eyes, he noticed her speaking with his parents. He could see his father handing her a small suitcase and some money. They hugged and shook hands.

Through the door, Heinz noticed that all civilians in the adjoining room were grouped into pairs and led out by officers. They walked down a narrow alley leading to the harbour, and Heinz's parents were among them. They did not look back. When the group turned a corner, it occurred to the little boy that his parents were leaving without him. Desperately trying to open the door, he had trouble turning the smooth doorknob that kept slipping out of his hands. When he finally succeeded, his parents had disappeared, and he could no longer see them.

Running down the lane, Heinz tried to catch up with them. Crying bitterly, he called for his mother and father not to leave without him. He could not understand why they would abandon him.

"I've been a good boy," he cried. "Why are you angry with me?"

A firm, gentle hand held and embraced him, and the woman who had smiled at him earlier pulled him to her chest and spoke soothingly in a language he did not understand. He continued to weep, asking for his mother and father, wanting to know why they were leaving him.

"You're taking Eva," he sobbed. "Why not me? Don't you love me anymore?"

After a while, he stopped struggling, resigning himself to his fate.

Henry LaVine had engaged a detective agency to determine what had happened to his parents and sister. Yesterday, he received the bad news. Upon forced reentry into Germany, his parents and sister had been murdered in a Nazi concentration camp.

Sitting at his desk, Henry cried, remembering the pain and sense of abandonment he had felt so long ago and still felt today. He had been too young to understand his parents' ultimate sacrifice. They had left him behind so he would live. Unable to get his mind off the letter, he decided to go home. But first he had to make one more stop.

There was a small synagogue two blocks away, and he entered. This was the first time since his arrival in the U.S. that he visited a temple. He thanked his parents once again for giving him life. Hot tears streaming down his face, he said *Kaddish* (Jewish mourners' prayer).

The characters in this story are fictional, but the story is based on true events.

Is Our Future Our Past?

John H. Adler

The Earth shook,
Smoke billowed high,
The so familiar look,
Are bombs falling from the sky?

But it came from below our feet
Assassins causing disaster,
Making our people bleed
And die at paces ever faster.

When will the dying end?
We have but one life to give,
We must have the right to defend
The land where we came to live.

This is not a soldier's war
Armies combating for gain,
We are only fighting for
Our biblical right to remain.

We are dying in the streets
Just like the pogroms of yore,
They're destroying our seed,
Survival is what we're fighting for.

Our eyes turn to the skies,
How long must the suffering last?
Won't anyone hear our cries?
Will our future be our past?

Sophie Soil

*B*orn in Iasi, Romania, Sophie Soil is a Holocaust survivor who experienced numerous traumatic Nazi-perpetrated atrocities. During the war, her father ended up in the Ialomitza concentration camp. He survived—barely—but was never the same. Sophie, her mother, and her younger sister also survived the war, though not without much deprivation and suffering. The family eventually ended up in Canada.

Sophie went on to become an accomplished poet and artist/craftsperson and won first and second place for her crafts at the Canadian National Exhibition (CNE). She also garnered many accolades for her poetry, prose, and short stories, which were published in literary journals and anthologies worldwide. Many of her written works have been short-listed for and recipients of numerous top prizes, including two Pushcart Prize nominations.

PublishAmerica released Sophie's two poetic biographical collections: *Bygone Daughters of a Lesser Fate: A Poetic Memoir* (2004); and *Ashes Left to Linger: A Poetic Search for Closure* (2005). Both publications are in the Yad Vashem library in Jerusalem. She wrote *Ashes Left to Linger* from the vantage point of a Holocaust survivor's daughter.

Sophie's personal healing journey also led her to the study of herbology, through which she earned her Chartered and Master Herbalist certificates. She currently writes alternative health material and lives in Toronto, Canada, with her husband of 56 years.

Me: A Portrait in the Raw

Sophie Soil

go back to your childhood years and try to remember
when you first heard the word *Shoah* and watched a tear
unfurl from your father's eyes; the word whispered like
some pleated sadness blossoming into a perfect sorrow;
unsavoury across his tongue, dark as grief; an aching stab
to your ear, a poking finger at your heart . . .

> and you not even knowing why.

did not that word initiated by a demon you can only guess at,
punctuated with a sigh, always catch you by surprise?
stir some want you hadn't explicated yet? a need to understand
the root, the meaning of the frown? the despondent pronunciation
loosened into the air like a released question mark, to deal with
whatever anguish it may spring; like a free-sprung heart-cry
infused with gravity and mourning, beyond

> whoever prays for quick release?

and what about *Shoah*: a word that means Holocaust? both the
cruelty of death pangs and the colour of blood spilled at a
street crossing; both the name of a family buried long before you
were born, and the colour on a survivor's soul, both ash-grey
and crimson; a red and grey far removed from beauty, now a
filler in two still-life portraits, an etch that needs to be
transported by a slew of lifetime tears; a bruise across a father's
heart with such dark traces, one *must* venture after it—yet step
right into peril; a peril strangely fire-like—so electric, it creates
its own evil glow, except that it's become a faint reticence, an
immediacy that pines for kin reduced to smoke and dust,

> whose name you are the bearer.

or is it just another memory transported into the portrait
I've become, regardless that it doesn't own a name?
a pain that never went away from him juxtaposed
directly onto me, underlining the spectrum of a
quasi-present, defined now only by the sorrow
that sustains it, birthing the purest of blue, or the
          greyest of grey feelings in the me of me . . . ?

Papa's Plight

Sophie Soil

half-naked, injured, bruised, and bleeding
from the beating, soaked in sweat, gasping for air,
imprisoned in a barren, hermetically sealed cattle boxcar
for the week's duration of the killing-voyage, the death train
clambered out an ominous tempo to the rhythm of papa's
pain and fright, as the mournful whistle hooted out the
tragedy of his kin's catastrophe. eight days back and forth
along the same short stretch of track without food or water,
then leaving the familiar territory of his city for the
black contour of killing camps, the pyramid of bodies piling
higher every day in the stifling proximity of crowded
space—for they wanted to be free from thirst and stench,
and so they entered the fading tangibility of the thousands
of dead scurrying toward the cruel sky
                        laid empty of every bit of empathy.

and soon, he, too, lay down to sleep his final sleep. . . . and
then his grandma's spirit came; an alighted vision
interrupting his vanilla death dream, saying, *"wake up,
it's raining, it's not your time to die yet."* stepping over the
pyramid of outstretched arms and legs and blank eyes, he
stretched toward the window bars, holding his handkerchief
toward the torrential raindrops, a white flagship of survival
hanging wet and limply in the soupy swill, then squeezed the
gathered raindrops on his dried up tongue against death's
imminent demand, gasping some solid breaths through a tiny
knothole. a single armed station guard on the platform
blew the whistle, mocking: *"hey there, Jew, have a piece of
cornstalk to choke on,"* handed over speared on his gleaming

bayonet; he sucking the cud's succulence; it dripping, dripping
life into his half-dead body . . . and it tided him through the
entire death ride as he straddled the corpses of his kin, the
iron dragon tugging and chugging blue murder

hurrying toward more than even this turbid scene
could possibly conceive—for it was harsh and
everything he feared. thousands perished there.
only a handful survived—he among them. . . . or
                                  what was left of him . . .

survived??? **no!!!** not this, this makeshift misalignment;
this quasi-animation pretending to be lifelike!!!

Renate Krakauer

Renate (Tannenzapf) Krakauer is a child Holocaust survivor from the Stanislawow ghetto in Poland. She was born in 1941, when Stanislawow was under Soviet occupation. Five months later, the Nazis invaded, and by the end of that year all the Jews were confined to the ghetto. A year later, Renate's mother smuggled her baby out of the ghetto and took her to a Polish peasant woman in a nearby village for safekeeping.

Following the war, Renate and her parents lived under Soviet occupation again and then escaped to the west (Poland and Germany), finally making their way to Canada in December 1948. Renate went on to work as a pharmacist, educator, and senior executive for the provincial government and postsecondary sector. She is now retired and lives in Toronto with her husband, Hank Lobbenberg. She has three children, two stepchildren, and three grandchildren.

Renate has had short stories published in various online and print journals, including *Parchment, Women in Judaism, The Storyteller, Foliate Oak,* and *Skive.* She has also had personal essays published in the *Globe and Mail, Dovetail: A Journal by and for Jewish/Christian Families,* and *Living Legacies: A Collection of Inspirational Contemporary Canadian Jewish Women.* In 2009 the Azrieli Foundation published her memoir, *But I Had a Happy Childhood,* along with that of her father, William Tannenzapf, titled *Memories from the Abyss.*

Escape From the Ghetto

Renate Krakauer

There is darkness everywhere. Where's my baby? I must find her! Oh, G-d, what have I done to deserve this punishment? Ah, there she is in the corner on a pile of rags–sweet dumpling, sweet skinny dumpling. They'll have to fatten you up at Irena's or those bad men will kill you—the beasts will know you're a Jewish baby. No, no! Don't cry! You're safe with me. Mama will protect you. I'll take you away from this hellhole. I'll be the shield; my bones are as tough as steel. I won't let any bullets get you, even if I have to stop them with my bare hands.

You're so hungry, poor darling. Here, suck on this rag. Soaked in sugar water, my sweet. I'll wrap you in the featherbed, and we'll fly away together. Out of the fires of hell. Away from these devils. Free as the birds. You'll see! Like a butterfly you'll be. Golden wings in the sun.

The devil in uniform guards the gate. Do you see his forked tail? His horns? His sharp pointy teeth? You mustn't worry. Snuggle into your Mama's bosom. There! Now the soft feathers make a nest around you. I'll waddle right by him. I meet his evil eyes and don't blink. I can see right into his black soul. I sidle past his thick brick back as bold as a peasant.

We're on the street. Oh joy! I rip off the hateful badge. What a desecration of our beautiful *Magen David* (Star of David). We slip and slide on wet cobble stones. That snake with wild eyes who shares our room stole my shoes. Her bite still stings on my forearm. No matter. With bare feet, I'm a dancer, a ballerina. I float, I fly, I leap. From doorway to lamp post. From street corner to tunnel. Under balconies. Over bridges. You and I are like a beam of light in this drizzle; we're transparent.

My darling, close your eyes. You don't want to see those nosy Poles peering at us from every window and doorway. They want to send us back. Never! They'll have to shoot me first. If they try to take you from me, I'll scream! I'll bite! I'll kick! I'll be fierce like a lioness.

Ooh, the smooth cobbles are gone. Gravel and stones hurt my feet. The rain has stopped. Heaven isn't crying anymore, but it's still grey and grim. I fear the peasants trudging by . . . men in caps pulled low on their foreheads with their bundles of twigs on their backs . . . women in kerchiefs unravelling sweaters with baskets of potatoes. I have to wait until they pass.

I keep my gaze on my feet. Fear freezes my stomach. What will I say if one of them stops me? Thank G-d they're gone. I'd better get off the road into the fields. Not much protection here, either. I hear the rumble of wheels, and the earth shakes. The Nazi troop carrier drives by, and I dive down on the ground. Poor Hannele. I almost smothered you in my haste to hide. Let me shake the dirt and hay off my treasure.

Sh, sh, no need to cry. Mama's here. Let's hurry to where we can't be seen from the road. Oo . . . oo . . . ooh . . . without shoes the stubble hurts my feet, like an unshaven man when he kisses you. Ah, the potato field is better. I pray no one will see us. We're so exposed here. I sink into the soft wet earth with every step. My eyes and my toes search for a leftover, just one little potato . . . even a rotten one . . . to my growling stomach it would be a delicacy. I reach the bushes by the riverbank without finding a single potato.

I wonder where Marek is now. I hope he's safe. See, Hannale, here's where we used to secretly meet before we got married. My first kiss was here, under that weeping willow tree. Nobody could see us under its canopy. Don't cry. Someday we'll all be together again. Now this can be our resting place—just you and me. Here's some water from my hand. And look, a little bread from my pocket. I'll make it soft with water. The milk in my breasts dried up long ago. I splash water on my face, my arms, my legs. So icy. So clean. I wash away the blood from my poor, sore feet and bind them with strips of cloth ripped from my slip.

Must press on. One foot in front of the other. Don't think. Push through the fatigue. Push through the pain. Push through the hunger. Through the trees now. Soft ground, soggy leaves. Rotting smell. Animal smell. Tree branches tearing at my hair, my face, scratching my arms and legs. They can't touch your delicate skin, Hannale. I won't allow it. Thank G-d, here's a dirt road. And the sun! Like G-d's eye poking through the clouds to check on me. But it doesn't stay. This blood-soaked land pulls it down to the horizon.

It's getting dark, and I'm a statue, frozen, outside and inside. My baby attached to my body like a leach. I don't have enough strength left even to collapse. My eyes are getting blurred.

What are the smudges over there? Blink. Still there. Blink. Smoke from chimneys? Where there's a chimney, there's a fire. Warm. For the baby. The first door. I knock with my last ounce of energy.

A woman answers the door. Smell of potatoes cooking. Warm air from the cook stove. I hand over the baby. Why is she staring at me?

"Oh, my Lord Jesus, Roza Rotenberg, what are you doing here?"

The woman crosses herself. I fall against her, and she drags me to the table and sits me down on a chair. She's cooing at the baby. Such good soup she gives me, with big chunks of potatoes and carrots. And a tin pail of warm water to soak my feet. She feeds Hannale like a baby bird, spooning gruel and milk into her hungry little mouth. The baby sleeps in a wooden box lined with a blanket. Now I see it is Irena, whose mother, Marta, was our housekeeper. G-d has directed my feet to her doorstep. It's a miracle. She gives me her husband's old boots.

"Where's Stashek?" I ask. My fear rekindles as I wonder how her husband will feel to see me here. Can I trust these Polish people, even Irena? What if all they want is money, and when they find out there's none left they'll betray my most precious ones?

"He's gone with the partisans," says Irena. "But you have to hide in the hayloft. It's too dangerous for you to stay here. I'll keep the baby and bring you food."

"What about the boys? What will they think about the baby?" Irena's sons are only three and five years old and liable to blurt out Hannale's identity to a Nazi soldier.

"Don't worry. They're asleep. They haven't seen her before and don't know anything about her. I'll just say I found a little orphan baby in the hay and they'll believe me. I'll call her Halinka."

The hot soup thaws my frozen heart. I start to cry. "How can I thank you?" I can't afford to allow even a shred of distrust into my mind right now or I'll surely go crazy.

"Never mind. Now dry your feet, put on these old socks and boots of Stashek's, and let's go."

Irena leads me to the barn. Before I crawl up the ladder, I hug her. Once settled in, I cover myself with straw, and for the first time in months, I fall into a dreamless sleep.

[This story is one of many fictionalized versions of Renate's experiences in the Holocaust that she has written based on stories her parents told her and on broad reading of fiction and nonfiction Holocaust material. It is a modified version of a chapter from a novel she is crafting.]

Hava Nissimov

*H*ava Nissimov was born in Warsaw, Poland, in 1939. During the Holocaust, she and her mother escaped from the Warsaw ghetto and she spent about three years hiding with a Polish family in a village (most of which were spent crouching behind a cupboard). Almost all of her family members, including her father, were murdered in the ghetto and in concentration camps.

After the war Hava immigrated to Israel with a youth transport and lived in *kibbutzim* (collective communities) and attended children's institutions. She later served in the army and then earned degrees in education, literature, and writing. Throughout her career, she also assisted with various causes, including Enosh (the Israel Mental Health Association) and the Claims Conference, aimed at helping Holocaust survivors make a claim for reparations. Other Holocaust-related volunteer initiatives include founding an organization to help child survivors and providing lectures at schools and the army.

Having enjoyed writing since she was a child, Hava authored two books: *A Girl from There* (Mikteret Publications), a collection of her memories from the Holocaust; and *Longing for the Uterus* (Eked), a poetry anthology pertaining to the Holocaust, relations with her mother, and love. Some of her poems and short stories have also appeared in literary journals.

Hava resides in Holon, Israel. She is married and has two sons, one daughter, and three grandchildren.

A Girl from *There* (Excerpts)

Hava Nissimov
(Translated by Linda Stern)
(Illustrations by Ofra Amit)

A white baby | Mother-woman tells me: During the bombing of Warsaw, I am a baby, a few months old. The nanny goes down to the bomb shelter with me, and my mother still waits in the house. When she joins us in the bomb shelter, she takes me from the nanny's arms. At that very moment, the house shudders, a bomb explodes very close by, and the nanny's arm is hit by shrapnel, in the exact place where my head had been lying a fraction of a second earlier. Later, her arm is amputated. My head and entire body are covered with white lime wash. My mother doesn't know if I am dead or alive. She goes upstairs to the house as the bombing continues, fills the bathtub, and puts my entire body in the cold water. I immediately start kicking my legs and waving my arms. I smile.

A new girl | From today I am a new girl. My mother puts a small chair on the table. She sits me up high on the chair. She cuts my hair short with a fringe. I look in the mirror: the fringe is a bit crooked. Then she dyes my black hair blonde. Also my eyebrows. But she doesn't manage to colour the eyelashes.

I am wearing a new chain around my neck with a small, pretty crucifix. I also get a completely new name.

From today I am another girl, a Polish girl. A Christian. I mustn't tell anyone I am Jewish.

My mother teaches me to cross myself like the Christians do.

HAVA NISSIMOV

Sack | I am put into a sack that is tied up.
It is dark inside the sack, but it has tiny holes and I can breathe.
Someone takes me on his back and walks.
Then drives.
And walks again.
I am taken out of the sack after a long time, in the house of some Poles
in a village where I hide out for three years.

Behind the cupboard | I sit with a Jewish woman behind the tall brown cupboard that has been moved away from the wall, leaving a narrow dark space.

I sit on a small log of wood.

The woman is the mother of another little girl, who is in hiding with some other Poles.

We sit there for hours, days, years. I am three years old, four, five, and six. Sometimes we are behind the cupboard, only during the daytime, and occasionally at night; it depends on the visitors or the neighbours who come to the house and whether they stay over or not.

On the chair opposite me sits the woman. She is permanently angry. She sucks sugar cubes that are white and sweet.

HAVA NISSIMOV

One after the other. I don't have any. But I want.

I pinch her hard, but she doesn't make a sound, because it's forbidden. There are strangers in the house who might betray us to the Germans, and then we will all die. So say the Christian mother and the Christian father, and also the son—the Christian brother—who are the Polish family whose house I am being hidden in since they brought me here in a sack, on the back of a man, in the night.

I know I mustn't make any noise, but the white cubes with the tiny holes are so very sweet. I pinch the woman again, until she gives me a cube. I put it straight into my mouth and suck it.

She is angry: "Bad girl." But later, when I get bored, she teaches me things; for example, how to rub your nose upwards with your fingers, again and again, and you rub some more, until the sneeze goes back in. It disappears.

Because it is forbidden to sneeze. It is also forbidden to cry.

But I never cried in my life, even when I was a baby. So said the woman who was my mother, when she came back.

Dancing | A six-year-old girl dances in a yellow, endless field, crisscrossed with blue cornflowers. Coloured butterflies fly in the sky. A scent wafts through the air.

I am wearing a red dress. A cackling white goose chases me in the yard and pecks at me. I am running. Hopping. Hiding among the fruit trees. I finally choose the biggest apple, pick it, and bite into its shiny red cheek, but I am disappointed by the floury taste. With my hand I dig a hole in the ground and bury the bitten apple under the tree. Cover it up with twigs and leaves. I hope nobody finds out that I wasted it.

Years later, my aunt, my mother's sister, comes to get me. The war is over.

The gate opens, and my aunt and cousin come toward me. My cousin gives me a picture book as a present.

Mother-woman returns | I'm told she's coming back from Germany today.

A woman who is my mother.

It's already dark, and she isn't here yet.

I've been in bed for ages. I'm facing the wall.

I hear a knock and the squeak of the door opening.

I'm still facing the wall. I don't turn around, I pretend to be asleep.

Everyone is talking excitedly. Aunt, uncle, and the woman who came.

They think I'm asleep, and they don't wake me up.

A little while later, someone comes into my bed.

Not really close, but next to me.

I know it's her.

I don't turn toward her.

I don't see her.

My face is turned toward the white wall.

I shut my eyes. I listen.

She breathes.

I breathe.

So it goes on, all night long.

Coffee, Tel Aviv! | I sail with some other children in a big ship to *Eretz Israel.*

I am put into a cabin with a family who will take care of me during the crossing. They give me some lemon when I feel nauseated and when I throw up.

When we are on the high seas, we are asked to destroy any items we have that have Polish written on them, because we are illegal.

I have a lot of important things with me that I have kept:

a diary, a photograph album, a collection of postcards . . .

I tear them all up into tiny pieces.

On the last morning of the crossing, I awaken to a voice declaring, "Coffee, Tel Aviv, Coffee, Tel Aviv," which meant we had arrived in *Eretz Israel* and that breakfast was ready.

My name was changed to another, a Hebrew one.

Nobody asks; they just give it.

I don't like the name.

HAVA NISSIMOV

Bald | I am a "Diaspora girl." That's what the children on the *kibbutz* (collective community) call me.

I understand it is not something good.

The children in the group look like non-Jewish children to me.

They are blond and have two parents.

They also bully me, like the Polish children in the Polish school, only a bit less because the teacher doesn't let them.

But all of a sudden the teacher discovers I have lice.

Paraffin is poured over my head, which becomes full of open sores.

I am put to bed at night in the house of the family who adopted me.

I cry in pain the whole night long.

The man, the father, puts his head up close to me and shouts,

"Be quiet, be quiet already! I have to get up for work in the morning!"

But he isn't my father, and I go on crying.

The next day, they shave my head—I am bald.

The children make fun of me and dance around me, delighted.

Pit | A girl imprisoned inside a woman, and inside her is a pit.
The pit is deep and empty, and it's surrounded by steep walls covered
with flakes of dust.
The dust drops off and chokes her.
The pit contracts or expands and yawns open.
It sometimes fills up with rare moments of joy.
Sparks, coloured soap bubbles that blow up for a fraction of a second
and then burst.
Falling in love, giving birth, writing a song.
The pit is deep enough to hide in,
you can shout into it and no one will hear.
The pit is a thirsty place.
Flowers and feathery grass grow there,
the grass is very short and the flowers are budding,
and again it is so dry that they wither as they reach their prime.
The grass with the soft buds—desiccating.
Suddenly, without warning, the joy bursts through,
tremendous waterfalls irrigate the parched earth,
drowning everything that was still alive.

HAVA NISSIMOV

Goodbye to you, little girl | Both of us went back in time and returned, you and I:
the girl inside me and myself.
Both of us know that not everything is possible anymore.
It never was.
We have to hurry and do whatever we can, because the road is getting shorter.
We were often saved from death, but we won't be saved from the jaws of time.
Yet even now we won't stop searching.
Here and there we will go on picking a flower. We will love. We will dream.
This is not our final journey.
Together we will continue wandering among the unsolved questions, among the forests of fear and longing.
In a never-ending attempt to patch up the torn web of memory.

Maryla Neuman

*M*aryla Neuman has had a busy life as an active member of her synagogue and community in Golden Valley, Minnesota. Yet, she has tattered pockets in her soul. A happy childhood followed her 1923 birth in Poland. Then in 1941, when the country fell under German occupation, she experienced the Lwów (Lemberg) ghetto, hiding on a farm, two prisons, and two concentration camps.

Following her move to the United States in 1949, Maryla went on to raise three children. Sadly, she lost two of them in the prime of their lives. As difficult as the camps were, she feels that they were not nearly as heart wrenching as losing adult children. Auschwitz came and went, but losing a child is forever. Her friends ask how she finds the strength to lead an active life, and she has no answer.

Maryla continues to work as a member of the Sisterhood of Temple Israel in Minneapolis, where she also speaks with youth about her Holocaust experiences. Her goal is to give school age children a piece of living history. Their positive letters serve as evidence that they are learning and growing from their sessions together. She feels privileged and rewarded to talk about her experiences with youth.

Bye Bye, Daddy

Maryla Neuman

They're all gone. The Nazi butchers killed them all. *Tatusiu* (daddy), *Mamusiu* (mommy), my little sister, Basha, cousins, uncles, aunts—all gone.

My father, Isak Kornblum, was a handsome man. He was not very tall, and he was a very quiet, loving man. You don't learn much from quiet people—only from their example.

There's not much to say about my father. Mother was the power of our life—of her marriage and of our upbringing. When I talk about my family, *Tatusiu* becomes the background to my strong, active, and talented mother. What can I tell you about daddy? He was gentle, and he liked to read. He liked quiet. *Tatusiu* worked hard, and he loved his two girls. And we loved him.

We always ate our evening meal together as a family. Each of us reviewed the events of our day. After supper, on warm evenings, we walked together and enjoyed the fresh air. In the winter, *Tatusiu* took his two little girls on sleigh rides. Basha, the tomboy, was more daring than lady-like me.

Tatusiu owned a sweets shop, where one could buy baked goods, ice cream, coffee, and sweet drinks. Basha and I often watched him at work, while we enjoyed goodies from the shop—mostly ice cream. How can one not love a gentle daddy who owns a sweets shop?

My sheltered life changed when the Nazis arrived. I was 18. Us Jews lived in fear and were degraded every day. I remember the armband we were required to wear every hour and in every place—the armband with the Star of David.

After about four months, we were forced to live—no, to exist—in the Lwów ghetto for more than a year. Each morning I was transported to an *Arbeitslager* (a labour camp), to make ammunition for the Germans.

Eventually, I was able to escape from the ghetto, and for the next six months I lived in hiding.

Then, in the summer of 1944, time ran out for me: I was arrested with false papers. The *Gestapo* (German Secret State Police) sent me to the Lackiego Street prison in Lwów, where I assumed that I would die. I was 21 years old.

I was actually familiar with the Lackiego prison—but only from the outside—because our home was only a few blocks away. As a girl, I often walked past this ugly brick campus, afraid of what might jump out at me. I certainly had no interest in entering.

However, as it turned out, the situation was not as bad as I had feared. False papers and an uncertain identity meant that I was a political prisoner. The fact that I was Jewish became a secondary crime. The Germans preferred everything to be very orderly. If you didn't have the proper papers, you became an interesting problem—perhaps a spy. Political prisoners were treated better than Jews, because they might have information. Spies were valued a few notches higher than Jews.

I was in a cell with three other young women. Thick, cold, grey walls made this an unpleasant home for a claustrophobic. Our small cell held two cots, which four of us used collectively. We shared stories and bemoaned the scarcity of food. There was not much to do, so we slept and conserved energy.

A window near the ceiling tempted my curiousity. None of us were tall enough to see outside. Our bare cell had no chair or ladder on which to climb. I jumped up and saw a large courtyard where men were walking in a circle. I jumped again, and this time, I cut my lip as I bumped into the wall. The big gash bled. To this day I have a scar on my lip.

As I lay on the cement floor, I told my cellmates that I had seen my father. I heard them discussing my misfortune: "The poor girl has lost her mind in the crash."

The *Gestapo* had taken *Tatusiu* from us about a month before the rest of our family was forced into the ghetto. One evening, he simply didn't come home from his errands. When people were hauled away, we usually assumed that they had been shot, hanged, or gassed. It had been almost two years since I had seen my daddy, and I missed him every day.

The throbbing pain and oozing blood did put doubts in my mind. Perhaps I hadn't seen my father. When the spinning in my head slowed, I pulled myself up along the wall. I eyed the window and planned my jump. When I was ready, I leaped as high as a wounded girl could soar. For a moment, I could even hold on to the window bars. There was my daddy. I screamed, "*Tatusiu, Tatusiu!*"

My comrades caught me before I hit the floor. They were sure that I was crazed. Nevertheless, they tended my wound. It was still bleeding, and I could feel it swelling.

Although the Lackiego Street prison was run by the Germans, our guards were Polish and spoke with us freely. One brought the news that my father was truly in the prison, that he had heard my shouts and knew that I was alive. He had been in the prison since his abduction and had been assigned work that used his talent with tools. Now I was crazed again, but this time with joy. What an unbelievable story. Like a miracle. By now I assumed that *Mamusiu* and Basha were dead. But my T*atusiu* was alive and close by.

If only we could make contact—but it was not to be. After about two weeks, I was moved to the Montelupe prison in Krakow. Don't ask me why the Germans kept moving prisoners around Europe. They could have killed us more efficiently. All I know is that off I went on a truck with other women to my second prison.

Montelupe prison was more spacious. We female prisoners lived in a poorly lit dormitory-like room and slept on individual cots. A thin forest-green blanket did not keep us warm, and two small daily meals did not keep us adequately nourished. Nevertheless, we were not treated badly—considering the circumstances—and we had room to move about. We were even given opportunities to walk outdoors in the fresh air. Again, political prisoners were treated much better than Jewish prisoners even if the political inmates were Jews. There were men at Montelupe as well, but we didn't see them often.

Not quite four weeks after our arrival, we were told that we would be moved again. We were ordered to march in a single file outdoors, where trucks were waiting. We didn't know what would happen next, but we were frightened to death. Yes, death was always present. The relaxed Montelupe atmosphere suddenly became cold.

We marched down some stairs and out a door that led into the bright sunshine. We saw a German *Obersturmführer*, or some such high-ranking officer, standing before us as we made a neat line. The officer was tall, had a stern face, and carried a *peitsche* (whip). He wore a pistol in a holster on his hip and held a large drooling dog on a short leash. A line of bedraggled men marched forward and turned to face us.

There, looking at me, not six feet away, was my father! Not thinking, I dashed up to the German officer. I kneeled at his feet and begged, "Please, this is my father. I have finally found him. Please, leave him with me."

I have seen people shot for less. Disobedience was not tolerated by the Germans. "*Zurück!*" shouted the *Obersturmführer*, ordering me to stand back in line.

By now I was out of control. I touched his shiny black boots. I cried and pleaded. Now was my chance to have my *Tatusiu* back. "*Bist du verrückt?* (Are you mad?)" I remember the officer shouting at me.

Surely, this brazen act was mad. "My father, my father," I pleaded.

I think that he slashed me with his whip. Suddenly, I found myself back in the women's line—but surprisingly, still alive. I looked at the row of frightened men. My daddy looked thin and pale. He was crying. I could see tears roll down his face. He dared not lift his hand to wipe them. Daddy looked so utterly frightened. Frightened for himself? Frightened for his little Maryla? I'll never know. That was the last time I saw my father.

There were 10 women on our truck as we sped off to Auschwitz.

The Price of a Shmatte

Maryla Neuman

I had no idea what awaited me at Auschwitz. At the time, I didn't know that there were two options upon arrival: the gas "showers" or hunger, filth, and humiliation. The gas showers, of course, meant immediate death. The rest of us were the "lucky" ones.

Anyone who looked old, weak, or in the slightest way deformed, was sent to experience the cyanide pellets. Who made the decision? Sometimes it was Dr. Josef Mengele himself. Other times, it was his sadistic henchmen, who understood his criteria. I had two points in my favour: I was a young woman of 21; and I had been arrested with false papers and, therefore, a political prisoner. To the Germans, that—not my Jewishness—was my primary crime.

I befriended a girl my age who had rather large breasts. We stood naked before the judge. Was it Mengele himself? My new friend was sent to one line, and I was sent to another. I later learned that the people in her line, the longer one, were sent to be gassed. Those of us who "passed" Mengele's test were sure that her large breasts were outside the judge's rule of "normal."

I was directed to the end of a line that led to a small shack. Women—we were all women—were crying. We were crying because when we stepped off the trucks and railroad cars, we had seen the camp. Anyone would cry. The camp resembled a neglected insane asylum. People were wandering around like bewildered beasts, just wandering aimlessly. There was no system to their walking. They looked as if they didn't know what had happened to them. The ground was muddy, people lost their shoes in the muck, and they were bald. At first I couldn't tell that they were all women. They wore crazy, poorly fitting clothes and each of them clung to a metal cup as if it were her link to life. We later learned that the cup, their only possession, was, indeed, key to staying alive.

I didn't know what to do. At the time, I still didn't know about the gas chambers. But the smell was unbearable. It was the smell of dead bodies.

I smelled it as soon as I got off the truck. Later, Auschwitz old-timers explained the smell of burned bones.

When I arrived at the shack, I received my tattoo—my new identity. I became number A-24201. Apparently, the numbering of inmates had reached such a large figure that the compulsive German pigs had to start a new numbering series: the "A" series.

After the tattooing ceremony, everyone's hair was cut off. Women screamed. To many of them, their hair was their beauty—their woman-hood. I was pushed into a different line, and my beautiful long, blonde braids were spared. Very few of us were given special treatment. We were the political prisoners.

Next, I was assigned to a barracks-like building. Wooden boards served as our mattresses. I didn't see any blankets. The beds were three-decker bunks, each one about the width of one single bed. We squeezed six, sometimes eight, to a pallet. When one of us turned, we all had to turn.

I was assigned to a group of workers, all political prisoners, all with hair. There were about eight of us. One was a Russian military captive, and two were captives from the Ukraine. One was a prostitute, who may have said something against Hitler, and another was a captured underground worker. A few Poles were part of our group. I was the only Jew. Our primary "work" was to pick up stones as part of a "cleanliness detail." We were each given a pail and, as a group, were assigned an area from which we were to pick up gravel. Once our pails were full of stones, we emptied them in an assigned location. When that location had enough stones to satisfy the guards, we were told to pick up the stones and bring them to another location. We were transporting the stones back and forth. Busy work! Does that make sense? Does keeping us alive make sense?

In fact, there was little effort put into keeping us alive. Our diet consisted of a cup of *Ersatz Kaffee* (imitation coffee) in the morning, along with a piece of dark bread. A cup of thin soup was our evening meal. Anyone who lost her cup starved. The cup was life itself.

The evening meal began when a huge barrel of soup was delivered near our barracks. A lead Jew, a *Kapo*,[1] an *Aufseherin* (a female guard in the camp), had a ladle. We lined up, and each of us received one ladleful of

---

[1] *Kapos* were Nazi concentration camp inmates who supervised other prisoners. They were offered this work in exchange for extra food and other privileges.

soup in our cup. When the barrel was empty, there was no more soup that day. Those at the end of the line sometimes went without. The stronger ones pushed their way to the front.

Every person at Auschwitz was in a constant state of hunger. The bland soup over which we fought might have had some traces of potato, perhaps a cooked cabbage leaf or two, and occasionally another vegetable. It was "health food." There was little incentive to fight over the "dinner," except that we were starving.

It was still dark when they woke us up each morning. I think that it might have been five o'clock. Who knows? Who had a timepiece? There were no calendars or watches. The weather gave us a rough hint of the passage of weeks and months. Orthodox Jews desperately tried to keep track of days so that they could say the *Sabbath*[2] prayers. Apparently, G-d didn't help them count the days.

We hated mornings. An *Aufseherin* came with a club and beat the boards on which we slept. Sometimes she was called *Oberseher* (overseer). She shouted, "*Aufstehen. Aufstehen!* (Get up!)" If we didn't move fast enough, she beat us with her club. What was there to get up for? We were too hungry to sleep, and during the day there was nothing but boredom and humiliation—and more hunger.

"*Aufstehen!*" The first ritual of the day was the count off. "Stand up and be counted" became an idiom with a new meaning. Those who couldn't stand for the count were shot on the spot or sent to be gassed.

One day, we stood for two hours while we were counted and recounted— as if somebody could run away. How could anyone run away? The whole camp was surrounded by barbed wire, much of it electric. Who could escape?

There was one girl, a rather popular girl in the camp, who had been in Auschwitz for a long time. I think she was from Warsaw. She was nice. Somehow she acquainted herself with an SS officer, and that created an opportunity for her to run. Of course, they caught her. Where could she go? The guards brought this poor girl to a large square and made us all stand in rows for a long time. Then, to teach us a lesson, they hanged her

---

[2]The Sabbath is a weekly Jewish holy day from sundown Friday until shortly after sundown Saturday that is meant to be treated as a day of rest from the regular activities of the week.

while we watched. It was a terrible, terrible disappointment to us all. We had wished for this girl's success so that we, too, could have some sense of optimism. The lesson learned from the hanging was that there was no reason to hope.

We looked for an airplane overhead, but none came. We asked each other why the Allies didn't bomb us. A bomb would tell us that they knew we were here—that they knew there was an Auschwitz. But no one seemed to know or care. When I was first captured and locked up in the Monte-lupe prison, I hadn't known there was an Auschwitz. I didn't know until I arrived. Who could imagine an Auschwitz?

The *Aufseherin/Oberseher/Kapo* was one of us—a Jew, a prisoner. The Germans trusted these women; they earned that trust by beating us and betraying our secrets. Often, the *Aufseherin* was more brutal than the German guards. That's how they stayed alive and earned a little extra food. They were typically Polish Jews like me. They could be Romanian Jews or Czech. I never saw a German *Aufseherin*. Perhaps the Nazis didn't trust the German Jews. Perhaps the German Jews didn't want to beat up other Jews. Who knows?

Not one woman ever menstruated. We speculated that the Nazis drugged the coffee. Diarrhea was common, and sometimes a woman soiled herself. That often earned a beating or a bullet.

We were never issued clean clothes. We wore what we could steal from the piles of clothes left near the gas "showers." An elegant dress was as welcome as a torn skirt and blouse. Did the dead know that they were bequeathing their clothes to the living inmates?

I was always hungry and dirty. I arrived at the camp in the late summer of 1944. When winter came, I was cold. The freezing inside my body wouldn't stop. It seemed to penetrate my bones and wouldn't leave. It was uninterrupted, perpetual cold. Those who had boots could walk in the snow with some comfort. Those who had sandals suffered frostbite.

One cold day, I was standing in front of my barracks waiting for the morning *Ersatz Kaffee*. The coffee was never hot, and I was very cold. Snow on the ground did not help my spirits, but there, lying on the ground, was a piece of a German army blanket—not a whole blanket, just a piece. I picked up that *shmatte* (rag) and wrapped it around my waist.

The *Aufseherin* became enraged. Insubordination! Sabotage! She could score points with the authorities if she played her hand correctly.

The *Kapo* called a uniformed SS officer. The SS guards wore pistols in holsters and always walked with two dogs. And they were still afraid of us.

The SS officer came at me with her two dogs. I thought the dogs would swallow me—they were huge. "*Raus* (Out)," hollered the officer. I stepped away from my group. The officer then took me to the square at the entrance of the camp—the front gate where the sign reads, "*Arbeit Macht Frei* (Work Will Set You Free)." She took me to a spot where the ground was covered with gravel and made me kneel on those tiny cold stones. She told me to hold my arms up over my head. I kneeled there on the gravel for many hours. When my arms started to come down I was beaten with a *peitsche* (whip).

Hour after hour, I kneeled as the sharp little stones cut into my knees. My shoulders ached, and I became dizzy. Gravel, snow, cold, bright sun, leather whip. I fainted three times. I don't know why the officer didn't just shoot me.

After many hours of being exposed to pain and cold, I was sent back to my barracks.

John Freund

John Freund was born in June 1930 to a middle class Jewish family in Czechoslovakia. In 1942 the Nazis transported his family to the Terezin (Theresienstadt) ghetto, and at the end of 1943, to a family camp in Birkenau, Poland. In May 1945 John returned to his hometown, Budejovice, and found only one aunt from his father's side still alive. He moved in with her and attended high school in Prague.

Following the war, the Canadian Jewish Congress, along with other agencies, assisted in bringing child survivors, including John, to Canada. With the help of a subsidy and a part time job, he went on to complete secondary school in Toronto, Ontario, and then enrolled in an accounting course that qualified him as a Chartered Accountant.

In 1990 John attended a reunion in Israel with some of the surviving "boys" with whom he lived at the family camp in Auschwitz-Birkenau. Ninety boys had been selected to stay alive and serve as slave labourers within the camp, while their families were sent to the gas chambers. About 35 of them survived. John proceeded to find the survivors around the world and compiled their stories and photographs in his book *After Those Fifty Years: Memoirs of the Birkenau Boys.* He has been married for over 50 years and has three daughters and 10 grandchildren.

Hurrah! Here We Are Again

John Freund

Inside the Third Reich

It was a hot, oppressive day in early August 1944. Dry scorched gravel and dust blew around the long-frame barracks. This day was no different from other days in the Birkenau concentration camp near Auschwitz. For many months now, long trains of cattle wagons were arriving daily full of people and leaving empty, ready for another load. This was the last stop on the long journey. Many died of dehydration or illness on the way. Those who arrived here were all lined up along the railroad tracks and, with a few exceptions, were marched to their death by gas.

The large factories with huge chimneys spouting fire and smoke just outside the Birkenau camp were the furnaces burning those killed by gas. The stench and burning smoke spread over a large area.

In Camp D, known as the Mannerlager, there were 3,000 men. They were young, having been taken out of the transports consigned to death in the gas chambers to do mean work inside the camp complex. Several hundred of them were engaged in the task of disposing of the bodies of those killed in the gas chambers. They were known as the "Special Commandos." Other work crews were assigned to nearby ammunition factories or to maintenance of the railroad.

Tension was great inside the camp on this Thursday. Rumours persisted and fed anxieties. There was going to be another selection. That meant that all those in the camp were to line up in the nude, and Dr. Mengele[1] or his assistant, with a flick of his finger, could consign anyone

---

[1]Josef Mengele was a German SS officer and a physician at the Auschwitz-Birkenau concentration camp. He supervised the selection of arriving transports of prisoners, determining who was to be killed and who was to become a forced labourer. He also performed medical experiments on camp inmates.

to the gas, to be murdered with the new arrivals in the gas chambers. There were rumours of military defeats over the Germans. The Americans, it was rumoured, had landed a huge army in France.

On this hot day, two of the inmates of Camp D took a step that sealed their fate. This is the true story of Manny and George.

Manny was 26 years old. He had been a good student in his native town of Krakow. His ambition had been to study physics, but the war had changed all that. The German Panzers overran the town, killing all who stood in their way. Manny, like all other Jews, was surrounded, separated from his family, and deported to a concentration camp. He was moved from one camp to another until he came to Birkenau in southern Poland.

When Manny arrived at the Mannerlager, he was assigned to work on railroad maintenance. Two tracks led from Auschwitz for about four kilometres to Birkenau. There were several sidings to prevent a scheduling backlog. This is where sealed cattle wagons brought the Jewish civilians to their wholesale slaughter. The rails required frequent repairs.

George was a young man from a small border town in Czechoslovakia. His good looks and manners concealed his great anger. He was angry when his beloved country was invaded by the Germans with their Nazi ideology. His anger exploded when a German soldier who demanded something in a language George did not speak but learned to despise had pushed him off the sidewalk. He was angry because German invaders had closed the university he was going to attend.

George could no longer contain himself. He spat into the face of a flag-waving Nazi during one of the frequent parades in his town. He was immediately seized by two SS guards and beaten. Then, without a trial, he was shipped to a concentration camp and ended up in Birkenau.

Manny and George met in the Mannerlager, in the railroad commando. Full trains arrived and empty ones left. It was not enough to kill the innocent, but the killers enhanced their manliness and hatred by their brutality. Uniformed SS men and German prisoners, usually murderers, ruled inside the camp.

Manny and George worked side by side. They marched out of the gate of the Mannerlager every morning at 6:30 to the sound of marching music played by inmate musicians. Twelve hours later, tired, they returned. During the day, while working, they talked, argued, and dreamed. Out of this came a plan, an insane plan. They considered their chances of survival to tell what they saw each day. "When the last train departs, it will be our turn." On that they agreed. They planned to escape. Few others had tried it; only one or two were successful.

There was a small wooden shed for storing tools near the tracks. There, piece by piece, they stored the civilian clothes that they would use for their escape. They accumulated food to last a few days, a flashlight, and a couple of knives. They had no access to a weapon for defending themselves.

The appointed day came. It was a routine working day. At six thirty in the evening the working crews returned to the gate. They marched in rows of five past the gate. The band played marching music. The SS guard counted the group as it passed and checked the total list, prepared on departure in the morning.

"Halt. Stop!" screamed Corporal Barda, the most brutal of the SS men. He counted again. His face was red with rage. "Name, group, and number of inmates," he shouted at the foreman.

"Group B, railway maintenance commando, 38 men," answered foreman Bloch.

"There are only 36 here now!" cried out Barda in great agitation. By now, he was joined by other men.

"Where are the missing swine?" With his fist, Barda hit the foreman across his face. Bloch stumbled to the ground. Two other SS men grabbed him, kicked him, and dragged him up.

The camp commander had been summoned; he ran to the telephone in the guard booth to call Birkenau central command. It did not take long. Sirens rang out. Then an ominous wail filled the air. Motorcycles had started moving in the direction of the railroad. We heard dogs with murderous howling barks.

There was absolute silence inside the camp. The inmates of the Mannerlager shuddered in fear. Who escaped? What was going to happen to them when they were caught? What would happen to all of us if they were not? The Nazis were trained in group punishment. When former escapees were caught, they were pulverized and drowned in their own blood.

George and Manny hid in the tool shed. They were not missed by the others who were too hungry and tired to notice their disappearance. They had to act quickly. They changed into civilian clothes and filled their pockets with food and small tools. They had enough money to buy old bicycles if they could only get away fast enough to mix with people in the nearest town. Daylight was against them. In the winter in complete darkness, their chances would have been better.

It was just past seven when the sirens were heard. The two escapees were one kilometre away along the railroad tracks. They were running and hiding behind posts and railway cars on the spur line. This was a no-man's land. Flat and dry, like a moonscape. The heat was intense. No wonder the Germans chose this place for their crimes.

The escapees needed one more hour to get to safety. Both men were young and still fairly strong. But the impossible was outside of their reach. The loud roar of motorcycles approached the tracks quickly, and the dogs were not far behind. Against hope, George and Manny climbed inside a pile of coal to hide. The hungry, angry dogs ripped into the men. They tried to fight them off with bare hands.

It was after eight o'clock. Three-thousand men in the Mannerlager stood in rows of five between the barracks. The daily counting usually took place right after the return of the working crews, and then supper was given. On this night, they had been standing for almost two hours. There was to be no meal. The enraged SS men charged at anyone who moved out of line and kicked or slapped at random. Yes, here were the enemies of The Reich—unarmed, starved, and fearful. Their wives, children, and elderly parents had been murdered by gas. Their only crime was that G-d had given them life and that they were Jews or other undesirables.

Around eight thirty a sudden hush fell over the camp. The marching band at the gate played "Home Sweet Home," and the two men appeared. They were tied together by their legs. Their faces were black from coal and sweat. They marched slowly, followed by SS men with weapons pointed at their backs. They carried a sign crudely written on a cardboard. It read: *HURRAH WIR SIND SCHON WIEDER DA* (Hurrah Here We Are Again).

They stopped at barrack 13, the punishment cell. It was the only barrack with a courtyard. To be more precise, there was a stone wall between it and the rest of the camp so that others could not see! The gate was opened, and the men were thrown in. The inmates of barrack 13, about 200 of them, stood in rows of five, now at full attention as the small party entered. The camp commander closed the gate.

The commander called for the "bench." The bench was immediately produced and set down in the center of the yard. Shivers ran up the backs of all present. The penalized man would be bent over the bench; his arms and legs would be tied to it. With his pants down, the condemned man would be flogged, and he would have to count out loud each blow that fell upon him. Each blow with a log would be like an electric shock hitting his entire body. After 15 blows, the flesh becomes raw; after 25, blood flows. This was the Middle Ages in modern times.

The punishment that day was extraordinary. For defying the Third Reich by trying to escape; for defying the great leader "*Der Führer*" by trying to escape; for claiming a right to life by trying to escape. The Nazis were angry. For Stalingrad, for Normandy, for their ultimate defeat, the Nazis were angry!

George was first. He was brave and vowed to himself not to make a sound that would appear pleading. He received 125 blows. Several SS men took turns doing the beatings. George counted to 75 and then screamed. He collapsed and was thrown aside and left to bleed.

Manny was next. He knew, just as all those watching this spectacle did, that his punishment would be worse! He had defied the Great Reich. He had defied the Great Leader and was a Jew. All the animal hate of the camp commander and the other SS men, all their anger for the bombed German cities and the final defeat of the Thousand-Year German Reich was now directed at this slight man.

Manny was stretched out on the bench. His arms and legs were tied to it. Four SS men, big and well-fed, took turns hitting, and they hit hard. After 125 blows, the real punishment began. He was thrown to the ground. With long poles, his entire body and head was beaten. One of the poles broke, and the angry SS man kicked, stamped, and beat with his fists. Manny's clothes were completely ripped off. He was bleeding heavily, his eyes were punctured, and pus was coming out of his head. His face took on a frightful aspect. This was no longer a man but a bloody rag. Inhuman sounds were emitted from his torn lungs.

"*Genug!* (Enough!)" shouted the commander. "Get a doctor."

A doctor arrived. The two men, close to death, were put on a stretcher and taken into the barrack. With crude medicine and dressings, the doctor spent the whole night with them.

George was up in a week hobbling on crutches. Manny was close to death for several days and was attended to by the doctor. The doctor, one of the inmates said, had been told by the commander that if the beaten men die, the doctor would also die. Manny and George were guarded day and night. They were given extra rations of food.

After three weeks, Manny could get up and take a few steps with a cane. In another 10 days, he was well enough to march. And march he did. So did George.

It was the middle of September. The chimneys of Birkenau were no longer spouting the ugly smoke. The last group, the hundreds of thousands of Hungarian Jews, had gone through the chimneys. The work was done. The Russian army was approaching. The prisoners could hear the artillery and see distant fire at night. The Nazis destroyed the crematoria so that the world would not know.

George and Manny were walking again. Gallows were set up near the gate in the Mannerlager.

Two men in pyjama-like uniforms were marched to the gallows. Several high-ranking officers arrived from Berlin to witness the cowardliness of the Third Reich. Their buttons, decorations, medals, and high-polished boots attested to their superiority. The commander read the decree signed by Heinrich Himmler, Chief of the German Police and Minister of the Interior, the great criminal equalled only by Hitler.

In a civilized society, the condemned are given comfort by a clergyman, a cigarette, or a moment to clear their minds. These sadistic butchers were not satisfied to just hang the two. They wanted everyone to see. The entire camp had to march past the gallows to see for themselves—as if it was really necessary—the unmasked cruelty and inhumanity of those who wanted to rule the world.

I was 14 at that time, and I survived to bear witness. That is why I have described the incident in Birkenau of the two men who were marched into the camp with a sign reading *HURRAH WIR SIND SCHON WIEDER DA* and were later executed.

Dorothy Fleming

Dorothy Fleming (née Dorli Oppenheimer) came to England from Vienna, Austria, on a *Kindertransport* (Children's Transport) in 1938 at the age of 10, accompanied by her four-year-old sister, Lisi. Their parents sent them on the transport to help them escape the Nazi horrors, and they were fortunate to be taken in by a loving Jewish family in Leeds. Luckily, their parents also later escaped, and the family reunited in 1941.

Dorothy later married a fellow Jewish refugee from Vienna, and they had three children and later six grandchildren and four great-grand-children. Dorothy became a widow in 2007 and

Dorothy Fleming at age six in 1934.

lives in Sheffield in England, where she spends much time in her retirement sharing the *Kindertransport* story.

Changes

Dorothy Fleming

All of a sudden the atmosphere changed;
At home it grew quiet, the laughter all gone.
At school we were outcasts:
"Don't talk to them—they're Jewish!"
The teacher said; she who'd liked me before.
The friends who wrote in my autograph book
Were no longer friends, wore uniforms now;
Bund Deutscher Mädel—girls from Hitler Youth,
In my school, in my town, strangers to me.

All of a sudden the atmosphere changed;
No longer talk of music, of plays, and of fun.
Now it was permits and visas and death;
Friends going missing, lucky ones left,
Less lucky those who were taken away—
Who could know where and for what?
Streets full of danger, new banners and flags
Frightening because no one explained
What it all meant, what would come next.

All of a sudden the atmosphere changed;
"There are people in England who'll give you a home
Until we get out and join you again—
You'll get the chance to practice your English
And live with an uncle and auntie in Leeds
And take care of your little sister."
Train journey of fears and surprises
We remember the smiling and kindly Dutch
And arriving in smoky London; for some it was all too much.

All of a sudden the atmosphere changed;
In Yorkshire now, long way from home.
Strange names and bedrooms and breakfasts.
Phone calls from Vienna to Chapeltown, Leeds:
"Are you sure you're looking after your sister?
Behaving yourselves and learning at school?
Is Lisi still crying, still wetting her bed?
We'll come to you soon, just wait a bit more
And thank Uncle Theo and give Tilly a kiss!"

All of a sudden the atmosphere changed;
Settled in Leeds now, the plaits an attraction.
Sister's calmed down, and school can be fun,
Dancing round maypole, learning some folk songs,
But arithmetic's agony, all those long sums!
Parents are coming! Longed-for reunion
Big hugs and kisses—and then they are gone! And
All of a sudden the atmosphere changed.

War comes and evacuation—travelling all over
This surprising new country of ours.
Where can we settle? Father's interned.
Now he's an enemy alien, who loves this country so much.
At last we're all together in Wales.
War work for Daddy and new schools for us;
No longer refugees, evacuees or any ees,
Just two girls growing up and seeing that
All of a sudden the atmosphere changed.

Many years later, we suddenly found out
That *Kindertransport* had been what saved us.
We'd been the lucky ones, our parents survived;
Most of the children were orphaned.
Terrible memories suddenly stirred
Some could hardly believe it;
Friendships renewed, experiences shared
With families now and emotions bared—and
All of a sudden the atmosphere changed.

To Those Who Want to Know

Dorothy Fleming

Ask your questions now,
While those who could answer still live.
Ask your questions now
So that those who remember will give
You all that they can
While they still can.

Ask your questions now;
Don't imitate fools like us,
Who still regret what was not said.
And now the ones who knew are dead,
So ask your questions now.

Ask your questions now
Of relatives both far and near,
Who hold the family's history dear
And want to make the mysteries clear,
If only you were there to hear—
So ask your questions now.

Ask your questions now
To find out how it used to be,
What was kept and what was dropped,
When some of our old customs stopped
Being honoured, and then you'll see
Shining out—your history!
So ask your questions now.

Ask your questions now,
About births and deaths and matches made
For marriages and goods to trade,
Travels to and from this place,
And veils that hid a hopeful face,
Promises so rashly made—
Ask your questions now.

Ask your questions now
About the words they used to use,
The jokes they told, the spread of news,
How their world would treat the Jews.
Were they scared, or proud, or wise,
Saying truthful, hating lies?
Ask your questions now.

Ask about the games they played,
Their learning tasks, the way they prayed.
Ask what happened to the sick
And whether help came slow or quick.
Ask what work they did and how
Payment came—was it like now?
Ask your questions now.

Find out from where your family came.
Is Mum and Dad's tale just the same?
Are there heroes, villains, stars,
Do you have an Aunt from Mars?
What were the sad and happy times?
Was anyone accused of crimes?
Ask your questions now.

With all the knowledge you acquire
You'll find you're one whom all admire.
A family tree could grow from this,
Or database if you insist.
Much fun and understandings flow
By listening to those who know,
So ask your questions now!

Francis N. Dukes-Dobos

Francis N. Dukes-Dobos was born in Budapest, Hungary, in 1920. He was 21 years old when the Nazis sent him into forced labour. Two of his five sisters were deported to Auschwitz. After more than three years in forced labour, when the war was almost over and his worker battalion had been stationed in Budapest during retreat from the Soviet troops, he escaped and hid in the Swiss Consulate.

Following the liberation in 1945, Francis enrolled in medical school. After graduation he became a clinical scientist at the National Institute for Occupational Safety and Health (NIOSH) in Hungary. Meanwhile, he also married Elizabeth Kaufman (now deceased) in 1946, and they had one daughter, Anne.

During the Hungarian Revolution in 1956, Francis and his family escaped to the United States, where he became a research associate at Johns Hopkins University. He was later employed by the U.S. government at the NIOSH research facility in Ohio. In 1966 the World Health Organization in Geneva, Switzerland, invited him to work as a visiting scientist for two years.

When Francis retired in 1985, he moved to Clearwater, Florida, with his second wife, Carol, and worked as an adjunct professor at the University of South Florida. Over the years, he had published over 70 scientific papers, some of which have been cited worldwide. He also served as president of the B'nai B'rith lodges in both Cincinnati and Clearwater. Francis passed away in February 2010.

Surviving the Holocaust

Francis N. Dukes-Dobos

To the Martyrs of the Holocaust

I survived the Holocaust in Hungary
As a forced labourer for more than three long years,
While others taken to the Russian frontiers
Did not survive the cold and hunger, which was fierce.

My sisters, uncles, and cousins
Were killed in Polish concentration camps,
Some shot by Hungarian Nazis
Into the blue Danube from its icy ramps.

There were some righteous people
Who saved the life of a few,
But bystanders feared their own life
And only watched as Hitler's power grew.

We prayed and hoped that reason
Would win over greed and hate,
And so it happened—but for
The twelve million, all too late.

Frieda Traub

Frieda Traub (née Goldenberg) was born as in Zlotchev, Poland, in November 1921. She was married to Simon Traub of Krakow, Poland, in December 1941. They have three children—Ronald, Victoria, and Deborah—seven grandchildren and four great-grandchildren.

Frieda and Simon, along with Ronald, Frieda's father, Moses Goldenberg, and her brother, Mark, survived the Holocaust by taking refuge in the homes of non-Jewish families in villages near their hometown. In 1948 Frieda and Simon immigrated to Canada from a post-war refugee camp in Austria.

Frieda now resides in Toronto, Ontario, living on her own since her husband passed away in 2006 at the age of 97. She remains active and enjoys walking, exercising, writing poetry, and cooking. She also loves watching her favourite shows on television and has a great sense of humour.

Saved By Miracles
A Personal Recollection of the Holocaust

Frieda Traub

The year was 1939. I will never forget it, because it was the beginning of a big struggle that millions of people went through and never survived. I was fortunate enough to see the end of the **PHANTOM** over the country that I was born in, Poland. For us Jews, life in Poland was never very easy, but—until the war—we managed somehow and lived a quiet life.

The first heartbreak I had at the beginning of the war came when my older brother was taken away to the Russian army. Since that day, we have never heard from him again, but we still hope that someday he might come back. We do not consider him dead. He is still alive in our hearts.

Two years with the Russians passed by, until one morning, after the biggest bombing in the history of our town. Dressed like paper soldiers with white gloves stained with blood, THEY had arrived, the murderers of six million Jews. They conquered Poland from border to border, ruling over the country for the three longest and most difficult and unforgettable years of our lives. Before we met them, we often read and heard about them. But we never knew that people of the twentieth century could be as barbaric as they were. It was 1941, and I was married and expecting a child in six months. It was certainly not the right time to bring another Jew into this world, but I believed it was meant to be like this. It was the will of G-d and in His hands.

The day the Germans arrived, our home was in ruins because of the bombs. It needed repairing, but—for us Jews—it was better to hide and not be seen. Not only were the Germans our enemies, but also some of our friends and neighbours, whom we had trusted. Because they were of different faiths, they tried to rob us and destroy our lives, hand in hand with the

Germans. Where do you turn and what do you do at such times? Lost and heartbroken, we turned to the people who we once considered friends, and they agreed to help us.

The first days of the German occupation marked the death of several thousand people. Just because the Russians had killed a few Ukrainians before leaving the town, thousands of Jews paid for it with their lives.

One day, sitting in the house, miserable, cold, and hungry, we heard a knock on the door. We rushed to open the door expecting to find murderers who had come to take our men, but instead they were two little boys with sticks in their hands. Our men had to obey them, since it meant certain death from the Germans if they had not come. My younger brother was still a kid, so they left him to take care of me. This was when the miracles started to save our lives.

My husband was being led by the two boys to the place where he was supposed be killed. A German soldier, needing a radio repaired, stopped him, not realizing that he was a Jew, and asked if he knew of a place where it could be fixed. He hopped into the car and went to the place where he thought it could be done. Our small town had only two radio technicians, and they both happened to be Jews on their way to be killed. Right away, it occurred to my husband that two lives could be saved by fixing that radio. He talked the German soldier into taking him to the horrible scene of the murder of many innocent people, where he might be able to save the lives of two people. Luckily, the soldier's desire to have the radio fixed was so great that he listened to my husband and they went.

The boys were saved, the radio was fixed, and the soldier brought my husband home. It was only two hours, but to me it seemed like a lifetime. We did not know what would happen next, but in the meantime, he was back and that was all that mattered that day.

As for my father, the only thing we could do about his situation was to sit and pray for a miracle. My father was not fortunate enough to be picked up by any soldier. He was pushed straight to the grave and stood in a long line waiting for his bullet, praying to G-d and still hoping that he would somehow be saved. All of a sudden, a big storm came, and the murderers were forced to leave their places until it subsided. In the meantime, my father's arm was touched by a man he knew from his business who said, "Mr. Goldenberg, the killers are not around." These words, giving him courage, sent him running over the hills and through waters. With G-d in his heart, he returned to the house safely. On this horrible day, though, we lost uncles and cousins who were the pride of our family.

After that day, a mass grave lay still on the top of a hill, and no Jew had the courage to ask why. Everybody was ready to go through the same thing, sooner or later. My family and I had a great trust and belief in G-d that somehow we might succeed in living though it, but this seemed foolish at that time. How can you survive if you do not know what the next moment will bring?

People from our town went crazy. They formed a special organization to help out the Germans, hoping that their lives would be saved. They were Jews that we had known all our lives, but at that time they turned their heads. The Germans tried to get whatever they needed from them, and if it was not delivered on time or in full, the next morning they would send down a few trucks to take as many Jewish people as they could find to kill them. Fortunately, my husband had many friends from his profession. Dentistry was still required for all the men and women in the country. For a set of teeth, they used to smuggle in a bit of food to our house, so we did not starve like many others.

One morning, my child was born, but I did not experience the joy of having my first child born and welcomed into the world. Everyone just shook their heads as if to say, "What was he born for—to die?" But as I mentioned before, G-d was in my heart and I believed in miracles.

A week later, we prepared for the circumcision. The man who was to perform the rite was a Jew with a beard and had to come early in the morning, under the cover of darkness, or face certain death if he were caught. The ceremony was performed, and we had a newborn Jewish son in our family. We hoped with all our might that perhaps, because of the innocent baby, our lives might be spared.

Six months went by without mishap. One evening, there was a mass killing in town. We were in the house, not knowing that the city was surrounded, making it impossible for a Jewish soul to go out to the country seeking refuge. As soon as we heard what was going on, we took the baby and were willing to risk our lives in order to escape. Dressed like a country girl, I left the house with my husband and baby with a prayer on our lips. We walked, hoping that no one would stop and question us. Finally, we arrived outside the city. We thanked G-d for that and started to walk through the fields toward a place where we thought a Ukrainian woman might let us stay in her barn over that awful night. But this did not happen as easily as we thought.

While walking peacefully in the dark, we suddenly found ourselves under search lights some distance away. The murderers had spotted us and were ready to shoot. A cold chill ran through us, and we thought that this was going to be the end. At the same moment, the lights came on in the middle of the field, and we fell into a ditch that was right in front of us. The searchers lost sight of us. We came home the next day to find that another day of killing had passed and many more innocent people had died.

A few months later, the Germans were still trying to seize more Russian territory. Meanwhile, we poor Jews, sitting by our radios that we had secretly concealed, listened and hoped that we would get news of freedom. The relentless Germans were not pleased that there were still so many Jews left, so off they went on another mass killing. The method of killing was different this time. They were running short of bullets for fighting, so they started to use gas chambers as a death weapon. A few hundred people pressed like sardines in a room were suffocated by gas. Electrocution was also used. That day, my baby and I were nearly destroyed.

In the morning, while still in bed, we heard strange voices outside. Always afraid of death, we were suspicious of another bad day. A quick look out the window made us think that surely this was the end. My father and brother went into the hiding place we had built in the house and insisted that we should go in with the baby. But how could you risk the lives of a whole family if the baby did not behave? My husband and I thought that we must take a chance and leave the house immediately by trying to run out to the backyard and into the house of non-Jewish neighbours. The Germans did not search a Christian house as thoroughly as they did when they went into a Jewish home. I took the baby into my arms and sent my husband first to seek permission. The neighbours, not knowing what was going on, let my husband into the house. While the door was open, my husband came to take us across the yard to that open door that meant safety. The few steps from my house across the yard seemed like miles, because to be out in the open at that moment could have meant certain death.

I was in the house with my neighbours, who became hysterical when they looked out the window and saw what was going on. Being long-time friends, they were willing to risk their lives rather than turn us over. As soon as the door closed behind me, the murderers were in our backyard, where I had been just a few seconds earlier, and they made their way up the steps to search the house. The people they found, excluding my father and brother, were taken away that day.

In the meantime, we were expecting that at any minute they would come and search the neighbours' house. The lady of the house decided to put the baby and me behind a dresser in the corner and put my husband in the closet. There was a knock on the door, and before anyone moved, they were in. My only concern was to keep the baby quiet.Shaking and trembling, I made sweet faces at my baby, and he just looked at me and smiled. He was so good. We lived through that horrifying day safely and were grateful to G-d for giving us the courage to take that chance. Our neighbours were greatly rewarded.

We went on living day after day frightened, punished, unhappy, and not knowing what the future had in store for us. The baby was almost a year old when the Germans decided to gather all the Jews that were left and place them in one section of the city surrounded by barbed wire (a ghetto). It was easier to finish the poor people this way whenever they had the desire to do so. We also had concentration camps, where the Jewish people worked like slaves to please the enemy.

Having some friends in the country, my husband started to look for someone who would take us out to his home and keep us hidden, for a reward, until the war was over. We did not think of going into the ghetto and waiting to be killed. It was not much trouble to find one woman who was willing to risk her father's life by allowing us to stay in his home. She transferred all of our possessions into her house for herself. Finally, one evening, we left our home and were brought into a little hut, where an old man was living alone with his dog. The daughter did not risk too much, she thought, because she was waiting for her father's death so that she could inherit some of the land that he possessed. She took whatever she could from us, and the rest did not bother her too much. This home was very far from other people, and it seemed to be a good hiding place.

We were sure that we would finally be able to have some peace. Yet, how can you have peace knowing that your father and brother are still in danger? The woman did not want to take the whole family in—only my husband, the baby, and me. We could not rest, since we felt we had to do something about this. The old man seemed quite friendly and even started to like us a bit. He believed in G-d and prayer, and we began to tell him that the rest of our family was in danger. If he could save another two people, he surely would be greatly rewarded. It seemed to us that he feared his daughter and did not want her to discover what he planned to do. But he gave in, and we brought my father and brother and put them in a separate room, which we decided to keep secret from the daughter. It was so peaceful there that we really considered ourselves fortunate to find such a retreat, but again we were very much mistaken.

One morning, after a few weeks, we noticed people working and cutting down trees in the forest not far from us. That was really the first time that we saw people around that place besides our benefactors. We didn't know what was going on, but we thought something was up. The next morning, we knew a lot more. A heavy knock at the door woke us up. The poor old man came face to face with two German soldiers. Imagine how he felt and our anxiety at that moment. They did not enter, but they informed him that there was going to be some shooting and that it would not be safe for him and the dog to remain in the house. There went the peaceful place and the hope of surviving.

In the corner of the barn, we had dug a subterranean hideaway large enough for five people to fit in during times of emergency. The old man took his dog and his coat and left the house. We sat in our grave-like shelter, nearly suffocating, and tried to hear anything we could from outside. There was a lull, as if before a big storm. My husband could not stand it any longer. He crawled out from the hiding place into the barn. Through a little crack in the boards he saw all the tragedy of a human race. What he saw then he would never forget. Even when we talked about it so many years later, he could not get over the shock of the gruesome sight.

It was only half a mile away from the hut where we were hiding. This mass grave of the poor innocent men, women, and children from the ghetto of our town still exists today. This was the end of our Jewish community. They had gathered them up into one place in the city in order to end their lives quickly and easily, when the time came. We were shocked to see the way those barbarians had arranged the killing. They dug out a big grave, brought people on big trucks, told them to get off, undress completely, and put their clothes on the empty truck. Then, they lined them up beside the grave, and one by one, each got a bullet in the back of the head. The bodies fell on top of each other. Some were dead, some half-dead, and mothers with children in their arms suffered doubly. When we saw what was happening, although we were used to seeing death on every step we made during the German occupation, we could not believe our eyes. It was unfathomable that this could happen to human beings and that people could do this kind of thing to others.

This went on for quite a few days. We did not have peace day or night. Although we had closed the blinds on all the windows, that horrible scene followed us while sitting, standing, or lying. We prayed and hoped that maybe we would be lucky enough not to be among those outside suffering, but little did we know what the good people that gave us a helping hand had planned. The old man's daughter thought that it was time to finish us the way others did. They had the best opportunity in those days. Just point a finger at us in the empty house, and we would be lost forever! The idea was to take our lives in order to keep our possessions, although we would not ask for anything back anyway.

One morning, they gave us away, and the murderers were after us. The Nazis had the name of the old man and were ready to come for our lives. Walking through the village, they stopped to ask a little farm boy for directions to the house. The boy did not hesitate for long and told them that he would walk them over to the place. Luckily for us, there was another farmer in the village by the same name. Off they went to his house, where there was no sign of a Jew, although they turned the place upside down.

We did not know all day what was going on in the village. At night, the old man came over to tell us the good news and insisted we leave his place immediately. The way he was thinking, he was perfectly right. The next day, they might come to look for us in the right place. In the middle of the night, we left to go nowhere.

Walking through the forest, we got tired and sat down for awhile. At first, we did not know that we were sitting right beside the grave of the mass killing, but when the moon came out we noticed where we were. We decided to go back to our house in town and try to work out something with the people that were living there. It was extremely risky, but a chance we had to take. With a one-year-old baby in my arms, I could hardly walk. Weak from lack of food and air, I really did not know how I was going to make it. The night was so dark that we could not find our way to the city. While standing at the beginning of two roads and not knowing which one to take, we prayed for help. We then started to cry like little children that were lost and looking for their mother.

FRIEDA TRAUB

All of a sudden, the moon started to shine on the road from our right side. Not having any other choice, we decided to risk walking along that road. We walked and walked. With a prayer on our lips, we arrived at our home. We knocked lightly on the window that had once belonged to us, and the man that lived there woke up and looked at us through the window. He thought that he was dreaming when he saw us standing like ghosts, begging to be let in at least overnight. He happened to be nice and opened the door from the cellar to let us in. We were safe again, but for how long? We waited until the morning to see what was going to happen next.

Early in the morning, the lady came down to ask us what we had come for and from where. We told her the story of how we had survived. But could she understand our situation? I would not have blamed her if she did not. She was afraid for her life and that of her family. Standing there looking at us and my little child, seeing how scared and lost we looked, she seemed to feel sorry for us. We were surprised by that look and thought that, after everything, they still had a little pity left in their hearts. Still, she could not decide what to do until her husband returned from the market.

Upon the husband's arrival, not being able to sell his own coat in exchange for bread and seeing us begging for help, he completely forgot how dangerous it would be to keep us. When we saw their situation, we thought that money would be the only solution. We did not hesitate to show them some of our remaining possessions and promised them an easier life if they let us stay with them for a while. The couple gave in, and we started a new life, sitting in a special hide-out place and waiting for freedom. It seemed so close. Any day now, we all thought, but little did we know that the war was going to go on for another 22 months.

Summer, fall, and winter came, and again for the same length of time we suffered cold, heat, and lack of food. It is really hard to believe, if you have not experienced it, that a person can stand such agony; yet, we did and waited. A few incidents happened while we were there that showed us that G-d was with us, and finally one day we heard the Russians bombing and shooting. We prayed with all our might that we would live through the last few days and survive.

All of the people from the city were supposed to leave to go to the country, because it was very dangerous to stay behind. The poor people that kept us for such a long time thought they would fail to bring us back to normal life. They left us alone, against their will, in the house with some bread and water. They went away because they were told to do so. Alone in one dark corner of the cellar, we sat and listened. What we heard did not please us very much. The Germans formed a hospital upstairs in our house and brought in wounded soldiers to be treated. Luckily, the Germans were afraid of the dark and never came down to the cellar.

We tried to keep the baby quiet so they would not hear us. A few days more and we would be free! What a thought at that time, what hope! The bombing and shooting was terrific, but it seemed that the more they were trying to destroy our house on account of the hospital, the less they succeeded. It was going on for a week. Five people, including my father, brother, husband, and me with the baby, had one piece of bread and a little water, not knowing when it was day or night.

Finally, after three years without fresh air and sunshine, we could walk out and thank G-d for the miracles he showed us through all the miserable, shocking experiences we had. Just a few people in our town were that fortunate. There was not one complete family like us. There were only men without their wives or vice-versa, as well as children without parents. From the community of 15,000 Jews, only 100 were left. The town looked like a big cemetery. All of the people, including us, had to start to learn how to walk. My child was whispering for a long period of time, because he did not get used to loud talking. It was heartbreaking to watch this child come into a normal life.

After one year with another baby, a girl, we started to try to get away from it all. We wanted to live far away from those horrible memories. We picked Canada, having a few relatives there, and we were not disappointed at all. On July 28, 1948 we arrived in our new country. We have hoped and prayed that our children will never have to suffer as their parents did.

Manya Friedman

*M*anya Friedman (née Moszkowicz) was born in Chmielnik, Poland. She lived there with her parents, two younger brothers, and a host of close relatives. In 1938, one year before Germany invaded Poland, the family moved to Sosnowiec, a larger city not far from the German border. On September 4, 1939, when Sosnowiec fell under German occupation, Manya was only 13 years old.

Courtesy of United States Holocaust Memorial Museum, Photograph by Arnold Kramer.

Manya went on to work for a German company that produced military uniforms. However, in March 1943 the SS surrounded the shop and all labourers were sent to the Gogolin transit camp, and from there to the Gleiwitz concentration camp. She never saw her family again; they were deported to the Auschwitz-Birkenau camp.

In January 1945, as the Soviet Army approached, the prisoners were evacuated on a death march. After about 10 days, they arrived at the Ravensbrück concentration camp. Later, Manya was taken to the Rechlin camp, where she was rescued by the Swedish Red Cross in April. All alone, she tried to locate relatives in the United States. But it took her over five years to obtain an entrance visa.

Manya married a survivor from Poland and has two children and one grandson. She currently volunteers at the United States Holocaust Memorial Museum in Washington, D.C., where she conducts translations, works at Visitor Services, and is a member of the Holocaust survivors' writing group and the Speakers Bureau.

Do Not Forget Them

Manya Friedman

The news of the approaching German army spread like an uncontained fire in Chmielnik, a small town in central Poland. The defenseless population was devastated. Only one brave young man, with a rifle slung over his shoulder and a military cap askew on his head, patrolled the streets of his hometown with the illusion that he could singlehandedly defend and protect it from the approaching mighty power.

A streak of stubbornness and the cocksure attitude of the young men of his generation convinced him that he could conquer the world. Even the roar of the motorized military column heard from a distance did not dim his determination. He was willing to sacrifice his life in defence of his hometown.

The first tank, preceding the armoured column, with its machine guns ready to fire, entered the town and scattered the young man's body all over the pavement near his home. After his burial, pieces of his flesh were still found in that street. Thus, he became the first casualty in this small town invaded by the merciless German army—a lesson for the inhabitants seeing the price they would have to pay for resistance.

The young man left behind a mournful town and a bereft family: his parents, two brothers, two sisters, a brother-in-law, and his adorable baby niece. His older sister, with her husband and the baby, had only recently returned to this small town from the big city in western Poland in the hope that Hitler would be stopped before his army could reach central Poland. They were wrong.

During the deportation of local Jews and the Jews brought in from the neighbouring towns, the young man's sister was in line, clutching her baby girl to her chest, when an SS man approached and tried to take the child from her arms. She resisted and would not give up the baby. The SS man shoved them both into the group of people destined for death. The child's grandmother, thinking that she may be of support to them, stepped forward, and she, too, was pushed into that group to share the same destiny.

The deportations continued. Young people were sent to slave labour camps and others directly to the death factories. The two brothers and the brother-in-law of the young man in the street were among those sent to labour camps in Germany. None of the three young men returned.

The father and his youngest daughter, who was my age, together with others, were sent to a munitions factory, Hasag, in Kielce. One day, rumours spread about a forthcoming deportation. Some of the workers hid in the factory's attic. However, they were soon discovered. As they descended the stairs, each one of them was shot. Among them were the father and his daughter.

Historians, scholars of the Holocaust, and the world in general consider them among the six million Jews murdered in Europe. To me, they were my uncle (my father's oldest brother), my aunt, and my cousins. Each one of them had a name, and each had a face, which I recall often amid my haunting memories.

After my memory is gone, and I can say no more, do not forget them.

A Headstone in the Air

Manya Friedman

Every year, thousands of tourists visit the Bonaventure Cemetery in Savannah, Georgia. The cemetery comprises acres of land located on the Wilmington River and is a unique burial place dating back to the eighteenth century. Beside the famous Georgians that are interred, there is an unusual collection of statues telling the story of the people whose graves they adorn. There is also an assortment of mausoleums and headstones. The most touching are the statuettes on the graves of young children, one reading: "Papa's Sweetheart." The moss draped, mighty, old oaks stand erect, protecting the elegant statuary and headstones. The cemetery is listed on the National Register of Historic Places.

At the beginning of the twentieth century, one of Savannah's Jewish congregations purchased land at the cemetery and established a Jewish burial section. The congregation also erected a burial preparation chapel. This chapel was recently renovated and includes a place for services, benches for mourners, and marble plaques engraved with the names and dates of some of the deceased. In accordance with Jewish law, the Jewish section is less ornate. However, it is easily recognizable by the many pebbles covering the headstones and graves, an indication that they have been visited by relatives and friends.

After walking through the rows of graves, reading the names and dates of several generations buried here, I came across an unassuming headstone. What caught my attention was the number of pebbles on the headstone and on the ground around it. The inscription read: "HERE LIETH A THIRD OF THE ASHES OF 344 CREMATED SACRED SOULS, VICTIMS OF THE NAZIS, INCLUDING THE REMAINS OF SCHMUL, SON OF Y'CHEEL SZCERKOWSKI WHO WAS KILLED ON THE THIRD OF NISSAN 5705 – MARCH 17, 1945 BROUGHT HERE FROM ALEM, HANOVER, GERMANY." The father of one of the victims brought the ashes to the United States.

I kept lingering at that grave, reading and rereading the inscription, while envious thoughts started to circle my mind. Here was a group of people killed by murderous Nazis, but at least their ashes were buried where people can come to pray for their souls, meditate. . . . My thoughts went back to my own parents and my two younger brothers. How I wished that there was a marker somewhere indicating their place of burial. Instead, I can only envision the smoke from the chimney rising toward the sky and a handful of ashes from the ovens of Auschwitz-Birkenau scattered around in the fields and blown away by the wind.

How can I place a pebble, a sign of visitation, on a headstone in the air?

Simcha Simchovitch

Simcha Simchovitch was born in Otwock, Poland, in 1921. During World War II, he fled from his home with two friends when German planes invaded his hometown in September 1939. He lived in the Soviet Union and then briefly returned to Poland after the war. However, his parents, siblings, and friends had been murdered.

In 1949 Simcha immigrated to Canada with his wife. He earned a degree in humanities from Woodsworth College at the University of Toronto, as well as a Master's degree in Hebrew Literature from the Jewish Theological Seminary of America in New York. Until his retirement in 1998, he worked as the librarian and curator at the Reuben & Helene Dennis Museum of Beth Tzedec Congregation in Toronto.

Over the years, Simcha wrote over 15 books in Yiddish, English, Hebrew, and Polish, including his memoir, *Stepchild on the Vistula*. He also translated to English works by late renowned Yiddish poet and songwriter Mordecai Gebirtig in a book entitled *The Song That Never Died* (Mosaic Press, 2001). His books have won various awards, including the Dr. Hirsh and Debra Rosenfeld Award for Yiddish Literature from the I.J. Segal Culture Foundation in Montreal (in 1991 and 2004) and the Harry and Florence Topper/Milton Shier Award for Creative Yiddish Writing from the Canadian Jewish Congress (in 1990 and 1997). He continues to live in Toronto and is a member of the League of Canadian Poets.

The Remnant

Simcha Simchovitch

After eight-thousand Otwock Jews
were sent to their deaths in Treblinka,
some four-thousand more remained in hiding.
Day by day they were traced, discovered
in attics, cellars of the empty ghetto.
Others came out themselves from hiding
driven by hunger, thirst, and despair.
They walked together in gloomy silence
to the ghetto police station.

Upon the ground, in a wire enclosure,
guarded by their own Jewish policemen,
mothers and children sat squeezed together,
fathers and sons, young and old.
Some cried to Heaven, even deplored
the Almighty who has no pity
on infants and youth, lovely daughters.
Others sang pensive Yiddish folk songs,
Yom Kippur[1] prayers, chapters of Psalms,
recalled aloud their former good deeds
or regretted their life-long thrift
to save for a rainy day somewhere in the future.
The children beside them sat silent and humble,
crying no more for food or drink.

---

[1] *Yom Kippur* is one of the holiest Jewish holidays during which Jews undergo a 25-hour period of fasting and attend synagogue in order to repent for their sins from the past year.

Twice a week, early in the morning,
ten German gendarmes arrived.
With them were Polish policemen
and behind—the *Judenrat*'s[2] guardsmen
with caps and armbands, truncheons in hands.
One by one the Germans entered
the fenced area of the doomed Jews,
demanding jewellery, money, and gold.

Men and women knelt in front of them
as if before ancient, monstrous gods.
They handed over hidden possessions—
wedding rings, watches, earrings, money,
imploring mercy for their offspring,
the fruit of their loins and wombs.

A team of gravediggers arrived,
Jewish inmates from the camp in nearby Karczew.
Hurriedly they were told to dig
a deep wide pit with a heaped up sand hill.
Now the gendarmes began to drive
the first ten Jews from the enclosure.
Some hurried through the short distance,
some held tightly each other's hands,
others walked slowly, silent, proud,
or cursed aloud the murderous race.
Now at the sand hill they were forced
to lie face-down upon the clear sand.
Then came the order, the fiery salvos,
and bullets smashed heads and backs.
Here the Karczew inmates were ordered
to shovel the bodies into the pit.

---

[2]The *Judenrat* was the Jewish Council established by the Nazis that comprised Jewish community leaders who were still prisoners and were forced to carry out German orders in the ghettos. The *Judenrat* was first instituted in Poland and later in other German-occupied countries.

The sand hill was cleared now, ready and waiting
for another lot of Jews,
blameless as the clear morning
that shone through the tall pines
of the Otwock villas around them.
Not far away from the mass grave
stood the Germans, combat boots shining,
the sweat dripping from beneath their helmets,
they hurriedly gulped from beer bottles,
engrossed in the slaughter of the remnant Jews.

And further on, behind wired fences,
a crowd of townspeople was assembled,
to witness the unholy spectacle
of the final end to the Otwock Jews.

Rested from a night's sleep, having taken breakfast,
women in light summer dresses,
men in short sleeves, in summer hats.
Many of them will now inherit
Jewish homes and their possessions,
their children will play freely
in Jewish courtyards, villas, streets;
their maidens will adorn themselves
in the wool and silk of Jewish daughters;
erased forever will be the memory
of all who lived here, laboured hard to build
such a fine resort town.

From afar they may have distinguished
former neighbours, colleagues, friends.
Here walks to her death, Yentl, the pretty daughter
of Isaac Mokotowski, the wealthy merchant,
owner of a brick house beside the bazaar.
Her sister-in-law walks bravely beside her,
both lovely women in the prime of life.
Only two days ago they both took refuge

in the ghetto police station,
trusting that there they would be safe.
Next morning, Kronenberg, Commandant
of the ghetto's police detachment,
drove them into the wired enclosure.
(The Germans will later shoot him, too,
together with Tola, his pampered wife.)
Now both Mokotowski women hurry
hand in hand to their destination,
at the golden sand hill they quickly embrace
and, under the hail of bullets,
roll together into the mass grave.

And so the annihilation continued,
twice a week,
from August to September 1942,
in the midst of the Second World War.
. . . And the Jews of Otwock were no more.

On That Day

Simcha Simchovitch

The last fires are blazing in the streets,
my home is drowning in a sea of blood.
The wings of flames carry and scatter
the last cries of agony and despair.

The world is silent, dumbstruck at the carnage,
the Earth did not shudder nor move
from its orbit,
Heaven did not split asunder;
G-d himself hid His face
on that day.

Tamara Deuel

Tamara Deuel was born in Kovno (Kaunas), Lithuania, in March 1930. During the Holocaust, she lived in the Vilna ghetto and was then sent to several camps, including Kaiserwald near Riga, Latvia, and Torun and Bromberg in Poland. After escaping from the death march at the end of the war, she went to Bucharest, Romania. She later sailed on a ship to Israel with the help of the Youth Aliyah organization.

Tamara Deuel in Israel circa 1965.

Over the years, Tamara crafted hundreds of paintings and sculptures. She donated her paintings to a number of museums around the world, including: Yad Vashem (Israel), From Shoah to Establishment of the State of Israel Museum (Kibbutz Yad Mordechai), Yad-La'ad Museum (Moshav Nir Galim), Massuah Institute for the Study of the Holocaust (Kibbutz Tel Yitzhak), and the Auschwitz-Birkenau State Museum (Poland). She passed away in 2007 and is survived by her husband, two children, and two grandchildren.

In Memory of
My Parents and Six Million

Tamara Deuel
(*Translated from Hebrew*)

What is the right to life,
why a time to die?
But what is time . . .
years, hours, moments.

Years ago, no more than thirty, forty,
the vicissitudes of fate
found innocents in their multitudes.
They lost the right to life,
and crying out
why thus, why now, before the time?

Their cries echoed
and falling on deaf ears were lost.
And in their death, life was decreed
and years to those who would survive.
Among these multitudes were two
who gave a gift
the day that I was born.

The gift of being, basis and the form,
character, values, and a name,
which I preserved in gratitude and pride.
This right to life to children I passed on
in later years of sun filled days
in summer and in spring.

Oh G-d
please listen to my prayer
that my children
never know the grief I saw.
Not see flames destroy whole cities
or faces filled with panic,
escape impossible to find.
That their only food not be
a dried up piece of bread
through days with no more hope
and nights no semblance of sleep,
dread from terrifying dreams,
and memories too terrible to hold.

And in my depth I swear
until my dying day
that I will not forget and not forgive
in remembrance of all of those
and the two who are so dear
who gave me life
the day that I was born.

TAMARA DEUEL

Memories and Contemplations

Tamara Deuel
(*Compiled from some of Tamara's letters to others*)

I was born in the 1930s. Both my older sister and I remained in Israel since we first arrived here. Several years ago, my sister passed away. We both have families—children and grandchildren. I gave my children a normal life like everyone else here by not involving them in my past.

One day out of the blue, more than 20 years ago, I started painting, and I have continued ever since. I had never painted as a young child. I do not feel that it is therapeutic. The importance of it is the transfer of my experiences and feelings in memorializing the Holocaust and the death of my parents, grandparents, and the six million Jews who were killed.

All of my paintings have one name: "Kaddish," which is the Jewish mourners' prayer. I do not plan my paintings. They flow through me during the process. A very religious man saw them and said, "They are all souls," and then later added, "All those who deny the Holocaust should see your paintings." Yes, I feel that they are souls in my paintings, and the expression of the paintings helps people to understand the feelings and conversations.

It is impossible to have good memories about what I went through in the Holocaust, except for one incident that I remember. It was when the women, who were captured along with me, cut a three-centimetre piece from the meagre bread (we got four pieces a day) that each received and built a cake out of it for me on my birthday. This showed the humanity and caring of those who were with me.

Besides the Kaiserwald concentration camp near Riga, Latvia, my sister and I were in a number of smaller camps. Two of the other camps that I can remember are Torun and Bromberg, both of which were sub-camps of Stutthof in Poland. We worked in a factory as slaves. My head was shaved, and during the freezing cold winter I was wearing only a thin dress and a cloth jacket. Once, I looked out from the back of the truck, which took us to the factory, and saw all of the children my age going to school, running, playing, laughing, and throwing snowballs. I could not understand why it was that I was so different.

I somehow knew that I would survive. This knowledge, along with the love that I had received from my parents and grandparents during my childhood, helped me hold on to hope, keep going, and maintain my humanity and sanity. I now know that I have a very strong faith in G-d, but I still cannot comprehend why we went through this tragedy. I believe that there is a reason for everything, and I have been convinced that the State of Israel would not have come into existence without the Holocaust. It is a matter of belief.

I feel that it is a duty that I have as a survivor to memorialize the Holocaust. Art is the best way for me to transfer my feelings and experiences, and perhaps the only way I can because I do not talk about this experience. Every survivor must leave behind a story of what happened, and this is my way. We are given grief and sadness, but at the same time we are given love and beauty. And for our continuation, we should not hold on to the pain, at least not with all of our power. We should believe and live the life that is given to us with love and beauty and start to climb out of the darkness.

Despite everything, I am very optimistic. I am continuing my life and not reliving the past, although the past is the basis of my life. There are many things that the positive world is giving that I enjoy. Every day we wake up to a new day, new beliefs, new hopes and opportunities. We never know what to expect with every new day, but the hope and the desire gives us a new challenge, and by that we can experience the most beautiful aspects of life.

I hope that the tragedies that happened and continue to happen due to the blindness of hatred can make people sit down for a while, think, ask themselves why, and then find the answer. It is a sin to discriminate. G-d created all of us equal. The beauty and love in the world was given to everyone and should caress everyone and cause joy rather than suffering.

Thomas Raphael Verny

Thomas Raphael Verny was born in Bratislava, Slovakia. In 1942 he and his parents escaped to Budapest, where a Christian family hid him, from age six to nine, until the liberation in 1945. Following the war, he was reunited with his parents and they returned to Bratislava. But in 1949 they escaped once again, this time from the Communist totalitarian regime. They ended up in Vienna, Austria.

Three years later, the family immigrated to Toronto, Canada. Thomas went on to become a gifted psychiatrist, academic, writer, communicator, and accoucheur for prenatal and perinatal psychology. He is the author of seven books, including the 1981 international bestseller *The Secret Life of the Unborn Child* and the recently published *Pre-Parenting: Nurturing Your Child from Conception.* He also penned 45 scientific papers. He is the founder and first president of the Association for Prenatal & Perinatal Psychology and Health, as well as the founder and first editor of the association's journal of the same name.

Thomas compiled and edited *Gifts of Our Fathers,* an anthology of short stories and poems about fathers and grandfathers. He also had his own poetry published in *Footwork, Paterson Review, Sublime Odyssey, Rage Before Pardon: Poets of the World Bearing Witness to the Holocaust,* and *Everyman: A Men's Journal.* He currently lives with his wife in Stratford, Ontario, where he practices as a psychiatrist.

Hidden

Thomas Raphael Verny

I felt good as I drove downtown on a warm and pleasant Saturday morning, thinking of how I would spend the rest of my day. While searching the airwaves for some music to fit my relaxed mood, I suddenly heard the strains of a familiar Israeli song. It had an unmistakably haunting Middle Eastern quality, and it reached right into me. Although it was not a sad song, I started sobbing uncontrollably.

Why was I crying?

—∿—

Several years earlier, I was in New York attending the first Hidden Child Conference. Everybody was crying but me. I wanted to cry, to scream, to shout, to rage. Yet, I could not. I listened, spoke to a few people, but I could not feel anything deeply. Speakers spoke eloquently about their wartime experiences, explaining where they were hidden, who saved their lives, how they were treated or, more often, mistreated. A man told of being hidden by a Catholic priest in Poland who ranted and raved against Jews and yet chose to save this Jewish boy.

One woman told of the time when she was seven and her parents proposed to send her into the woods, while they were going to stay in their village and wait for the Nazis. She asked her parents, "Why did you give birth to me if you want to abandon me now?" They fled together and survived.

Another woman spoke of how she and her family were hidden under the floor of a barn. Before they went underground, the father showed them a bottle and said, "This will be our memory bottle; into this bottle we shall place the blue sky, the smell of fresh grass, the songs of birds in the trees. We may not leave this place for a long time. So when we want to remember the outside world, we shall open the bottle and it will all come back to us."

We heard horrendous stories of Christians betraying Jews out of hatred or envy, or for just a bottle of vodka. We also heard tales of tremendous courage, where, at the risk of losing their own lives, Christians rescued Jews. A special celebration was held for some of these rescuers, who attended as guests of the conference.

One woman, who was a member of the Belgian underground and saved hundreds of Jewish children, told the audience, "I remember you—your sad eyes, your dark curls, and your somber faces. You were my children; I am proud of you." After her brief talk, several women she had rescued excitedly crowded around her. They hugged and kissed her, laughed, and wept, and they would not let go of her.

From the noisy hallways, I escaped into a small meeting room to attend a workshop on "Losses" chaired by Psychiatrist Robert Krell, who was also a hidden child. We were asked to begin by saying what each of us felt we lost as a result of being persecuted. Participants took turns, spoke haltingly, movingly, and often broke out in tears. They spoke of losing "my family," "my friends," "my ability to play," "my feelings," "my ability to enjoy life," "the love of my parents," "autonomy," "spontaneity." One woman said, "I don't know how to parent my son." An elderly man added, "I felt shame for being Jewish."

All of us hidden children seemed to share the common belief that compared to those who were murdered in ghettos or concentration camps we suffered very little. As we told our stories, the realization gradually dawned on us that we, too, suffered, that our fears and our terrors were legitimate and deserved recognition. No one in hiding had escaped unscathed.

In the midst of this outpouring of grief an intense little woman opposite me suddenly started screaming, "This person is a psychiatrist; she is not a hidden child and has no business being here! She is taking notes. We don't want to be studied." The vehemence of this attack shocked me. I, too, had been taking notes, and now I felt guilty. As inconspicuously as possible, I tried to hide my notebook while the room erupted with demands that the psychiatrist be removed. I felt like I was in the middle of a lynching mob.

Several participants pointed out that this psychiatrist had worked for years helping victims of the Holocaust. I pleaded for tolerance and understanding. It was all in vain. Most of the participants, caught up in a maelstrom of emotions, were not capable of listening to reason. Reluctantly, the chairman asked the female psychiatrist to leave, and leave she did. The woman who led the attack and three or four of her most vocal supporters beamed with pride and satisfaction. The discussion resumed where it left off.

"My G-d, how awful," I thought. These people who have suffered so much could, in a split second, turn from victim to victimizer. Am I wrong to despair about humanity? Apparently, suffering by itself is rarely ennobling.

—∿—

In the lobby where we congregated between sessions, large bulletin boards carried notices often accompanied by faded photographs, seeking information about lost family members or friends. The whole wartime experience in all its horror was right there before me. There were pictures of bewildered, frightened adults standing on the edge of the abyss of destruction, helpless to protect their children or themselves. Children, many, many children, looked sad and lost. All of these people, as if frozen in time, their photographs taken maybe hours or, at the most, weeks before their deaths.

My eyes locked onto a photo of two young girls, perhaps eight and 10 years old, beautifully dressed in white blouses, black skirts, white socks, black patent leather shoes, and white gloves. They were holding hands on a street that could be any street in Amsterdam, except for a small detail: they look like any two children going to church on a Sunday morning. These little girls wore a yellow Star of David on their chests, and that made them targets for ridicule or destruction for any Nazi with a truncheon or a gun.

I thought of the parents of these two girls, of the plans and the hopes they had for them, the sacrifices they were willing to make for them, and the pain that still lay ahead of them. What bothered me most as I contemplated these pictures was the humiliation, the degradation, and the sadistic suffering inflicted on these poor innocent people before their deaths. A soldier shot on a battlefield dies with dignity and dies quickly. These people and the other six million Jews were starved, beaten, herded into cattle cars, experimented on, turned into living skeletons, or gassed into oblivion. If I saw an SS guard now, I think I would try to kill him with my bare hands.

Where was our Father in Heaven when this was going on? How can anyone still believe in a G-d of goodness and righteousness?

It was time for me to see Judith Kestenberg. She was one of the primary organizers of this conference, and it was she who knew of my wartime experiences from a previous contact and had invited me to attend. She was then (now long deceased) a psychiatrist and psychoanalyst who had studied the effects of the Holocaust on children for many years. She was in her 80's, a tiny grey-haired lady with stooped shoulders, but with incredible charm and energy. Judith struck me as the archetypal wise old woman. In the next two hours, I related to her my wartime experiences in Budapest as a hidden child from age six to nine.

She listened to me with deep interest and genuine caring. When I looked into her eyes, I could feel that she really saw me. I was slipping into what felt like a trance. In that moment, nothing existed but her and I; we were the only two people in the whole world.

I told her everything I remembered, and what I did not remember I tried to imagine. All the while, I was emotional but not upset. Toward the end of the interview, I asked her whether I could read her a poem that I had written about the Holocaust. I had read this poem to a few close friends before, but when I read it to her I broke down and cried vehemently.

Where Jackals Run and Vultures Fly

I.

After a day of skiing the snowy mountains,
we rest in our comfortable beds,
caressed by the quiet night
and our love for each other.

Over morning coffee
we retrace our adventures in dreamland:
Sherlock Holmes and Watson
in hot pursuit of psychic mysteries.

You tell me of your dreams,
of missing trains and failing exams.
I, too, have dreams of trains and exams:
the trains headed for the camps,
the examinations to select for the gas chambers.

How I envy people like you,
who can take a shower
and not think of Auschwitz—

who can dance to the strings
of the Blue Danube
and not hear
machine gun fire from the banks
of that bloody Danube—

who can look at a distant ski chalet
with its smoking chimney
and think of intertwined bodies
sipping brandy and exchanging kisses,
while I see vultures
circling the smoke stacks,
attracted by the nauseating stench
of human bodies burning.

II.

How I envy people like you
who can merrily play with their dogs
and not think of German Shepherds snarling
and biting, tearing children to shreds—

THOMAS RAPHAEL VERNY

People who can walk through forests such as these
and not think of decaying flesh
in the thousands of mass graves
still to be discovered
under their feet.

I envy your blond, hard-muscled father
and your cute, freckle-faced mother,
who could always walk to church
with their heads erect
in their Sunday best,
prayer books under their arms,
protected by an invisible shield
from the vultures and the jackals
jeering at me,
throwing stones at me,
only a child,
and calling me *a dirty Jew*
on my way to prayers.

Most of all I envy you,
your clear green eyes.

Mine will always be clouded,
having watched
for two-thousand years
the jackals and the vultures
do their terrible work.

And my darkened eyes cannot forget.

—∽—

As these memories flash by, they remind me that war or peace, the high-
ways and byways of life, are still dangerous. Life is a minefield. Just think
of what one song on the car radio can do to you.

Susan Warsinger

Susan Warsinger (née Susi Hilsenrath) was born in Bad Kreuznach, Germany, and was the eldest of three children. During *Kristallnacht* (Night of Broken Glass) in November 1938, Nazis broke into her home, smashing windows and destroying furniture. The family was forced to hide in the attic, and her father was arrested and taken to jail.

In 1939 Susan and her brother Joseph were separated from their parents and smuggled to France. In 1940, while the German army invaded Paris, the children fled with other Parisians to Versailles, where they were housed in the Hall of Mirrors. Later, with the help of Oeuvre de Secours aux Enfants (OSE), an organization that assisted in saving children, they were sent to the Château des Morelles at Broût-Vernet.

With assistance of the Hebrew Immigrant Aid Society, Susan and Joseph were able to immigrate to the United States in 1941 and were reunited with their parents and younger brother, Ernest. Susan went on to receive a B.S. degree in Education and an M.A. degree in Human Development from the University of Maryland. She taught in the Maryland Public School System. Since her retirement in 1993, she has served as a volunteer for the United States Holocaust Memorial Museum as part of its Speaker's Bureau and as a tour guide of the Permanent Exhibit for visiting law enforcement officers. She has three daughters and nine grandchildren.

Belonging

Susan Warsinger

My biggest dream upon coming from France to the United States was to become an American citizen. I thought that if I was a citizen then all of my memories of the Holocaust would disappear.

When I attended public schools in Washington, D.C., I did not get a sense of belonging. I felt the other students were secretly making fun of me because I was an immigrant and could not speak English properly. Much later, I went to the University of Maryland and did not get a sense of belonging there either, because I thought my peers were superior to me. Many of my boyfriends were also refugees from Europe, so they gave me no sense of belonging.

After meeting my future husband, who was a third generation American, I started to feel safe. I married this tall, handsome man who had been in the United States Army. However, I still remembered my experiences in Europe, even though I tried to put them in the back of my mind.

In 1952 I became pregnant with my first child while working in the Executive Office of the President on Pennsylvania Avenue, located next to the White House. The office was situated where the State Department had been during the Holocaust. The Bureau of the Budget, my place of employment, occupied the first and second floors of this grand old building, which was complete with marble staircases and small elevators. The Joint Committee of Economic Advisors and the conference rooms were on the third and fourth floors.

I was in the ninth month of my pregnancy when it was necessary for me to ascend to the third floor for an errand. Since I was not in shape to climb the marble staircase, I went to the small elevator next to my office, which was not used very often. I pushed the "up" button, and when the doors opened, there was our President, Harry S. Truman, with one of his security guards. All three of us were shocked upon seeing each other. The security guard probably thought that he needed to adjust the elevator so that when he was escorting the President, the doors would not open upon request of the public. I thought President Truman, who seemed to have a lot of charm, wanted to tell me that it was okay to have interrupted his journey up to the fourth floor.

For me, that instant was a major turning point. Even though I had been a citizen of the United States for some time, I wondered how a child who had been in the Holocaust could come face to face with the President of the United States. There must be some order and perfection in the world after all. The incident took only a moment. The guard asked me to please wait for the elevator to return. However, before the doors closed, President Truman wished me good luck with my baby.

I knew then that my husband, child, and our future children would be safe and thrive in a society where we belonged.

Liz Lippa

iz Lippa (née Elisabeth Neumann) was born in Vienna, Austria, in January 1938. She was six weeks old when the Nazis marched into Vienna and destroyed the lives of her family. Some of them were fortunate enough to escape. Liz was one-and-a-half years old when her family fled to Montevideo, Uruguay.

In 1946 Liz had the great fortune of coming to the United States, where she went on to raise six children, attend college, and create a wonderful life for her family and her 12 grandchildren. She currently resides in St. Louis, Missouri, and is forever grateful for her blessings.

Memories of
Yom Kippur Morning

Liz Lippa

The house is still; absent are the usual morning sounds.
My mother is not in the kitchen, making breakfast.
This is the morning of *Yom Kippur*[1]—the day of fasting.
My mother's headache has already begun,
And she is lying in bed, hurting.
She says it is from not having her usual morning coffee,
But I know it is more than that.

This is her day of mourning for all that she lost;
For all that was taken from her by the Holocaust.
For her parents, who were killed in Auschwitz,
For her aunts and uncles, cousins, nieces and nephews, and friends,
All lost and never recovered.
For her life in Vienna, city of art and music.
City of her and her children's birth,
Her language and culture, left far behind.

She had escaped and survived and went on with her new life.
She did not whine or complain about her life.
But on *Yom Kippur,* the day of atonement,
On this most holy day, she mourns for all her losses,
For all her loved ones, gone forever,
And for the life she was never to live.

---

[1] *Yom Kippur* is one of the holiest Jewish holidays during which Jews undergo a 25-hour period of fasting and attend synagogue in order to repent for their sins from the past year.

She allows herself to lie in bed and have her headache,
And to be unavailable for ordinary duties and discourse.
She will get up in time to go to the *Yizkor* service;
The memorial service for all whom we have lost,
And there she will dutifully say the prayers
Prescribed by her religion and its customs.
She performs her obligatory ritual, and it brings her healing,
But the real mourning had occurred in the morning,
Lying in bed, feeling the pain in her head and in her heart.

The Banyan Tree

Liz Lippa

I was born in Vienna, Austria, in 1938, and I have always missed my family. I was six weeks old when Hitler marched into Vienna and annexed Austria to the Third Reich. I was one-and-a-half when my family fled to Montevideo, Uruguay. Growing up in South America, I did have my parents with me, and I had a brother, an aunt and uncle, and a cousin. However, I knew that I needed more than that.

When I moved to the United States in 1946 and heard my new friends talking about other kids in the Jewish community who were related to them, I always envied them. It seemed to me that it gave them some special legitimacy to be connected as family to people around them. I thought it would be so great to have people scattered around the city who were my family. I wanted to bump into someone downtown or at a movie or restaurant, and to tell my companions, "That's my aunt" or "He's my cousin." When I would hear about family reunions where there would be as many as 100 people, I could hardly imagine how magnificent it would be to have that many relatives!

When we lived in South America, my family consisted of seven people, and we all lived in the same house. When we came to the United States, four more people were added to the family group, but it still seemed quite meager. I knew that there were a few more aunts scattered around Europe, Asia, and South America, but I never knew them or got letters, presents, or birthday cards from them. My mother and father each had seven siblings, and almost all of them had been married. I heard my mother talk about uncles, aunts, and cousins she grew up with in Vienna who were now missing from our lives. Where was everybody? What happened?

What happened was the Holocaust. People were snatched out of their everyday lives in Vienna, and many of them were murdered. Those who survived were scattered around the world and in no situation to start a family. As a result, I didn't have the cousins I was meant to have, and I felt the emptiness in my soul.

When I was a teenager, I went on a vacation to Florida, and there I saw my first banyan tree. This tree sprouts roots that look like fronds and hang down from its branches. When these fronds reach the ground, they dig in, form new roots, and eventually become new trunks that get thicker and stronger and then send out their own branches that will again send down new growth. This tree can grow to take up acres of land, and it is quite a phenomenal sight. In some parts of the world, people live in these trees, by hanging partitions and dividing the spaces into rooms. In Florida I saw a number of banyan trees that took up a whole yard next to someone's house. However, most of the banyans were much smaller. Their growth was controlled. Humans had cut off the fronds before they could reach the ground and set down roots that would become trunks.

I was tremendously touched when this was described to me. I remember fighting back tears and feeling a deep grief well up inside. I remember thinking that this tree was the perfect metaphor for what had happened to my family, as well as to so many other Jewish families in Europe. Hitler and the Nazi regime had cut us down and deprived us of our destiny. I bought a few postcards with pictures of this tree, and I taped one to my refrigerator when I got back home. It was like a memorial to my missing family. I have continued to hold a special affection for the banyan tree.

I am so grateful that I was able to pass down my own root fronds and that they all took hold and continued to sprout more fronds, which are now growing to be strong trunks. I have also been fortunate enough to witness this growth. I have six children and 12 grandchildren, and I am the first woman in four generations to see my grandchildren grow up. Furthermore, I am the only person in my family who has been so blessed, and not a day goes by that I don't appreciate this miracle. It is my personal revenge and victory.

I know that all of the Jews who have been able to survive and produce children after the Holocaust have the same feelings. We treasure our children and our grandchildren. They are the proof that we will endure as a nation.

Ann Szedlecki

Ann Szedlecki in Israel circa 1950.

$\mathcal{B}$orn in Lodz, Poland, Ann Szedlecki escaped to Siberia with her older brother, Shoel, in December 1939. She was only 14 at the time. Two years later, Shoel succumbed to tuberculosis, and Ann was completely alone. She spent a total of six years within 500 kilometres of the Chinese border, doing odd jobs and trying to avoid getting arrested. She eventually secured a job delivering mail, which enabled her to survive, as well as to frequent the local movie theatre. In 1946 she returned to Lodz and discovered that she was the sole survivor of her large family.

In 1950 Ann relocated to Israel with her husband. Three years later, she moved to Toronto, and in 1966 she established her own ladies wear business, Albion Style Shoppe, which she successfully ran for 26 years. Over the years, she was also a contributor to the *Canadian Jewish News* and several other national Jewish publications. She was a speaker for the Holocaust Centre of Toronto. The Azrieli Foundation published a memoir of her wartime experiences, *Album of My Life*, in 2009 as part of its series of Holocaust survivor memoirs. Ann passed away in 2005 after a brave battle with colon cancer.

The Last Dayenu

Ann Szedlecki

The annual rites of spring began when the housewives dumped the old
straw from the mattresses and replaced it with fresh smelling straw.
Passover couldn't be far off. My mother's homemade wine was distilled,
drop after drop running through clean linen, leaving a deposit. The linen
was changed a few times until the wine was clear. A large jar held cut-up
red beets and water filled to the top that was going to ferment. Vinegar
was not allowed, because it is a product of wheat—*chametz*[1]—and there
was also our *borscht*.[2]

Our large laundry basket, by now well scrubbed and lined with a large
white sheet, was ready to store the *matzah* (unleavened cracker-like bread
eaten on Passover). We had Passover dishes and cutlery, but we didn't have a
Passover set of pots and pans. Our dishes were made kosher[3] by a man who
pulled a wagon containing metal vats with hot water. By dipping the pots
and pans in the water, the cookware was declared kosher for Passover.

My public school, Number 132 in Lodz, which only Jewish girls
attended, was located on 19 Wierzbowa—Willow Street. Classes were
taught in Polish. For *Rosh Hashanah* (Jewish New Year), we were asked
to bring some items to be distributed amongst needy students. The same
went for Passover. The food tank was an old tradition. We never knew who
was being helped; all I knew was that I was the giver. This tradition was
instilled in me from an early age.

---

[1]Bread, grains, and leavened products that are not consumed on the Jewish holiday of
Passover.

[2]A soup, often made with beets, that is popular in many Eastern and Central European
countries.

[3]Kosher foods are those that conform to Jewish dietary laws such as not including ingredients derived from non-kosher animals or from kosher animals that were not properly
slaughtered and not mixing meat and dairy.

For Passover, I was outfitted in new clothing: new ribbons for my braids; new underwear and socks; a dress; and, finally, new shoes. My mother always took me shopping, but in the spring of 1939 she could not spare the time.

We had a new addition to our family. My 23-year-old sister had given birth to a baby girl, Miriam, making me an aunt at almost 14. My mother was busy helping my sister cope with the baby. The task of buying me shoes fell to my aunt, Tauba Glika, my mother's middle sister, who was childless. Sarah Rivka, my youngest aunt—she was also childless—had been thrown out of Germany a year before. She had enough problems of her own and couldn't participate in our Passover preparations.

Upon entering the shoe store, my aunt immediately asked for a pair of flat, black patent-leather shoes with a strap, the kind I had worn since age five. My eyes were drawn to a pair of blue suede pumps trimmed with pink leather X's and, most importantly, a three-centimetre heel. My mind was made up. I wanted those shoes. A battle of wills ensued. It was to be those shoes or none. I emerged victorious, much to the delight of my sister, who applauded me for asserting my independence. By the way, she liked the shoes so much that she also wore them sometimes.

The wooden floor of our kitchen was scoured with sand to get out the oil stains left by the sewing machines. The kitchen was my father's working area, as well as my mother's cooking domain. The only other room was a dining room, minus our beautiful black dining set. The table and chairs had been repossessed by the city for non-payment of taxes. It was just as well, there was no place for the set. The other half of the room had two beds: one lounge for my brother and a metal child's bed for me. It was really getting too short.

Red wax was applied to the floor and allowed to dry. Finally, a heavy polisher was pushed manually to give the floor a shine. After all of these preparations, we followed our father through the house on the evening before the first *Seder*.[4] With candles in our hands and a feather in his, we went through every corner of the house to get out the last bits of *chametz* trapped in the crevices. The *chametz* was to be burned the next morning.

---

[4] A ritual feast that takes place on the first night of Passover. Jews outside of Israel hold a *Seder* on the first two nights of the holiday.

By noon the next day, everything was ready for the festivities: the beautifully ironed white tablecloth; the polished sterling silver candlesticks; and the armchair, where my father was going to sit leaning on a huge pillow. On the table we had china, cutlery, napkins, wine glasses, and a beautifully embroidered *matzah* cover in front of my father's seat. On the round plate, there was a roasted egg, a shank bone, bitter herbs, and other foods that are blessed at the *Seder*. Mouth-watering smells emanated from the kitchen. My stomach was growling, but it would have to wait.

My sister, her husband, and the baby arrived. There were six adults, but only four chairs. The lounge chair was put against the table for me and my older brother, Shoel. The women lit the candles and said the blessings. We opened the *Haggadot*,[5] and the *Seder* began. My brother asked the Four Questions, even though I was the youngest (except for the baby). I checked Elijah the Prophet's cup to see if he drank from it.

Everything went smoothly until we reached "Dayenu."[6] As far as I could remember, I had always giggled when I heard this song. This year I was almost 14 and an aunt. I had hoped that I had outgrown the laughing, but there was no such luck. As we came closer to "Dayenu" my father's blue eyes, beneath bushy black brows, fixed on me as though asking me to behave. I got up from the table, hand on my mouth. When I reached the kitchen, the giggles I was holding back erupted.

A short while later I rejoined the family. The *afikoman*[7] was on top of the wardrobe and easy to find. My sister, her husband, and the baby left quite late. I had trouble falling asleep. I was waiting for the morning to arrive so I could put on all my new clothes to impress my friends.

The aroma from the kitchen woke me up. My mother was preparing breakfast for me. It wasn't very fancy. During Passover, she served either *matzah brie* or *bubbaleh* (dishes made with *matzah* and eggs). In those days,

---

[5]Books read on Passover containing the story of the Israelites' Exodus from Egypt and the ritual of the *Seder*.

[6]A song at the end of the *Haggadah* about being grateful to G-d for the blessings He bestowed upon the Jewish people during the Exodus from Egypt and their journey to the Land of Israel. *Dayenu* means it would have sufficed.

[7]A half-piece of *matzah* that is broken at the early stages of the *Seder* and set aside to be eaten after the meal. In many families, the *Seder* leader hides the *afikoman* for the children to find.

we didn't worry about cholesterol. Tea with lemon followed. My special treat was sponge cake with wine. Pouring the wine over the cake, I waited for the liquid to be absorbed. It tasted heavenly, just like a tort.

After breakfast, I joined my girlfriends in the courtyard. We played hopscotch, and my new shoes got scuffed. I used a brush with special bristles to fix the shoes.

My aunt, Sarah Rivka, the Berliner, came to join us for lunch. Afterward, she took me to see a movie, *The Great Waltz*. My aunt was a very attractive woman in her 40's. Beautifully dressed, she drew admiring glances from the holiday crowd filling the main streets on this warm, sunny spring day full of promise.

On the way home we passed Rumba, the new ice cream parlour. It was crowded. I was tempted to go in, but I resisted. I remember being so proud walking beside Sarah Rivka. I didn't want the day to end, but it was getting late and the preparations for the second *Seder* were in full swing.

I wondered how I would react to "Dayenu" that night. To be honest, I don't remember. But it would be many years before I heard "Dayenu" again. By then, I didn't find the song funny. The beautiful time we shared as a family was shattered and taken away from us so tragically as a result of the Holocaust. Only fond memories remain.

Dr. Miriam Klein Kassenoff

*D*r. Miriam Klein Kassenoff was born in Kosice, Czechoslovakia. In 1941, when she was a young child, she fled German-occupied Europe with her parents and infant brother. After seven months spent in hiding and on the run, her family arrived in the United States.

Miriam attended Yad Vashem's International School for Holocaust Studies in Jerusalem, Israel, and also graduated from the Vladka Meed Holocaust and Jewish Resistance Teachers Program. She co-authored two books with Dr. Anita Meyer Meinbach: *Memories of the Night: A Study of the Holocaust* (1994) and *Studying the Holocaust Through Film and Literature: Human Rights and Social Responsibility* (2004).

Currently, Miriam is Co-Chair of the Education Committee of the Holocaust Memorial in Miami Beach, Florida, Director of the Holocaust Teacher Training Institute at the University of Miami School of Education, and District Holocaust Education Specialist for the Miami-Dade County Public Schools. She is also a member of the Association of Holocaust Organizations and the World Federation of Jewish Child Survivors of the Holocaust, and she sits on the Florida Governor's Task Force on Holocaust Education.

In recognition of her commitment to Holocaust Education, State of Israel Bonds in Miami and Miami City Commission previously honoured her as a Woman of the Year. In 2008 she garnered the Professional Educator of the Year Award from the Miami-Dade Council for the Social Studies.

Where Are the Children?

Dr. Miriam Klein Kassenoff

The shoes
All those shoes
I've never seen so many shoes

Who were they?
Where are they?
Why are they so little?
Where are the children?

Who would kill so many little children?
Who would take such innocents?
Who were in these shoes?
Who was Julika? Her name is engraved on her shoe—
For me to know her

Where is that little ballerina now?
Does she cry for her lost dancing shoe?

I can see the laces and the buckles
And the bows—

But

I can't see the children. . . .

Where are they?
Who are they?
Where are the children?

Sonia Pressman Fuentes

Sonia Pressman Fuentes was born in Berlin, Germany, to Polish parents. Along with her parents and brother, she fled the Nazi regime in Germany in 1933 and, after some months in Belgium, arrived in the United States in 1934. She went on to graduate from Cornell University and the University of Miami School of Law. She co-founded the National Organization for Women (NOW) and was the first woman attorney in the Office of the General Counsel at the Equal Employment Opportunity Commission (EEOC). She spent 23 years as an attorney with the federal government and 11 years as an attorney and executive with multinational corporations.

In 1999 Sonia published her memoir, *Eat First—You Don't Know What They'll Give You: The Adventures of an Immigrant Family and Their Feminist Daughter.* She has received numerous honours and awards for her endeavours as a feminist activist, including induction into the Maryland Women's Hall of Fame, inclusion in the Jewish Women's Archive online exhibit of 74 American Jewish women who made significant contributions to women's rights, and recognition by the Veteran Feminists of America as one of 36 feminist lawyers who made significant contributions to women's rights from 1963 to 1975. She resides in Sarasota, Florida, and is a feminist activist, writer, and public speaker.

Return to Germany

Sonia Pressman Fuentes

In 1978 my husband, Roberto, and I began planning a trip to Greece. Neither of us had ever been there, and we looked forward to exploring its historic ruins and taking a cruise around the Greek Isles.

In the past, on foreign trips, I had given a number of talks for the United States Information Agency (USIA) as an "American specialist" on the second wave of the women's rights movement. (I was a founder of the National Organization for Women—NOW—and the first woman attorney in the Office of the General Counsel at the Equal Employment Opportunity Commission—EEOC.) I called Michael Bennett, my contact at the USIA, to see if the agency needed anyone to speak in Greece.

"No," he said. "We don't. But we do have a request for someone in France and Germany. One week in France and two in Germany. Would you be willing to go?"

I was taken aback by Michael's request. Germany? The land I'd escaped from over 40 years ago? The country of *Heil* Hitler, marching boots, and swastikas? The country soaked in the blood of my people? Could I go there? I told Michael I'd need time to think about it and then consulted Roberto about the USIA's request.

"Up to you," said Roberto.

For years I'd had a strong desire to return to my birthplace, to see where I would have spent my life if Hitler and his band of murderers hadn't come along. But when I had thought about it, I had envisioned a quick trip into Berlin, followed by an immediate departure. The USIA, however, was asking me to stay two weeks—something else again.

On past USIA trips, I'd enjoyed sightseeing and local entertainment in my spare time. But how did one enjoy oneself on the site of a charnel house? I'd always found it challenging, meaningful, and exciting to speak abroad about women's rights. But were women's rights relevant in a country where millions of Jews as well as non-Jews had been slaughtered?

I decided to consult local and national Jewish leaders. The first person I called was Rabbi Stephen Pearce of Temple Sinai in Stamford, Connecticut, the Reform temple to which I belonged. A handsome young man in his early 30's, Rabbi Pearce empathized with my reluctance to go, but added, "It's not just *their* country. There's Jewish history in Germany, too." I hadn't thought of that.

"If you do decide to go," Rabbi Pearce continued, "I hope you'll report to the congregation upon your return."

I agreed to do this if I went but wondered what there would be to report. After all, the Jewish problem had ended with the war in Germany in 1945, hadn't it? What would there be to report now—over 30 years later?

I spoke with Jewish leaders in organizations such as B'nai B'rith. The consensus was that Germany was a new land with new people. Israel was trading with Germany, so who was I to resist? I decided to go. But because of Rabbi Pearce's request, I asked the USIA to include in my itinerary meetings with Jewish leaders and a visit to a former concentration camp.

Before departing, I called my brother, Hermann, who was 14 years my senior, and asked if he remembered any of the addresses of the places where we'd lived, where my parents had operated their stores, and where we owned an apartment building. To my amazement, he reeled off all the addresses, some of which were now in East Berlin. I resolved to try to find them all, if possible.

On November 2, 1978 I flew to Paris. (Due to his work commitments, Roberto was to join me later.) To my surprise, on the night of my arrival, the Jewish question came up. I was having cocktails with a small group of feminists at the home of the woman who was head of the American Cultural Center. A French reporter for the news magazine *L'Express* mentioned that she had recently interviewed Louis Darquier de Pellepoix, the 80-year-old Frenchman who had been the Vichy government's commissioner for Jewish Affairs.

Darquier de Pellepoix, a major French war criminal who had been convicted in absentia but was never punished, lived in Spain. He told the reporter that the genocide of the Jewish people had never happened; that the 75,000 French and stateless Jews he deported from France to death camps had been resettled in the East and only lice were gassed at Auschwitz-Birkenau. The following day, his statements were on the front page of *L'Express*.

The reporter also mentioned that the French had never come to terms with their collaboration with the Nazis. While the NBC-TV film *Holocaust* had been shown all over Western Europe, it had not yet been shown on French TV. A Frenchwoman had, however, started a private fundraising appeal so the film could be shown there.

Roberto joined me in Paris, and from there we flew to West Berlin, arriving on the night of November 8. The German assistant to the head of Amerika Haus met us at the airport and told us that by an odd coincidence we had arrived on the eve of the 40th anniversary of *Kristallnacht* (Night of Broken Glass).

Forty years earlier, Hershl Grynszpan, a 17-year-old Jewish student, had shot and killed Ernst vom Rath, an official in the German Embassy in Paris, in retaliation for the treatment his family had received at the hands of the Nazis in Germany. Hitler and Propaganda Minister Joseph Goebbels used the incident to incite Germans to wreak vengeance against the Jews. As a result, mob violence began on the night of November 9, 1938 and continued into the next day as the regular German police stood by and crowds of spectators watched. Nazi storm troopers, along with members of the SS and Hitler Youth, beat and murdered Jews, broke into and wrecked Jewish homes, and brutalized Jewish women and children. All over Germany, Austria, and other Nazi-controlled areas, Jewish shops and department stores had their windows smashed, thus giving the terror its name *Kristallnacht.* The Nazis killed 91 Jews, burned 267 synagogues (177 were totally destroyed), demolished 7,500 businesses, and arrested over 25,000 Jewish men and sent them to concentration camps.

We had missed the march commemorating that night but were in time to see the exhibition at the Jewish Community Center, the *Jüdische Gemeinde zu Berlin,* on 79/80 Fasanenstrasse. The Center was a modern building in the heart of West Berlin. As we approached, we noticed what appeared to be the ruins of another building cemented onto the front of the Center. We wondered about the significance of this.

The Center was thronged with people from the march. The exhibition consisted of pictures of Berlin's magnificent synagogues as they had looked before the Nazi desecration, the shambles that had remained after they had been bombed and ransacked, and how those that had been reconstructed looked today. One of the "before" pictures showed Kaiser Wilhelm visiting one of these synagogues in an earlier period. One of the "after" pictures showed the remains of the synagogue that had stood on the site of the Center. Two pieces of those remains were attached to the front of the building.

A poster announced that the following Friday there would be a joint synagogue service in which a rabbi, priest, and minister would participate. This would be the first joint Jewish-Christian service in a Berlin synagogue in recent history.

We left the Center and walked around the city. I felt as if I had stepped back in time to the '20s and '30s. It seemed so much like the Berlin of the past about which my parents had spoken. Both West and East Berlin were a curious commingling of past and present for me.

One day in East Berlin, as I was crossing the street, I saw two uniformed men coming to get me. I cringed until I realized they weren't *Gestapo* (German Secret State Police), just two East Berlin policemen crossing the street. Despite such experiences, I loved being in Berlin—staying at the Hotel Frühling am Zoo on 17 Kurfürstandamm, walking on streets on which my parents had walked and seeing street names that had resounded throughout my childhood: Alexanderplatz, Kottbusser Damm, Koepenicker Strasse, Gipsstrasse, and Unter den Linden.

A friend in the States had recommended a West Berlin restaurant named Xantener Eck. We went there one night for dinner. In Germany, if there are no empty tables, the maitre d' seats you at one that is partially occupied. On this night, we were seated with two men in their early 40's who we later learned were in the printing business.

As we pored over the menus, one of them recommended several entrees to us in halting English. With his English and my German, we were able to converse. When he learned I was Jewish, he immediately said, "I feel no guilt. I was born in 1937." He then embarked on a tirade against Jews and Israel and referred to the head of the Jewish Center we had just visited as a fascist.

"Why does he have to be a Jew first and a German second?" he asked. "If I were a member of a proud people like the Jews, I would not take money from Germany, as Israel has done, as individual Jews have done, and as the Center continues to do. All people are equal: Jews and Christians, whites and blacks, Israelis, and Arabs. Why does the Jew think he's better than everyone else?"

I shifted uneasily in my seat.

"And look what they've done to the Arabs in Israel," he continued. "Two-thousand years ago, Celts lived on the land where my house stands today. Their descendants now live in France. They don't come back here and say they have a right to my house. What gives Jews the right to do this?"

His companion had paradoxical views. On the one hand, he seemed to share his friend's sentiments, if not his vehemence. But he also asked me whether I'd had any special feelings as a Jew returning to Germany. When I told him I had, he said, "You know, my father was involved during the Nazi regime. I have to live with that."

We spent several hours at dinner, during which we shared drinks and reminiscences with these men. When we left, we exchanged business cards, and they promised to visit if they ever came to the States. One of them came close to hugging me when we parted.

I was in a state of utter depression as we walked the foggy streets of West Berlin after this encounter. "Those men really liked me, Roberto," I said. "And yet, it wouldn't take too much for them to come for me again." The discussion in the restaurant brought home to me the fact that what had happened in Germany was still there in some of its people.

A day or two later, I shared the experience with a law professor and his feminist wife while having breakfast in their home. The professor said that he resented the burden of guilt that had been laid on Germans, but his wife did not echo his sentiments. His students did not like being reminded of this guilt, he said. They did not want to be made to feel responsible for events that took place before they were born.

We visited the Center again, this time for a meeting with the assistant to the director. I asked him about the conflict between the Germans' desire to forget and the Center's commitment to remind them. "Do they want to get rid of the past?" he asked. "Or do they want to continue it? It is in the interest of Germany not to forget. It has nothing to do with guilt or responsibility. Germany must cleanse itself of these things. It must be different in the future from what it was in the past. How can this be done without history, without knowing why it happened and how it happened?"

"How long must it take?" I asked. "After all, this happened 40 years ago."

"Forty years is not a long time in the history of mankind," he reminded

me. Germany was ridden with the tension between the collective obliga-
tion to remember and the personal need to forget.

We rented a car and spent days looking for the addresses that Hermann had given me in both East and West Berlin. I knew that Berlin had
been reduced to rubble during the war and that I might not be able to
locate any of the streets I was looking for, much less the buildings. But that
was not the case. We found all of the locations. However, the buildings
had all been demolished and rebuilt—except one—the apartment where
I was born at 83-A Linienstrasse in East Berlin. It was still standing intact.
There were lights on in some of the apartments. I went inside, knocked on
a door at random, and a woman came out.

"Is there anyone here who might remember a family named Pressman
that used to live here in 1928?" I asked.

"No," she answered. The oldest resident had moved into the building
in 1947. There was no one to remember us.

A friend in the U.S. had introduced me to a woman who had lived in
Berlin for many years. I visited her, and we had a wonderful time together.
We talked, as women do, about our lives, our husbands, our hopes for our
children. We hugged, and I turned to leave. She wouldn't have done it to
me, would she? I walked out her door. Why not? Why would I have been
the exception?

We left Berlin and spent the rest of our trip driving through the German countryside and into the other cities where I lectured on the women's
rights revolution in the United States: Dusseldorf, Heidelberg, Freiburg,
and Munich. I looked at the people; they looked just like anyone else.
What had happened to their ancestors? What madness had seized them?

In Freiburg, we stayed at a picturesque hotel high up in the mountains.
When I awoke in the morning and drew the curtains aside, an incredibly
lovely panorama was spread out before me. As far as the eye could see,
there were undulating valleys with picture postcard houses nestled among
them. I was struck by the beauty of this in the midst of the horror that
had been.

It was in Freiburg that I met with Margrit Seewald, a German program specialist with the U.S. Embassy in Bonn who had coordinated many
aspects of my programs in Germany, although we had not previously met.
The Embassy had asked her to travel to Freiburg for my program, and
she, Roberto, and I spent some lovely times together.

Then it was on to Heidelberg. At the end of my talk there, a woman came up to me and said, "You have made me feel so good that you, a Jew, came back to Germany and that you came back to talk about women's rights. I hope you'll come again."

In Munich, at Café Kreutzkamm on Maffeistrasse, I had lunch with two women who were leaders of Jewish women's organizations. One was chairperson of an organization named Ruth, and the other was with the Women's International Zionist Organization (WIZO).

"How can you live here?" I asked, "next to Dachau?"

The younger woman, in her 50's, had, with forged papers, survived the Holocaust by passing as a Christian. "Every person has his or her own story," she said. "We each have a certain degree of schizophrenia." She felt guilty about living in Germany and read every available book on the Holocaust, but she had not encouraged her son to identify with Judaism. He considered himself "European," she said.

The older woman, in her 70's, had spent part of the war years with her husband in a Jewish ghetto in Austria. They had returned to Germany, because German was the only language her husband knew. "I don't think about [the Holocaust]," she said. "I work with German women in organizations. They would be hurt if they felt I was different, and I don't want to be different. When so many people stretch their hands out to you, you forget. Germany is no different from any other country."

She had told her children and grandchildren about the Holocaust. Her son-in-law told his children about the camps once and never mentioned them again. He had enrolled them in an exclusive private school, where they were the only Jews. There, they were being educated as "cosmopolitans." She was nonetheless pleased when her young grandson came to visit, donned his *yarmulke* (skullcap), and accompanied her to synagogue. She was optimistic about the future of Jews in Germany.

In Munich, Dr. Michaela Ulich, a feminist who was preparing an American Studies program for German high school students, interviewed and taped me. Thus, I, who had to flee Germany for my life in 1933, would, through the medium of tape, have a chance to talk to the young people of Germany.

We left Munich and spoke about the future as we drove on Dachaustrasse into the past—to Dachau, the first of Hitler's camps. Dachau was full of tourists, most of whom were young Germans. In the midst of the crowd, one couple stood out—a man and woman in their late 50's walking arm in arm. Wherever I looked—whether at the gate with its ironic *Arbeit Macht Frei* (Work Makes You Free) sign, at the museum, on the ground where the barracks had stood, at the gas chamber (which had never been used), or at the crematorium—they were everywhere.

Finally, I could not stand it any longer. I walked over to them and said, "What is it with you people? Wherever I look, there you are."

The man responded in Yiddish. He was a German Jew who had been imprisoned in Auschwitz-Birkenau at the age of 14 for five years. He now lived in Israel with his Israeli wife and children. He had come to Germany to testify at the war crimes trial of a former official at Auschwitz-Birkenau and had done so the day before. Now, he was showing his wife a camp such as the one in which he had been interned. Tears welled up in her eyes as he told us that, on one occasion, he had been beaten six times with a whip such as was exhibited at Dachau; he had thereafter been unable to sit for two weeks.

He pointed to the chimney of the crematorium and told us that on his first day at Auschwitz-Birkenau, one of the officials had directed his attention to the smoke coming out of the chimney and said, "Tomorrow the smoke coming out will be you."

Roberto asked to see the number on his arm.

"Do you still think about it?" I asked.

"Think about it?" he said. "I wake up in the middle of the night saying this number." Like Primo Levi, he "felt the tattooed number on . . . [my] arm burning like a sore." [Primo Levi, *Survival in Auschwitz and The Reawakening: Two Memoirs*, trans. Stuart Woolf (New York: Summit Books, 1985), 370.]

I asked him how he could identify the camp official at whose trial he had testified when he hadn't seen him in 40 years. The passage of time was not an obstacle for him. "That is a face I will never forget," he said.

We left Germany and returned to the U.S. Shortly thereafter, I received a postcard from Margrit Seewald, who wrote: "Those last moments in Freiburg when I walked down the steps and you stood there at the top have impressed themselves in my mind. It occurred to me that my life could have been yours, and yours mine."

Perhaps.

Garry Fabian

Garry Fabian at age eight in 1942.

Garry Fabian was born in Stuttgart, Germany, in 1934. Two years later, his family fled to Czechoslovakia, hoping to escape Nazi persecution. However, by 1942 Garry was interned in the Theresienstadt concentration camp. He stayed in that "model" camp until May 1945 and ended up being one of only about 150 children of the 15,000 who entered its gates to survive. His self-published memoir, *A Look Back Over My Shoulder*, bears witness to the real story of what happened in that infamous camp. Remarkably, his parents also survived the camps and were able to build a new life in Australia.

Garry later got married and started a family, and he has two children and five grandchildren. He has been celebrating his survival and the gift of a second, post-Holocaust, existence through his active involvement with various Jewish and other community organizations in Australia for over half a century. He served as Chairman of B'nai B'rith in Victoria from 2005 to 2009.

A Look Back Over My Shoulder (Excerpts)

Garry Fabian

The story of my family and, indeed, myself is not more special than that of others, but it reflects the many stories of European Jewish families and what happened to them in the 1930s and '40s. It also offers a brief glimpse of the movement of those who survived the Holocaust and the rebuilding of their lives, both across geographical and cultural renewal.

There was an American television series in the early '60s called *The Naked City,* which dealt with law and order in New York. While the show was not very memorable, at the end of each episode a voice-over announced: "There are eight million stories in the Naked City—this has been one of them." There are millions of stories about the fate of European Jewry and the small remnant of survivors. Perhaps this story is also one of them.

The past often changes, even in our own memories, with the passage of time. Outlines become blurred, facts recede into the distance, and it is difficult to recall events with any degree of accuracy. It is important, though, to make a record as accurate as human memory permits for future generations, so that they know about the events that took place during a time of global upheaval, on a scale never before witnessed in human history.

Finding a starting point to any story always presents a challenge to the writer. Selecting an event marking a definite divide between the old and the new worlds of my life seemed to be the logical beginning of this narrative, which looks back over almost seven decades.

It was a cold wintry morning in July 1952, typical of Melbourne winter mornings. I stood up in the Melbourne Magistrates' Court, not because I had broken the law, but to become naturalized as an Australian citizen. In the '50s, these ceremonies were conducted in the cold sterile atmosphere of the Magistrates' Court. Later, they were held in the more congenial surroundings of the local town halls, with some pomp and circumstance.

The Magistrate in charge of the proceedings called on me to renounce my allegiance to my homeland, before taking the oath of allegiance to the Crown. . . . At this point, I must go back in time to trace the events of almost two decades preceding this morning.

Setting the Scene

My family on my father's side goes back over 400 years in Germany, and most likely considerably longer. The family came from the Pomeranian town of Kallies (Kalisz, now part of Poland). The first official record can be found in the town chronicle in Kallies. In 1602, it was recorded that, in consideration for services rendered to the local Land Graf (local gentry), "Jew Fabian was allowed to purchase a plot of land." This was a most unusual event, since Jews were generally not allowed to own land during that period.

While the records available to me are very sketchy to say the least, I understand that the family lived there until the time of my great grandfather.

My grandfather, Albert, moved from Kallies to Berlin as a young man and lived there until his death in 1935. He married my grandmother, Johanna Baron, and they had four children: Ernst, Manfred, Hanna, and Leo. Manfred, my father, was born on September 10, 1899.

On my mother's side, the family has been traced back to the late 1200s in the area surrounding Heidelberg and Manheim. However, this is from verbal snippets my late mother, Paula, told me, and I do not have any more details. My maternal grandparents, Salo and Augusta Frisch, had two children, my mother and her younger brother, Alfred. My mother was born in Heidelberg on August 30, 1908.

My parents were married in Berlin on June 26, 1932. After the wedding, they moved to Stuttgart, where my father was employed as a tobacco salesman. I was born in Stuttgart on January 11, 1934 and named Gerhard, since my mother admired the famous poet Gerhard Hauptmann.

Early Days

Our first stop is an event that took place almost a year before I was born. This event would alter the course of my life, as well as that of tens of millions of people around the world. The date was January 30, 1933, when Adolf Hitler became the power that was to rule Germany for the next twelve-and-a-half years. Life became difficult and restrictive for those who did not fit the image of the new order. If you happened to be Jewish, life became even more difficult, with severe restrictions and officially encouraged daily harassment.

I was blissfully unaware of the events that went on around me for the first four-and-a-half years of my life, and I only learned about them later.

An amusing incident took place when I was about 18 months old. My mother's cousin was visiting us in Stuttgart and took me for a walk in my pram. A couple of men stopped her in the street, and one said to the other, "Look at this child—blue eyes, blond hair, and distinctive features— the best example of a true Aryan." This is just a small illustration of the climate of prejudice that had developed in Germany in the 1930s.

After the proclamation of the Nuremberg Laws (antisemitic laws in Nazi Germany) in 1935, life became increasingly restrictive for Jews. In 1936 my family decided that there was no future for them in Germany, a country that had been their home for over 700 years. Together with my maternal grandparents, they purchased a surgical instrument factory in neighbouring Czechoslovakia and emigrated there. While the move made sense at the time, in hindsight it is obvious that they did not move far enough to escape what was to happen a few short years later.

We lived in Podmokly (Bodenbach) in the Sudetenland, the area adjacent to the German border. This region hit prominence in world headlines as the key factor in the now infamous Munich Conference, when British Prime Minister Neville Chamberlain ceded the area to Germany without the consent of the Czech government. He proclaimed that this agreement had secured "Peace for Our Time." Politicians have never been very good at predicting the future with any accuracy.

My recollections of these days are naturally very vague. As a child, I lived in a very small and, indeed, protected world of my own, and did not take a great deal of notice of the larger events around me. I can recall that we lived in a large yellow house, which had a garden that backed onto the River Elbe. I used to stand at the back fence in the summer, watching barges ply up and down the river. In winter, when the river was frozen over, I watched children skate on the solid ice.

My first real recollection of events can be compared to sitting in the sun with your eyes closed, half asleep, feeling the warmth on your face and seeing the bright light through your eyelids as a warm orange glow. Suddenly, a cloud passes over the sun, and it turns dark, with a cold wind blowing over your face. This cloud came over the horizon and was to stay for some six-and-a-half years. The date was September 14, 1938.

Halina Yasharoff Peabody

Courtesy of United States Holocaust Memorial Museum, Photograph by Arnold Kramer.

*H*alina Yasharoff Peabody was born into a liberal Jewish family in Krakow, Poland, and was the eldest of two daughters. At the start of World War II her father crossed over to Romania with other refugees when the Russians occupied Eastern Poland. He tried to return home, but the Russians caught him, accused him of being a spy, and sentenced him to 20 years of hard labour in Siberia.

Halina was nine years old when the Germans invaded the rest of Poland in 1940. Her mother ended up buying new identification papers for herself, Halina, and her sister, Ewa, from a Catholic priest. They then travelled to Jaroslaw, where they lived as Catholics with a washerwoman. Later, Halina's father sent a letter through the Red Cross notifying them that he was alive and with his sister in Palestine (now Israel).

When the war ended, Halina's mother was able to find her husband, flee Poland with her daughters, and join him in London, England. Halina went on to represent England in the 1953 and 1957 Maccabiah Games in table tennis. She lived in Israel from 1957 to November 1967, and then she immigrated to the United States.

Halina now resides in Bethesda, Maryland. She volunteers at the United States Holocaust Memorial Museum in Washington, D.C. and is an active member of the museum's Speakers Bureau.

The Happiest Day in My Life

Halina Yasharoff Peabody

Luckily, I have had more than one happy day in my life, so I am having a little trouble settling on just one. One such day was when I visited Israel for the first time. I was excited and apprehensive about the trip, because I knew so little about Israel. I wondered what the country looked like and how it would make me feel.

I was living in England at the time, having lived through the Holocaust in Poland amid the horrendous events of World War II. It was not easy for me, because I did not speak English and was not used to the customs, which were so different from mine. What helped me adjust was joining the Maccabi Youth Club and playing table tennis. Eventually, I became quite good at the sport.

When the 1953 Maccabiah Games rolled around, I was chosen to be part of the Maccabi team representing England and earned the trip to Israel. The Games take place every four years, like the Olympics, except that they are for Jewish youth from all over the world.

The trip took seven days by train and sea, and I had a chance to get to know athletes from other countries who were travelling on the same ship. I soon discovered that many of the participants were of Polish origin and, after the war, had settled in different countries that they were now representing. Most of the Polish athletes were Holocaust survivors, like me, so we had a lot in common. We became inseparable and enjoyed exchanging stories throughout the voyage.

On the last night of the voyage, as we approached Israel, I stood on the deck all night in order to catch my first glimpse of the country. I knew that Haifa was built on a mountain, and when the first glittering lights began to come into view, it looked a bit like Naples all lit up. By the time we docked in Haifa, it was already morning and the sun shone brightly.

Sylvia, my childhood friend who had settled in Israel after the war, met me at the port. Our families had known each other well before the war, since her family used to visit us every summer. My mother told me that Sylvia, who was a few years older than me, had thrown me out of my pram once and we used to joke about it.

Sylvia drove from the dockside up to Hadar, a neighbourhood in the middle of the Haifa hillside, and then to Carmel, which is at the top of the city. As we continued upward, I observed the surroundings with great curiousity. I noticed that as we climbed the buildings went from typical stone structures to more modern apartment houses. There were a lot of small shops and kiosks that sold drinks and watermelons. As the road wound around the mountain, the view of the town and bay below became more and more beautiful. Everything was enhanced by the brightly shining sun, a wonderful antidote to the gloomy English weather I had left behind.

I was overwhelmed by a feeling of coming home. I couldn't understand how this was possible on my first day in a strange country with a different language. I wondered if it was because everyone was Jewish and I wasn't a foreigner anymore. In England, I was made to feel like a refugee. The English accepted my family and gave us citizenship, but our neighbours never really made us feel at home. Here, I suddenly felt that this country was mine, even if I didn't know it yet. My Jewish identity became a source of pride rather than embarrassment.

When we arrived at Sylvia's apartment, we were warmly welcomed by her two grandmothers. They cooked us a marvelous meal, and we sat and ate on the balcony that surrounded the apartment. As I was looking down on Haifa Bay, I remember turning to my friend and asking, "What? We only have three ships?" Then I realized what I had just said. I had said "we" and meant that I, too, belonged here.

My experience in Israel continued wonderfully for the entire two months that I was there. I didn't win a gold medal in the Games, but I got a bronze in singles and silver in mixed and ladies doubles.

After the Games were over, I got to know my three cousins and my aunt and uncle, who had immigrated to Israel in the 1930s. Everybody I met became my friend, and everybody wanted to do something for me. When I travelled by bus alone in town, I would have the destination written on a piece of paper in Hebrew to show the driver so he could tell me where to get off. The whole bus would get involved and make sure to let me know. Everybody also had a "boy" for me—one with a refrigerator. In the early 1950s a refrigerator was a sign of wealth in Israel!

I was having such a good time that I really didn't want to return to England. But I knew that my mother was waiting for me. After all that we had been through together during the war, I knew I had to return home. However, I never stopped thinking and dreaming about going back to Israel.

Sadly, my mother succumbed to cancer and passed away in 1956. I was granted another chance to represent England in the 1957 Maccabiah Games. I had planned to stay in Israel for one year, but it turned out to be a happy 11 years.

I consider the first day I arrived in Israel to be one of the happiest and most pivotal days of my life.

Helen Drazek

*H*elen Drazek was born in the War-saw ghetto in Poland in 1941. She and her parents were the only survivors of a large, close-knit family that was entirely annihilated during the Holocaust. In a terrifying and extremely complex man-oeuvre, the Drazeks succeeded in escaping from the ghetto to the Aryan side of Warsaw. Good friends—an aristocratic Christian family—received them and provided them with false identity documents and safe shelter in their estates. The Christian family put their own lives at great risk and faced the constant threat of being denounced to the Germans by Polish collaborators.

The two families have maintained contact for over 60 years. The extraordinary rescuers were honoured by Israel's Holocaust museum, Yad Vashem, with the designation of Righteous Among the Nations. Helen's parents gave video testimony of their incredible war experiences to the USC Shoah Foundation Institute.

After the war the Drazeks moved to Paris, France, and later to Brussels, Belgium. In 1952 they immigrated to Montreal, Canada, where they opened a fur boutique and were involved in various commercial enterprises. Helen attended McGill University with her husband, Philip, an engineer and Holocaust survivor from Belgium. She went on to become a French language specialist, administrator, and principal of a private school. Helen and Philip reside in Toronto, near their two married children, who have blessed them with wonderful grandchildren.

The Screams of Silence

Helen Drazek

A silent scream resounds within our hearts
Echoing of a time bereft of voice
An age of evil and of death now still
Mute of all sound and barren of all noise.

The horror that befell us swiftly came
Supreme sacrilege, gruesome heinous crime
Obscene depravity, despicable and vile
Darkest infamy committed in all time.

The nightmares of those years engulf our minds
The memories of that hell remain intact
Sordid images of terror, pain, and blood
Every breath drawn, a death defying act.

A silent scream stifles our words and thoughts
Recoiled in shock, numbed beyond shout or cry
Locked in our grief, imprisoned in our hearts
Tormenting us until the day we die.

A hollow tune still sounds inside our heads
A melody of silence, harsh and shrill
A symphony devoid of pitch and tone
The notes are mute, the instruments are still.

The shrieks of horror are long past and gone
The cries of agony resound no longer there
The wails of war have died without a trace
Only the screams of silence fill the air.

A burning fire rages through our beings
A blazing torch, a sacred legacy
The holy souls of murdered innocents
Engraved forever in our memory.

A silent scream pervades our tortured souls
Heart-piercing wail, odious demonic curse
Reverberating mutely through eternity
Preserved forever in the universe.

Holocaust Hoax

Helen Drazek

It was a hoax
It did not pass
They did not kill
They did not gas

They did not hang
They did not shoot
They did not burn
They did not loot

We did not starve
We did not ail
We did not bleed
We did not wail

No Zyklon B[1]
No cattle car
No partisan
No Babi Yar[2]

No Treblinka
No Terezin
No Warsaw ghetto
Lodz, Lublin

---

[1]Zyklon B was the poisonous gas used to kill prisoners in gas chambers at the extermination camps.

[2]Babi Yar is a ravine northwest of Kiev, Ukraine, where German SS Officers murdered about 100,000 people, including over half of Kiev's Jewish population, Roma (Gypsies), Communists, and Soviet prisoners of war.

No Mengele[3]
No pointing hand
No tortures, tests
No numbers brand

Our loved ones live
They are not dead
They were not slain
It's in our head

We were not there
We did not see
We are not here
This is not me

<hr />

[3]Josef Mengele was a German SS officer and a physician at the Auschwitz-Birkenau concentration camp. He supervised the selection of arriving transports of prisoners, determining who was to be killed and who was to become a forced labourer. He also performed medical experiments on camp inmates.

Edith Pick Lowy

*E*dith Pick Lowy was born in Czechoslovakia. During the Holocaust, her family fled to Poland hoping that from there they would be able to find safe refuge in another country that would welcome them. However, Edith ended up in Poland's Wieliczka ghetto, then in hiding for a short while, and later in two labour camps. Afterward, she was transported to four

Edith Pick Lowy with the striped outfit she had worn at the Buchenwald concentration camp in Germany.

concentration camps: Plaszow in Krakow, Skarzysko-Kamienna (Werk A and Werk B camps), and Buchenwald in Germany.

Edith was eventually liberated by the Russian army while on a death march, and she and other survivors were assigned to stay with German families in nearby communities for recovery. Her father, who was liberated from the main Buchenwald camp, found her there, and together they returned to their hometown in Czechoslovakia. The local community was very welcoming.

Edith moved to Israel in 1948 and joined the Israel Defense Forces. In 1958 she immigrated to the United States with her husband and their first daughter. Their second daughter was born in Washington, D.C. Edith went on to work as a teacher at the Charles E. Smith Jewish Day School in Maryland. Now retired, she continues to provide lectures about the Holocaust to various groups. She and her husband also have four grandchildren.

A Precious Gift

Edith Pick Lowy

It was in Europe, in Poland, and it was a time of war. Especially for the Jews, it was a long and terrible war. It had been five years since my family left our homeland, Czechoslovakia, and began our journey to an unknown life. No one imagined that the new life would be so very sad and cruel.

There I was in a place that had replaced my home—a CONCEN-TRATION CAMP. It had been two-and-a-half years since I had been separated from my mother. I knew that she had been taken away in a cattle train with many other Jews from our city, to an unknown destination. We heard terrible rumours about what happened to them, but I just could not believe what I heard. I did not *want* to believe it. I thought about her every day and I missed her. How I missed her!

My only brother, Erik, had been shot a year earlier while we were in a different concentration camp. They shot all the children up to the age of 16. I was 13 at the time, and I don't know how it happened that I survived. There was one other girl, a friend of mine, Lola, who had also survived. Her brother had also been killed. I can still hear the sound of the machine gun that killed them. This was the only time in my life that I wanted to die. How could Erik be dead? He was only 11 years old! But I had to live. I was all that my father had left. I had to live—for him.

Life went on. We were caged behind barbed wire fences. Every day we had to march in parade fashion to work in an ammunition factory, always being watched by Germans from both sides. There was no escape for us. We lived in barracks, many women or men in the same huge room. Our beds were hard wooden planks, and we were hungry—always hungry. Although my father was only working day shifts and my work alternated— one weekday then one weeknight—we managed to see each other every day. We lived for the short precious moments we had together.

One day, standing in line for food, I was holding a place for my father. The other prisoners did not mind because I was one of the few children in the camp and they protected me whenever they could. But on this particular evening, my father did not show up. I took my bowl of soup for him and went to his barrack. He was on his plank bed. He said that he had not come to pick up his food because he was too tired. I sensed that this was not true. We were so hungry that, if needed, we would crawl to get food.

I later found out, from his fellow prisoners, that on that day he had gone by the camp's kitchen and found a carrot in the trash can that he had picked up for me. He was caught, taken away, and terribly beaten. He did not come to the food line because he could not move, but he tried to hide the pain from me.

The camp life continued at a normal pace: families were together; seasons changed. For us, time was precious, yet it had no meaning. Each day was the same. Feelings of fear, sadness, hunger, and hope dominated our lives. It was winter again. In my other life, in my other world, back at home, besides the joys and beauty of winter, it would have also been my birthday time. But here, in this place, what was the point of remembering? It could only bring painful feelings from a once happy time. And even if you did remember, how could you celebrate a birthday in a place like this? We had nothing to give, no way to get presents. Most of us did not even know what day of the month it was. What difference did it make? And yet, my father knew. He remembered. And he must have thought about it for many days, maybe weeks ahead of time.

When we met on December 22, my father gave me a birthday gift. His eyes were full of tears. It was a simple steel comb, which he had made for me in the camp's workshop. I could not imagine how he managed to do it, since German supervisors were watching all the time and one could do only what he was supposed to do. What terrible risk did he take to make this gift for me? It was made crudely; the teeth of the comb were not completely even. Yet, for me, it was the most beautiful gift.

From that day on I carried the comb with me to work and I kept it in my plank bed at night. I always had it with me. Days passed, months passed, and I continued to treasure my comb.

Then, one day, an order came to evacuate the camp. We were hoarded into cattle trains, women and men separately, and shipped to the

Buchenwald concentration camp in Germany. When I arrived in this new camp I found out that my father was shipped somewhere else. I had no idea where he was. New horror and sadness came over me. We were ordered to put everything we possessed on a pile. We did not know what would become of us. I had a collection of poems and stories that I had written in the various camps, and I put them in a pile. But I decided that under no circumstances would I give away my precious comb. But how could I save it?

As I was standing in the crowd of terrified women, I decided to kick out a hole in the ground and dig with my fingernail until I could hide my precious comb. I thought that if I lived through the day, I would be able to find it and no one was ever going to take it away from me. We were led to large shower rooms, where we had to strip naked. They shaved our heads and gave us striped prisoners' clothes.

When we came out, after being processed, I tried to remember where I had buried my comb. I did not realize how difficult it would be to remember. Since I had buried the comb shortly after our arrival at the camp, I did not yet know its physical layout. It was crowded, and I had been so scared while hiding it. I looked for it and tried many times during my stay in this camp to find it, always frightened that some German or Ukrainian would see me and punish me. To my great sadness, I was never able to find the comb.

The war ended a very long time ago. Since then, I have received many gifts, which mean a lot to me. But I still feel sad at the loss of the gift that my father gave me, with so much love, in a place where there was nothing to give.

Your Life and Theirs

Edith Pick Lowy

It is not easy to talk
About the sad and painful time
In which a part of the German nation
Committed a terrible crime.

I was very young
When my life suddenly turned bad,
And my safe and loving world
Became painful and sad.

I am going to tell you
A little about my past,
About the time we know of
As the Holocaust.

Try to think of your world—
Your homes, family, and friends.
    The world of the children of the Holocaust
    Was surrounded by a tall, unfriendly fence.
    They became prisoners
    Away from home, family, and friends.
    They became prisoners
    Behind this dreadful fence.
    They were locked up in a world
    that was sad and unkind.
    They were locked up with only memories
    Of the world they left behind.

Try to think of your world
Of games, parties, and fun.
> For the children of the Holocaust
> There was no place to go or to run.
> They were kept prisoners—
> There were no parties in the world to see.
> They worked hard, and they hoped
> That soon, soon they again would be free!

Try to think of your world
Of all the different foods you can eat.
> The children of the Holocaust were always hungry.
> They barely remembered the taste of fruit, milk, or meat.
> They were kept prisoners,
> Although they committed no crime.
> They were locked up with their memories
> Of a once safe and happy time.

Try to think of your world—
Swimming in the ocean, running in the wind.
> The children of the Holocaust were victims
> Against whom wicked people had terribly sinned.
> They were kept prisoners
> Without understanding why.
> They lived with their memories of laughter
> In a world where it was easier to cry.

Try to think of your world—
Of baseball fields and swings waiting in the park.
> The children of the Holocaust lived in a world
> That was lonely and dark.
> They were kept prisoners
> In their strange world of sadness and fear.
> They prayed and dreamed and hoped
> For their freedom to be near.

Try to think of your world—
Of school, projects, and all you can achieve.
  The children of the Holocaust also
  Painted, sang, and wrote, and continued to live.
  But since they were prisoners
  Locked behind a monstrous door,
  They wrote, sang, and painted
  About the things they missed and longed for.

Try to think of your world—
Where flowers grow and butterflies and birds fly.
  The children of the Holocaust only sometimes saw birds
  Flying high and disappearing in the sky.
  But since they were prisoners,
  Their eyes followed the birds as far as they could see,
  Flying over the barracks, the fence, and a tree,
  And they wished—how they wished—to also be as free.

But when freedom came,
So many of them had died.
And I often ask: "Why?"
Why could not all have survived?

Today we have assemblies,
We plant trees and flowers
To remember the children who died
And to remind the world to destroy all evil powers,
So that what happened will never again be
And the world will be a place
Where you can always be safe and free!!!

EDITH PICK LOWY   255

Gunther B. Katz

Gunther B. Katz was born in Speyer, Germany, in 1929. In October 1940 he and his parents were deported to Camp de Gurs in France. Although they desperately tried to escape the Nazi trap and war, by attempting to immigrate to the United States, they were not successful. When they received affidavits for the move abroad while in France, they were sent to the Marseilles area. Gunther and his mother stayed at Hotel Terminus du Port, while his father was at Camp des Milles.

In August 1942 Gunther was separated from his parents prior to their deportation to the Auschwitz-Birkenau camp. Oeuvre de Secours aux Enfants (OSE), an organization that assisted in hiding and smuggling children during the war, saved him along with 71 other children. When Gunther was smuggled to Switzerland in 1943, he lost contact with all of his former friends.

In 1946 Gunther immigrated to the U.S. and lived with his mother's sister in Philadelphia, until he entered the United States Air Force during the Korean War. Following his discharge from the army, he earned a degree in Business and Restaurant/Hotel Management and worked in that field until 1972. In late 1996 he reconnected with some other survivors who had been saved by the OSE and were living in Los Angeles, where he and his wife, Susie, now live. Gunther and Susie have two sons and one granddaughter.

Memories for Our Hearts
Farewell Thoughts on the Occasion of Joe Brenig's Death

Gunther B. Katz
(Written January 15, 2004)

Joe Brenig with his granddaughter, Ariana, in December 2002.

It was on the afternoon of December 28, 1998 when we drove into the parking lot of the Miracle Springs Hotel in Desert Hot Springs, California. My wife, Susie, and I had come here to reunite with Theo Brenig, with whom I had been interned at Camp des Milles in France during World War II. We were also going to have the pleasure of meeting his wife, Ruth, his older brother, Joe, and Joe's wife, Avril.

As we looked for a parking space, we noticed that another car was also sizing up the parking spaces. "That might be them," said Susie. Eventually, we both found a spot we liked. As we got out of our car, I realized that Susie was right, and we had our first reunion right there in the parking lot after not having seen one another since 1943. The discussion soon turned to the plans for the evening, and we all decided that Susie and I would empty our car and then meet everyone in the spa for a little warm water to begin our time together.

When we got to the spa, Avril, Joe, and Theo were already in the water and we joined them. Theo's wife was not there because she was resting due to a very sore back. As we reminisced about the past, a question someone posed got me talking about the last day I was with my parents, on August 10, 1942, before they were deported to the Auschwitz-Birkenau camp. I recalled how I had fought the idea of being separated from my parents. Eventually, Andrée Salomon, a caseworker for Oeuvre de Secours aux Enfants (OSE), an organization that assisted in hiding and smuggling children during the war, convinced me that this was what I had to do. I continued to recount what happened that fateful morning.

Two buses that the OSE had sent entered Camp des Milles to take away 72 children under the age of 16. My parents walked me to the buses and we waited. Finally, the children were called to get on board. I noticed that an armed guard was standing by the entrance to each bus.

As my name was called, I started to get on the bus. My father grabbed me by the sleeve and pulled me back. He placed his hands on my head and recited the Priestly Blessing (*Birkat Kohanim*), which I had heard so many times before at much less auspicious occasions:

"May the Lord bless you and keep you.
May the Lord shine His face upon you and be gracious to you.
May the Lord lift up His countenance upon you and give you peace."

As my father said those words in Hebrew, the guard got tears in his eyes, turned away from the bus, and walked over to the wall of the camp.

At that point, as if shot out of a cannon, Joe jumped up high in the spa and yelled, "That was you!" I had no idea what he was talking about. He began to tell us that he had taken his brother Theo to the bus to say goodbye, because his parents had chosen not to go to the bus. As the guard turned away from the bus and walked toward the wall, Joe saw an opportunity to escape and jumped on. He was never able to say goodbye to his parents. He hid under a seat and declared his presence to the adult supervisor after the bus had been well clear of the camp.

Joe told us that he had even mentioned this incident on his *Shoah* (Hebrew name for the Holocaust) tape. But he only knew that a religious man had blessed his son, giving him the opportunity to save his life.

It was not until that very moment that I found out how my father's last religious act in my presence had actually saved a life. Joe's story put an entirely new spin on my memory of that sad August 1942 morning.

Since that day, Susie and I became good friends with Joe, Theo, and their wives. Every time I saw Joe, I felt that there was a little piece of my father standing before me.

As we celebrate Joe's life, I remember that as a result of my father blessing me he also blessed Joe and gave him an additional 61 years of life.

Farewell

Gunther B. Katz
(Originally written in German while in Grade 6 in Winterthur, Switzerland, 1943)

It was a day of parting so incredibly sad,
As our bus pulled away, no hope of reunion to be had.
We were taken away from our parents so dear,
Tears and sobbing could be heard far and near.

They were jammed into cattle cars, oh, so rough,
Prayers and pleading were not enough.
The old, the young, whether healthy or sick,
All were pushed or hit with a stick.
Bullets whistled when a poor soul tried resistance,
As Vichy police in large numbers showed persistence.

They were taken away.
Where? No one would say,
And I haven't heard to this day.
Shot in a lonely place so far away?
Drowned in a river deep and cold?
Or dead from illness, sorrow, fear untold?

But, oh, I hope to see them again
One day when war and death no longer reign.

Shula Robin

Shula Robin was born in Poland in 1920. Belonging to Zionist youth organization Hanoar Hatzioni, she was inspired to later go to Palestine (now Israel) to complete her education and to help build a national Jewish homeland. After graduating from Havat Halimud, a college in Jerusalem, she wanted to visit her family in Poland but could not because of the war. She ended up getting married and had two daughters.

In 1957 Shula and her family immigrated to Montreal, Canada, and she became a widow. Upon remarriage, in 1970 she moved to Toronto, where she has continued to reside. Over the years, she worked in a number of professions, including home economics teacher, lecturer, fundraiser, and impresario. She also enjoys creative writing and has published six books of poetry, including *Sunshine from Within, I Know Who I Am, I Begin to Understand,* and *Mixed Blessings.* In 2004 she released *The Tablecloth and Other Short Stories.*

Some of Shula's poems were set to music and performed at a concert. David A. Stein produced a short film for Bravo! based on her poem "At the Exhibition." In March 2004 Moviewitz Productions Inc. released two other short films, *My Heroic Sisters* and *I Know Who I Am.* In addition, Shula has recited her poems to a variety of audiences at public libraries, the Royal Ontario Museum, retirement residences, synagogues, and other public venues.

My Heroic Sisters

Shula Robin

You are not forgotten,
not abandoned by history,
my fearless, larger than life
Jewish heroines.

I was searching in the Bible
and ancient mythologies for
names of women of your stature,
but could not find any;
there are none compared to you.

Oh no, you were not a herd of sheep
going without resistance to slaughter.

Lola, you spring to mind:
young, beautiful, majestic dancer—
even the sadistic, cruel Nazi Beast
could not resist his sexual desire,
seeing you naked, before sending you
behind the door, into the gas shower.
You did the impossible, unimaginable:
took off your shoe, threw it to his face,
hurt his nose, destroyed his balance,
managed to grab his loaded weapon,
shot him
with a resounding salvo, until dead—
injuring his helper as well.
For that you perished,
burned, engulfed by raging flames,
for all to view and be afraid.

My unfortunate sisters:
Ala, Rosa, Regina, and Esther,
your only sin was being Jewish;
Young, graceful, smart,
despite merciless hunger,
you were selected to work at
Auschwitz munitions factory;
day after day you saw the chimneys,
day and night you inhaled
the stench of burning bodies.
The idea to blow up crematorium
number four was born.

Mortal danger staring
into your eyes, miraculously,
behind the backs of your
bestial supervisors, you succeeded
to smuggle enough gun powder and
secretly pass it on to the *Kapos*[1]
assigned to work in this
life devouring crematorium.
They blew it up!!
You were discovered, hanged
in full view of all prisoners assembled.
Your heroism inspired all of them.

Oh Ala, Rosa, Regina, and Esther,
you have saved countless lives.
With the destruction of the *Moloch*
devouring humans en-masse,
doomed prisoners, now were sent to work
in Germany's towns and villages
and survived!!

---

[1] *Kapos* were Nazi concentration camp inmates who supervised other prisoners. They were offered this work in exchange for extra food and other privileges.

Mala, my twenty-year-old sister,
you were so clever, astute—
working as a translator at Auschwitz, you managed
to omit from the lists names of those
selected to die.

You escaped from Auschwitz
desiring to live,
smell flowers, and eat,
but you were captured,
sentenced to hang. Instead,
you slashed your own wrists,
in view of a huge crowd hit
your notorious guard in his face,
shouting at the top of your voice:
"Soon you will also die and pay a price
for your horrendous crimes!"

OH Jewish maidens,
Troubadours will sing your praises,
a new tradition will be born—
during the holidays, your stories
will be told and retold from generation
to generation until the end of time.

—⚋—

The full names of the heroines are:
Lola Horowitz
Ala Gartner
Rosa Robota
Regina Sapirstein
Esther Wajcblum
Mala Zimetbaum

To the German Tourist's Daughter

Shula Robin

It was in June or July
1975
at Toronto General Hospital
when a cry for help
pierced the air
seeking a communicator
between a gravely ill
German tourist,
his daughter, and a doctor.

The young German woman said,
"I flew in from West Berlin
to take my father home
dead or alive.
Thank you again and again.
Your German is so fluent;
is your homeland Germany, too?"

"No, no,
I came to Canada from Poland.
Normally, my mouth never, never opens
in German
to people of my generation,
because of the inevitable question:
Is He the one, are They the ones
who turned my parents
to ashes, to soap,
and my brothers and my folk?"

"I know, I know," she cried out.
"With this guilt I will have to die!
Home in West Berlin,
watching with my husband
programs on television,
we whisper to one another,
'Do you think my gentle parents
did it, too?
Is it possible my beloved parents
murdered viciously,
counting, one, two, one, two . . . ?' "

The German woman's words
gave me a tremor,
a quiver,
touched deeply my soul.
Oh G-d,
we are both tormented souls!
I don't know your name,
neither do you know mine,
but we will never forget
one another
and the conversation
at Toronto General Hospital
in June or July
1975.

Untitled

Anonymous

In the late summer of 1938, looking out of the bedroom window on what seemed to me, a child of six years, a peaceful evening in Berlin (my parents protected me so well from what was becoming an impossible situation), I had the most vivid experience of G-d as of yet in my life. I heard, "Now you just go to sleep, and everything will be all right for you." That was the entire message, no more. "I don't feel threatened, so what is this all about?" I wondered.

A few months later, walking the streets of Berlin all night with my Father made a child of not quite seven years grow up overnight (in some respects!). The destructive behaviour of adults with bricks on lorries, setting fire to buildings, made me realize that there are no simple truths such as "children are naughty and must learn how to behave from adults." I had no cause whatsoever to doubt the integrity of my parents, though.

Another few months passed. My sister, then four years old, and I became refugees in England, living with strangers just a few months before the beginning of the war. My first task was to be an oasis for her. This persisted throughout my life, though a situation where she was an oasis for me came soon, still during the war. We were waiting, in a home for children, to be assigned to new foster parents. Supervision of me, an alleged adult at the age of 11, was almost completely lacking.

I became very ill after swallowing floodwater from the Thames while playing outside all day with other children, like every day, roaming around London as we pleased. My sister sold her dolls to get an apple a day to keep the doctor away. When he finally did come, he said there was nothing more to do; my immune system just managed to fight the illness. I had an experience in a dream where I saw a tunnel with light at the far end, and someone at the entrance said, "You keep out of here; there is still work for you to do."

This and other experiences on their own may not sound like much, but their collective effect had significant meaning that cannot be denied. On the day of my 50th birthday, nearly 28 years ago, I experienced an irresistible call: "Some scientists and journalists are beginning to write that as we learn to understand more about the universe (G-d's creation), it seems that G-d is being pushed aside to the few continually decreasing areas we do not yet understand. Therefore, the most likely outcome is that G-d does not exist or, at any rate, there seems to be nothing for Him to do as Creator. You are called upon to find the reasons for how and why this attitude is false. Don't preach; scientists prefer to hear arguments in their own language. But make it understandable for the general public, too."

"I have no idea where to begin," I replied. "I firmly believe in G-d, but as a trained physicist I don't see the point where my colleagues are off the rails."

"Never mind, I will show you what you need as you go along. You will also learn more in the ordinary course of your studies."

The outcome today is that there was certainly not a "Big Bang" to create the universe. G-d did that quietly, but with an effect more successful and amazing than any number of wild explosions. He did use cosmic fire at the right stage—against which our nuclear bombs look like little pin pricks, though terrible for humans on this tiny planet. An example of this would be tunnel construction—engineers use explosives in a controlled, effective way. G-d worked in a similar way to get the universe going, but not at the moment of birth, because no "Big Bang" could have produced the structures we see today in the universe. Why is it all so big? Why are we on Earth so insignificantly tiny? Are we really insignificant? We are if we cannot adjust our engineering to come to terms with G-d and understand His creation in the language of modern science.

G-d's creation is very clever in many senses, one of which is that we are free to destroy this planet, blow it up completely, if we fail to learn and practice better behaviour. That will not make any difference to other inhabited planets of other stars where the populations have learned to use their resources sensibly. We do not know yet if G-d has populated other planets, but modern science has certainly shown that the vast size and complexity of the universe is essentially necessary, even if only to make our environment here on Earth work.

Ghita Malvina

*G*hita Malvina was born in North Transylvania, Romania, in 1920 as one of six children to religious parents. During the Holocaust she was taken to various concentration camps, including Auschwitz-Birkenau, Buchenwald, Krakow, and Mauthausen. Then, as part of Kommando (labour squad) Leipzig Markkleeberg, she ended up at the Terezin (Theresienstadt) camp in Czechoslovakia until the liberation in 1945. Eighty members of her family, including her parents, were murdered in the war. She and three of her brothers survived.

After Ghita lost her husband in 1986, she immigrated to Canada and reunited with her only daughter and her family in Toronto. Over the years, she has enjoyed writing poetry and essays and painting, and she finds that writing provides a release for her soul. She is inspired by real life experiences and accepting the circumstances in one's life. She tries to express a view to mankind that freedom, love, and friendship are the most important things in the world and believes that each person on Earth can and has to contribute something good in order to make our world safer.

Many of Ghita's writings have been published in various newspapers, magazines, and anthologies. Some garnered her Editor's Choice Awards from the National Library of Poetry. In 2003 she published her first poetry book, *My Way,* containing works in both Hungarian and English. She has also volunteered for the Holocaust Centre of Toronto.

Never Again!

Ghita Malvina

I.

I will remember and never forget!
The darkness of the nights
The words which were all lies . . .
The people without feelings
People with cruel meanings.
I was afraid! So—desperate!
I cried all day!
I needed help some way.
                    I lost my Father!
I didn't know where my Mother was. . . .
Six children, Sisters and Brothers
                    They are my Family!
I cried: "Please—**help me**!"

II.

I will remember and never forget!
In concentration camps
My name was 18903.
A life without justice, or feelings
Treated like animals
Not human beings.
                    My eyes were on fire
My heart stopped beating
I was thirsty
and hungry.
My lips were dry—I couldn't cry!
                    I felt—I would die.

III.

I will remember and never forget!
The long trips in the **Trains**
The **Door**—to **fire** and **hell**!
Birkenau-Auschwitz-Mauthausen,
              The smell of **human flesh**!
The guarded barracks,
The surrounding electrical wires
The soldiers ready to kill
And—the long lines of thousands of people
Men, **women**, their **children**—together
Became—in a short time, through Zyklon B gas
Nothing! Only a hill of **human ash**!

IV.

I will remember and never forget!
The shrieking sounds . . .
Breaking the silence of the dark nights
Where the "Monster Tower"
Worked day and night . . .
Blending its piercing light
With the smell of flesh
Of the **death** of six million **innocents**.
I will remember and never forget!
The mountains of shoes and clothes
Hills of gold teeth, hair, and jewellery.
Were they my Sister's?
Were they my Brother's?
My Mother's, my Father's?
Every day, we passed them,
Singing on the way
To the factory where we worked. . . .
              Oh! Where were you
              High cultured **humanity**?
              Couldn't you **hear**?!
              Couldn't you **see**?!

GHITA MALVINA   271

V.

I will remember and never forget!
The winter days, the long ways.
From Krakow to Leipzig,
Buchenwald to Theresienstadt
Half naked to work in the *Gemeinschaft*.
My silent, secret prayers . . .
Always begging, nights and days . . .
                My G-d!
                Why do you punish us?
                Can't you **see**?
How many deaths will it be?
Show your **kindness**!
Break the darkness of the **walls**
With your light!!!
Give us life! Peace! Our homes!
Let us be—like other people
who live in **love** and **freedom**!

VI.

We will remember and never forget!
Future generations have to know that!
It is written in **fire**—with **blood**
May it never be forgotten!

Permissions

(continued from the copyright page)

"An Address to Students: Commencement Speech at El Camino College in Torrance, California, June 2006" first appeared in *If You Save One Life: A Survivor's Memoir* by Eva Brown and Thomas Fields-Meyer (Upper Story Press, 2007). Reprinted with permission of Eva.

"Burlap Sacks" first appeared in *Painted in Words: A Memoir* by Samuel Bak (Indiana University Press, 2002). Reprinted with permission of the author.

"The Library" and "The Emigration of the Jews Out of Germany" first appeared in *Joseph and His Daughter: From 1890-1980*, written and published by Inge Heiman Karo (1997). Reprinted with permission of the author.

"Negotiating with the Gestapo" by Rabbi Jacob G. Wiener first appeared in *Echoes of Memory* (United States Holocaust Memorial Museum, 2005). Reprinted with permission of the author.

"The Brownshirts Are Coming" by Fred M. B. Amram first appeared in *Prick of the Spindle: A Quarterly Online Journal of the Literary Arts* Vol 3.2 (June 2009). Reprinted with permission of the author.

"Role Reversal" by Anne Kind first appeared in *Beyond Lament: Poets of the World Bearing Witness to the Holocaust*, edited by Marguerite M. Striar (Northwestern University Press, 1998). Reprinted with permission of the author.

"Opera in Auschwitz" by Agi Geva first appeared in *Echoes of Memory* (United States Holocaust Memorial Museum, 2008). Reprinted with permission of the author.

"Mother" first appeared in *Person of No Nationality* by Ruth Barnett (David Paul Books, 2009). Reprinted with permission of the author.

"The Only Survivor" is excerpted from *Always Look Twice*, a collection of short stories written and published by George Liebermann (2009). Reprinted with permission of the author.

"Cellar" and "Lost" first appeared in *Island of Wakefulness* by Marietta Elliott-Kleerkoper (Hybrid Publishers, 2006). Reprinted with permission of the author.

"The Table" by Louise Lawrence-Israels first appeared in *Echoes of Memory* (United States Holocaust Memorial Museum, 2008). Reprinted with permission of the author.

An earlier version of "In Memoriam" by Pete Philipps first appeared in *Echoes of Memory* (United States Holocaust Memorial Museum, 2004). Reprinted with permission of the author.

"The Invitation" by Pete Philipps first appeared in *Echoes of Memory* (United States Holocaust Memorial Museum, 2005). Reprinted with permission of the author.

"Through a Child's Eyes" and "Is Our Future Our Past?" first appeared in *Laugh a Little Cry a Little: Stories of Jewish Life* by John H. Adler (Xlibris Corporation, 2007). Reprinted with permission of the author.

"Me: A Portrait in the Raw" and "Papa's Plight" are excerpted from *Ashes Left to Linger: A Poetic Search for Closure* by Sophie Soil (PublishAmerica, 2005). Reprinted with permission of the author.

Excerpts from *A Girl from There* by Hava Nissimov (author), Ofra Amit (illustrator), and Linda Stern (translator) (Mikteret Publications, 2007) have been reprinted with permission of the author, illustrator, and publisher.

"Hurrah! Here We Are Again" first appeared in *After Those Fifty Years: Memoirs of the Birkenau Boys*, written and published by John Freund (Toronto, 2009). Reprinted with permission of the author.

"Changes" by Dorothy Fleming first appeared in *Survival: Holocaust Survivors Tell Their Story*, edited by Wendy Whitworth (Quill Press, 2003). Reprinted with permission of the author and The Holocaust Centre in England.

"Do Not Forget Them" by Manya Friedman first appeared in *Echoes of Memory* (United States Holocaust Memorial Museum, 2003). Reprinted with permission of the author.

"A Headstone in the Air" by Manya Friedman first appeared in *Echoes of Memory* (United States Holocaust Memorial Museum, 2006). Reprinted with permission of the author.

"The Remnant" and "On That Day" first appeared in *Out of the Abyss* by Simcha Simchovitch (Toronto, 2003). Reprinted with permission of the author.

"Belonging" by Susan Warsinger first appeared in *Echoes of Memory* (United States Holocaust Memorial Museum, 2008). Reprinted with permission of the author.

"Where Are the Children?" first appeared in *Studying the Holocaust Through Film and Literature: Human Rights and Social Responsibility* by Dr. Miriam Klein Kassenoff and Dr. Anita Meyer Meinbach (Christopher-Gordon Publishers, Inc., 2004). Reprinted with permission of Dr. Klein Kassenoff.

"Return to Germany" is excerpted from *Eat First—You Don't Know What They'll Give You: The Adventures of an Immigrant Family and Their Feminist Daughter* by Sonia Pressman Fuentes (Xlibris Corporation, 1999). Reprinted with permission of the author. © 1999 Sonia Pressman Fuentes. More information on Sonia and her book can be found at http://www.erraticimpact.com/fuentes.

Excerpts from *A Look Back Over My Shoulder* by Garry Fabian (Melbourne: Makor Jewish Community Library, 2002) have been reprinted with permission of the author.

"My Heroic Sisters" and "To the German Tourist's Daughter" are excerpted from *I Know Who I Am* by Shula Robin (Toronto, 1996). Reprinted with permission of the author.

"Write!" by Dora Posluns has been published with permission of the author.

"Auschwitz 1944" and "Rosh Hashanah 1944 in Birkenau" by George Scott have been published with permission of the author.

"A Secret Trip to Berlin" by Rabbi Jacob G. Wiener has been published with permission of the author.

"Kristallnacht: The Night of Broken Glass" by Fred M. B. Amram has been published with permission of the author.

"Great-Aunt Mathilde" by Anne Kind has been published with permission of the author.

"The Selection" by Agi Geva has been published with permission of the author.

"Why Didn't the Boat Sink? How a Kindertransportee Kept Afloat" by Ruth Barnett has been published with permission of the author.

"Hilda Prays at Birkenau" and "No Town to Call Home" by Miriam Spiegel Raskin have been published with permission of the author.

"The Kiddush Cup" by Alfred Traum has been published with permission of the author.

"Acquiring a New Name and a New Family" by Gerda Krebs Seifer has been published with permission of the author.

"The Ring of Love" by Andy Réti has been published with permission of the author.

"Jewish Partisans" and "The Young Mother" by Fruma Gulkowich Berger have been published with permission of the author's son, Ralph Berger.

"The Great Action, 1942" and "The Holocaust Inferno" by Leon Krym have been published with permission of the author.

"Escape From the Ghetto" by Renate Krakauer has been published with permission of the author.

"Bye Bye, Daddy" and "The Price of a Shmatte" by Maryla Neuman have been published with permission of the author.

"To Those Who Want to Know" by Dorothy Fleming has been published with permission of the author.

"Surviving the Holocaust" by Francis N. Dukes-Dobos has been published with permission of the author.

"Saved By Miracles: A Personal Recollection of the Holocaust" by Frieda Traub has been published with permission of the author.

"In Memory of My Parents and Six Million" and "Memories and Contemplations" by Tamara Deuel have been published with permission of the author's family. More of Tamara's poems and her paintings can be found at http://photaspect.com/SQL/main.php and www.tamaradeuel.com.

"Hidden" by Thomas Raphael Verny has been published with permission of the author.

"The Banyan Tree" and "Memories of Yom Kippur Morning" by Liz Lippa have been published with permission of the author.

"The Last Dayenu" by Ann Szedlecki has been published with permission of the author's daughter, Lynda Kraar.

"The Happiest Day in My Life" by Halina Yasharoff Peabody has been published with permission of the author.

"The Screams of Silence" and "Holocaust Hoax" by Helen Drazek have been published with permission of the author.

"A Precious Gift" and "Your Life and Theirs" by Edith Pick Lowy have been published with permission of the author.

"Memories for Our Hearts: Farewell Thoughts on the Occasion of Joe Brenig's Death" and "Farewell" by Gunther B. Katz have been published with permission of the author.

"Untitled" has been published with permission of the author, who wished to remain anonymous.

"Never Again!" by Ghita Malvina has been published with permission of the author.

Acknowledgements

Thank you to my family for their love and support and for believing in me and this endeavour.

Many thanks to the Holocaust survivors and relatives of the survivors who helped to make this publication possible. These courageous individuals have so much to offer the world. It has been an honour to be able to connect with survivors from around the world and to further discover how significant it is when you can get to know such people and hear what they have to say firsthand, rather than just reading summaries of historical events. I will never forget.

I am greatly appreciative of the following dynamic and inspiring people for generously sharing their wisdom, advice, and feedback and reminding me that dreams can become reality: Dr. Samuel Gerstein, Donna Kakonge, David Silverberg, Steven Michael Berzensky, Helen Zegerman Schwimmer, Lillian Boraks-Nemetz, Barry Shainbaum, Annette Poizner, Darryl Salach, Jill Andrew, Marni Norwich, Pete Masterson, Michael N. Marcus, and Avrum Rosensweig.

Thanks to the many individuals who also kindly provided support by offering words of encouragement, helping to spread the word about the call for submissions, and/or providing additional feedback: Tanya Freedman, Maxwell Kates, Ruth Brainis, Matthew Sidon, Riva Waldman, Gili Haimovich, Katia Grodecki, Samantha Goldstein, Adam Becker, Emmanuel Lopez, Maayan Itzkovich, Lillian Freedman, Theresa Schrader, Janet Cordahi, members of Thornhill Toastmasters, Brad Dworkin, Warren Falkenstein (www.WigitalGS.com), Alison Burke, Lauren Stein, Riva Finkelstein, Julie Starr, Rabbi Sheldon Korn, and Shoshana Tanenbaum.

There were numerous organizations—too many to list—that also helped to spread the word about this endeavour to Holocaust survivors and their relatives, and I am very grateful to all of them.

Special thanks to the talented individuals who assisted in bringing my vision for this publication to life. I appreciate their creativity, patience, and attention to detail. That includes Hailey Eisen for helping with proofreading and some copyediting, Jim Zaccaria for the cover design and illustration, and Glenna Collett for the interior design.

A warm thank you to Michael Berenbaum for his insightful foreword and his support. Through his work, he has made significant contributions toward helping to raise others' awareness about the Holocaust, and I wish him continued success with his endeavours.

Thank you to the various individuals and organizations that granted permission to reprint some of the material in this publication, including the United States Holocaust Memorial Museum, Yad Vashem, and Pucker Gallery.

I am grateful to G-d for blessing me with the opportunity to facilitate the manifestation of this publication.

May G-d continue to guide humanity in creating more love and peace in our world.

About the Editor

B ased in Toronto, Canada, freelance writer and editor Shlomit Kriger enjoys sprinkling inspiration and moving others through the written word. She holds a Bachelor of Journalism degree from Ryerson University and specializes in covering dynamic and inspiring people and ventures for diverse news outlets and organizations. Her articles have appeared in such publications as *Canadian Jewish News, This Magazine, Thornhill Liberal, Jewish Tribune, Ryerson Alumni Magazine, Good News Toronto,* and *One80,* a youth newspaper for which she also served as an editor. In 2005 she coordinated the 6th Annual Creative Writing Contest for the Homeless through the humanitarian organization Ve'ahavta and assisted in producing a zine featuring the winning entries.

Shlomit has also crafted her own poetry, songs, and short stories since age nine. She weaves a literary kaleidoscope blending reality and illusion. Her creative pieces stretch readers' emotions and imaginations, as well as push them to dive deeper into societal issues. She recently earned a certificate in the Foundations of Expressive Arts Therapy from ISIS-Canada and continues to explore how the arts can be used to help people express themselves, become empowered, and heal.

Photograph by Charlene McIntosh.